Syria

"If you want to better understand the importance and complexity of Syria, this is your volume to read and to study. In plain, clear language, Ambassador Rajendra Abhyankar provides the reader unmatched information, understanding and insight into this fascinating and pivotal country."

—US Congressman Lee H. Hamilton, *Honoree of the Hamilton Lugar School of Global and International Studies, Indiana University, Bloomington*

"Well regarded scholar diplomat Rajendra Abhyankar deserves commendation for his comprehensive delineation of the almost unfathomable complexities of the changing dynamics of the war in Syria in his very aptly titled book *Syria: The Tragedy of a Pivotal State*. A recommended read."

—Indian Ambassador Ranjit Gupta

"*Syria: The Tragedy of a Pivotal State* by a polyglot seasoned diplomat, Rajendra M. Abhyankar, India's former Ambassador to Syria, is a meticulously researched and balanced analysis of the complexities of a new phenomenon, the 21st century endless wars by invitation, which are challenging the very core of UN-based international order. Ambassador Abhyankar cogently unpacks layer upon layers of ill-will and deception—by individuals, extremist groups and nations, near and far—which have turned a peaceful local uprising in Syria eight years ago against murderous Assad regime, into tragic battle ground in pursuit of rotten self-serving interests and global ambitions. *Syria* is a sobering account of the causes of devastation of a pivotal state and society. It offers a pragmatic future political map and humanitarian and reconstruction scenarios to end the war. Clearly written, richly documented, fast paced, succinct, timely, a must read for understanding the root causes of the endless mayhem in the Middle East, especially resolution of the Syrian conflict."

—M. Nazif Mohib Shahrani, *Ph.D., Professor of Anthropology, Central Asian and Middle Eastern Studies, Hamilton Lugar School of Global and International Studies, Indiana University, Bloomington*

"If reconstructing Syria, as we know since the end of the Second World War, is impossible, how did we get here? With details and lucidity, Ambassador Rajendra M Abhyankar offers a gripping, non-polemical, and non-partisan outsider view of the pivotal state, its seemingly endless crises, and its more troublesome future."

—Professor P. R. Kumaraswamy, *Jawaharlal Nehru University, New Delhi*

Rajendra M. Abhyankar

Syria

The Tragedy of a Pivotal State

palgrave
macmillan

Rajendra M. Abhyankar
School of Public and Environmental Affairs
Indiana University Bloomington
Bloomington, IN, USA

ISBN 978-981-15-4561-0 ISBN 978-981-15-4562-7 (eBook)
https://doi.org/10.1007/978-981-15-4562-7

This Palgrave Macmillan imprint is published by the registered company Springer Nature Singapore Pte Ltd.
The registered company address is: 152 Beach Road, #21-01/04 Gateway East, Singapore 189721, Singapore

An Endless War Challenges the International Order

for
Paulomi

Preface

My connection with Syria continued almost throughout my diplomatic career and I retain an abiding interest in the country and its people. The evolution of the endless civil war, with its twists and turns, became a fascinating subject of study. The country retains a unique character that impinges on every facet of international relations today. Yet it goes beyond.

Syria, situated in the Mesopotamian basin, has nurtured three religions—Judaism, Christianity and Islam—possessing holy places and landmarks of all three. It is thus a part of the universal heritage of humankind. Going back into antiquity, Syria is one of the most ancient inhabited regions on Earth. Traces of human civilization in Syria go back to roughly 700,000 years. Over the ages, Syria has provided a fertile ground for outside powers to settle their differences. What was then, we see now with four of five permanent UN Security Council and all major regional powers enmeshed in the civil war.

My interest in Syria started in 1992 when I was posted to Damascus as the Indian Ambassador. After having spent three years in Iraq, I was interested and excited at the thought of living and working in another Arab country. Little did I realise the great difference between the two countries. While Iraqis are the Prussians of the Arab world, the Syrians are the Belgians!

In nearly four years in Syria I was exposed to every aspect of the country, above all, their facility in assimilating influences from across the seas and making them their own. No wonder, since they are the worthy successors of the Levantines of old.

I continued my interest in Syria even after completing my diplomatic tenure in Damascus. As Secretary in the Ministry of External Affairs from 2001 to 2004, once again India's relations with Syria became part of my territorial remit. I was invited, long after retiring from service, in November 2011 to Damascus by the Syrian government. It was six months since the Arab revolution had hit Syria and among the first to provoke a violent response from the government. In April 2012, I again visited Damascus and Homs, by when the Syrian government had ignited a full-scale insurgency. It was following my visits to Damascus in May 2017 and May 2019 that I started this book project.

Syria is unique on many counts. It is the only country still wedded to the political ideology of Arab Ba'ath Socialism with its tenets of Arab unity, Arab solidarity and socialism. Iraq until 2002 was the other. Not surprisingly, with two dictators ruling in both—Hafez Assad and Saddam Hussein—inevitably there were differences even within this majority of two!

Yet as an Indian, I found the clear separation of religious authority from the authority of state the Ba'athist ideology's most attractive feature. Along with it went women's' empowerment with Syrian women working in all branches of government, industry and trade.

Syria today remains the only country in the Middle East still wedded to this ideal and the reasons are not far to seek. It has consolidated Syria's reputation as the only country in the Middle east where minorities, both Muslim and non-Muslim, can live in peace and enjoy their rights. Syria is a multi-confessional state: in addition to Sunni and Shia Muslims, there are Alawites, Orthodox and other Christian confessions, Druze, and Kurds. In the interests of the Middle East's diverse populations, we need to preserve this rarity.

The long running civil war has completed nine years with Bashar Assad having asserted, aided by Russian and Iranian military muscle, his authority over most of his country, except the province of Idlib. In so doing, he has established his indispensability in any future political dispensation. At the same time, Russian and Iranian political and military role in Assad's battleground success has created for them long-term interests that could make it difficult for Assad to assert his will.

Even more serious problems need to be faced starting with creating conditions for return of the five million refugees abroad and nearly six million displaced within the country. Whether Assad will be able to secure the required funding for these monumental tasks remains moot.

Syria has yet to emerge from its civil war even though the end game has started. Yet its continuing instability has provoked Turkey to seek its interest by invading the country. The situation remains fraught. It is unlikely that Turkey will emerge unscathed from this operation while it prolongs the agony of the Syrian people. Former Iraqi prime minister, Haider al-Abadi pertinently remarked that if Syria disintegrates the whole area will be under threat.

In the end, the Western countries chose expediency in labelling Bashar Assad illegitimate closing off any opportunity for a finding a workable solution to the Syrian crisis. It created a paradoxical situation in which the Western champions of democracy saw Russia defending the UN principle of non-intervention to an impotent United Nations Security Council.

Truly, Syria always was, and remains, pivotal to the future of the Middle East and of the international system. I hope this book succeeds to convey this sense.

Mumbai
January 2020

Rajendra Abhyankar

Acknowledgments

'The scariest moment is always just before you start' so wrote Stephen King, the famous novelist. How much more scarier is it when you have embarked on writing on a subject that is constantly in motion—that is a real live story. That was my situation as I started, in the summer of 2018, to write this book, after some false starts, on the tragedy that Syria has become. Moreover, a situation that continues to evolve after eight years.

In getting ahead with my book, I have counted on a number of institutions and people who have been a constant support. I start with the O'Neill School of Public and Environmental Affairs at Indiana University where I have been teaching since 2012. My grateful thanks go to John Graham, the former Dean, who was always supportive of my academic endeavours. I also thank Michael McGuire who as the former Executive Associate Dean gave me his time and assistance as I needed. I particularly refer to the excellent research assistants that were available to me as part of the School's support.

The O'Neill School is a remarkable institution—at the national level—with an outstanding faculty. In my view, its faculty is it most prized possession. A friendly body of great academics always willing to help. I consider myself fortunate in belonging to such an institution situated as it is in Bloomington, a haven of cosmopolitanism.

I thank the Islamic Studies Program at Indiana University, where I am adjunct faculty, for financial help to support travel to the concerned countries for research for the book and to help with the publication and publicity of the book. I also presented my ideas at a conference organised after my 2017 visit.

In Syria, I have to thank Dr. Buthaina Shaban, the Diplomatic Adviser to President Bashar Assad who has always been receptive to my queries and ready with helpful advice. I met Buthaina for the first time when I went in 1992 to Damascus as the Indian Ambassador. Since then our friendship has endured. Another eminent person from whom I have learnt a lot is Dr. Mohsin Billal, now a member of the politbureau of the Ba'ath party. We became friends during my posting in Damascus and I have always been able to see him whenever I have visited. In addition, many others have always been ready to help. I thank them all.

In researching the material for this book, I had dramatic help from my two brilliant research assistants, Farhana Khan and Amanda Lawnick. I am confident that both will do well as they move forward in life.

Farhana, apart from researching various issues and going deep into the structure of the book, also created Syrian Timelines covering the period from 2011 to 2019 that bring in a tabular form the day-to-day developments on the Syrian peace process. The tables are in the annexes to the main text. An outstanding piece of work from an outstanding person.

Amanda Lawnick's contribution to the book is no less significant. She painstakingly researched a huge amount of published material to create chapter-wise abstracts of all relevant articles and books that were of immeasurable help in my writing. They often came to my rescue when I was at a dead end. By any reckoning, it was an equally outstanding piece of work form an intelligent and outstanding person.

In my School, I have greatly benefitted from the unstinted secretarial assistance I have received from Jennifer Mitchner and Charlie Abbot. Jennifer was my secretary for most of my stay at the O'Neill School and I have thanked my stars to have such a capable person supporting me. Charlie has been of invaluable support in dealing with the practical details of my travels and other requirements.

At Springer, I thank Sagarika Ghose and Sundeep Kaur for taking on my work and providing encouragement when needed including being patient with the submission of the written material. I could not have expected better support in my endeavour.

Finally, my eternal gratitude to my wife, Paulomi, for giving me the time and space for completing this work as indeed all that have been written earlier. I dedicate this book to her.

Mumbai
January 2020

Rajendra Abhyankar

President Hafez al-Assad (1971-2000) and Ambassador Rajendra Abhyankar after his Presentation of Credentials, February 23, 1993

Up to the Minute: An Introduction

Syria: The Tragedy of a Pivotal State

Possessing a unique geography, Syria is at the crossroads of major world religions, empires and economic and mercantile networks. Its timelessness and antiquity have made it a pivotal state in the Middle East. It's enduring proclivity to engender and synthesize diverse, often contradictory, streams of thought, civilization, religion and politics have made it a battleground for opposing ideas, beliefs and practices. Lying at the junction of three continents Syria was called the bridge to Africa and the key to Asia. Over thousands of years, Syria was occupied by, hence exposed to, the great cultures and empires of the region.

The Syrian cauldron has awakened long-standing issues of sectarian and communitarian accommodation in the region, questions that have remained repressed for over five decades. Repeatedly, Syria has been the trigger and the terrain for forces determined to upset or destroy the existing order. It has brought to the fore the question of inclusiveness in the context of multi-sectarianism and national unity. With Syria's diversity of minorities, it has become imperative to preserve the feeling of goodwill between peoples of different faiths. This goodwill will be sorely needed with the arrival of the corona pandemic to Syria on March 22, 2020. While numbers are reported to be 112500 there is no certainty since very little testing is being done. With hospital facilities badly battered and doctors grossly inadequate and unavailability of PPE, sanitizers and ventilators, the country is in a dire state. With economic loss at $200 million per day, currency under severe pressure, excessive corruption, crisis in Lebanon and the effect of the US Caesar Act, there is a shortage of assistance forthcoming. The conditions in the areas outside the government's control are worse. Syria's humanitarian catastrophe just became considerably worse. Sadly, the future course of Syria's tragedy is unlikely to be deflected from its path.

An International Yet Ideological War

The Syrian civil war, now in its tenth year, is a war with global implications since all the participants, particularly four of the five permanent members of the UN Security Council, are on the ground in Syria. They have subordinated the cardinal principles enshrined in the United Nations Charter to their vested interest. In mimicking history, Syria has once again provided the battleground for opposing interests to settle their quarrels, Israel and Hezbollah, Iran and Israel, the United States and Iran and the United States and Russia. Another dimension of the civil war is the 'hybrid religious war'—both on ideology and on the ground—taking place between Iran and Saudi Arabia. In bringing all the major world and regional powers on a common battlefield, Syria has become the *septic focus* that would end the international system established after the Second World War.

Refugees

Its immediate visible impact has been in rendering nearly eleven million Syrian homeless—half of the country's pre-war population—about six million within the country and five million refugees, majority in Turkey, Lebanon and Jordan. My interviews of Syrian refugees at the Zataari camp in Jordan have exposed the reasons they had to leave their country, yet at the same time, their unanimous desire to return. The humanitarian crisis that Syria faces only compares to that resulted from the Second World War. Since March 2011, more than 465,000 Syrians, including 55000 children, were killed in the fighting and over a million injured. Their succour, return and rehabilitation to their homes will require an equally extraordinary international effort as it has taken to destroy the country.

The Shape of Future Wars

The Syrian civil war suggests that we could see, in the future, a combination of intra-state and inter-state wars in the same time and space. Four major and continuing axes of conflict can be identified, first, of Turkey with the Kurdish-dominated Syrian Democratic Forces and its ally the Kurdish PKK. Second, between the Assad regime with its external allies—Russia, Iran and Hezbollah—versus Turkey with Turkish-supported radical opposition groups in Afrin and Idlib. Third, Israel supported by the United States versus Iran and Syria across the Golan Heights and finally, Turkey versus Syria in the putative Turkish corridor along their common border.

In Syria and Iraq, the war against the Islamic State is virtually over and the Caliphate has been largely defeated as a territorially anchored and jihadist entity. Nevertheless, the organization has gone back to its original missionary incarnation with an estimated 3000 fighters in the Syrian desert. It is the author's contention that the Islamic State represents an extreme idea in Islam, yet an idea nevertheless. It can only be marginalized through a wider dialogue, under the aegis of the Islamic Cooperation Organization, among the world's Islamic countries.

Turkish Invasion

Bashar Assad has won back about 90 percent of his country yet he still needs to settle the issues of Afrin and Idlib. While the Turkish invasion, in contravention of UN principle of non-interference, has given him a bonus in re-establishing his Army's presence in the Kurdish area of the country, he still needs to restore Syrian sovereignty in the proposed Turkish 'cordon sanitaire' on the Syrian side of their common border. The civil war has suddenly taken a new turn that could increase the indispensability of both Russia and Iran. In rebuilding the country, Bashar Assad will need to give up the idea of 'victor's justice', as seen in Iraq, and emphasize the values of secularism and inclusivity that make Syria unique in the Middle East.

Why Syria Matters

Syria's pivotal nature stems from its enduring history and its incomparable contribution to human civilization in nurturing three great religions—Judaism, Christianity and Islam. Its multiple dimensions have contributed to regional and international stability. Syria's view of itself rests on the fact that it lies astride the civilizational confluence of four cultures: Arab, Persian, Turkish and Hebrew. Its population between eighteen and twenty-three million is a mosaic of ethnically, culturally and religiously distinct communities. The secular culture that it has bred makes it unique in the Middle East. Still Islam, in its different interpretations, remains a legacy of the Syrian people. The need to juggle relationship of land, kinship and politics has greatly influenced the evolution of the country and its people. For this reason, the evolution of the long-running civil war into a largely sectarian conflict bodes ill for the long accepted ethos of tolerance in the country.

Yet the Syrian civil war is multidimensional including sectarian strife and socio-economic grievances. It is a class conflict between wealthy ruling elite and marginal communities mostly confined within the Sunni Arab community. The Syrian government found it expedient to incorporate to its side the non-Sunni ethno-sectarian groups such as the Christians, the Druze, Alawite and Kurds to assert that it would protect them from 'Islamists' and 'terrorists'. It thus made religious belief the primary identity marker posing the dilemma between maintaining sectarian diversity while preserving national unity.

The country's archaeological historicity is unmatched. *Ras Shamra*, or Ugarit on the Lattakia coast, has yielded evidence of uninterrupted human habitation over five millennia. Even more, the sites of these ancient sites, even today, provide the nucleus of living spaces for the people. Nothing illustrates this better than Damascus and Aleppo. The Omayyad Mosque, in the centre of old Damascus, has been hallowed ground, since two thousand years, for the three religions each having left discernable traces in its architecture. Syria has six world Heritage sites and thousands of others spread out all across the land. For this reason, the wanton destruction of these sites by the Islamic State was intended to negate traces of human civilization and deny Syria's ancient historicity to the adherents of the three major Western religions.

It is equally remarkable that this religious interaction facilitated the growth of multiple sects through a melding of ideas from different faiths and their mystical strands. Modern Syria remains a melting pot of many unique sects like the Alawites, Ismaili and Druze.

Bashar Assad Survives

Bashar Assad's survivability in the long-running civil war has been remarkable. Apart from the efficient state structure and non-politicized army bequeathed to him by Hafez Assad, Bashar's ability to outplay regional and international enemies has been a surprise. His success owes greatly to the exploitation of ethnic and sectarian fault lines, by supporting opposing stakeholders, in Lebanon, Iraq, Turkey and Palestine. His ability to divide his opponents on the diplomatic table and the battlefield has been remarkable. Syria had sixteen army coups since 1949 until Hafez Assad's championing of the Michel Aflaq inspired Arab Ba'ath Socialism provided the answer the people were seeking. The Ba'ath Socialist political culture has emphasized homogeneity as a high virtue making the state cardinal in politics, society and public life. While it weakened the growth of liberalism, it made the leader supreme in all decision-making. Hafez Assad created a system of divide and rule and personalized his power to the extent that he alone became the embodiment of the state. The state melded the Syrian identity as a blend of Arabism and elements of Islam.

In asserting his staying power, the state made constructive use of the glory of the past. Great prominence was given to the archaeological sites in Syria and to the upkeep of the museums in Damascus, Aleppoand Palmyra. The attempt was to portray modern day Syria as the heir to the *Bilad as Sham* even though certain parts of those historic lands were not under Syrian sovereignty. Syria's past was moulded into an Arab Islamic, and even more, a pre-Islamic and pre-Arab past, that made it the cradle of human civilization. It provided the historical ethos for the modern Syrian state.

Hafez Assad's lifelong interest was power. With ruthless determination and indefatigable negotiating ability, he was able to make his small country pivotal to the resolution of every challenge in the Middle East. He had orchestrated a smooth transfer of power to his second son Bashar Assad through his inner coterie, all of them Sunni. With Bashar, the Ba'ath Party became a far-reaching instrument of state control of the economy, politics and society. He had to adapt his foreign policy while maintaining the continuity of his father's policy. Although in 1991 Syria joined the

US Coalition against Saddam Hussein, he was unable to reap great dividends. The economic and political changes that he sought were to be at a 'Syrian' pace that in the end proved fruitless to a population expecting far more. The upsurge for democracy was not seen for what it was—a demand to introduce democratic change—making Bashar's attempt to introduce constitutional changes, in November 2011 and April 2012, too little too late.

Yet Bashar retained support from key elements of Syrian society, the army and intelligence services, and particularly the Alawites. Like the Alawites, other minorities and some middle and upper class Sunnis have continued to regard the Assad family as a bulwark of stability in the face of Islamic radicalism in the region. The Assad regime has survived for forty years by a combination of guile and cozying up to powerful countries like Russia and Iran.

The Arab Revolution

Syria was well placed to stand against the whirlwind of the Arab revolutions that in 2010 flowed out of Tunisia engulfing Egypt and threatening Bahrain. Already the high hopes for a free and democratic Arab world had spawned civil wars in Libya, Yemen and Iraq. Yet they led to rule by strongmen and made the Army the inevitable arbiter of the peoples' fate. Even monarchies were forced to make concessions and Tunisia, the cradle of the 'Arab Spring' remained its sole success.

It also saw the assertion of the power to intervene by the absolute rulers of the Gulf Arab states, particularly Qatar, UAE and Saudi Arabia. Bashar's resistance model in March 2011 was in keeping with the period of political confusion seen in the states afflicted by the Arab Spring. It was only by 2014 that the formalization of Syria's counter-revolution by its 'deep state' took place. By then Egypt had seen the assumption of power by Abdel Fattah al-Sisi, the return of the old guard, Nidaa Tounes Party, in Tunisia and the fragmentation of the Gulf Cooperation Council.

Thus, the Syrian case became unique with Bashar Assad staying the course overcoming relentless opposition from numerous radical Islamic groups, all supported by foreign powers. Syria dispelled the intoxicating sense of an Arab public coming together to confront its despotic leaders consolidating resistance by entrenched groups and interests. Nowhere is it better illustrated than by the effort of the Gulf States to avoid an Arab revolution seen from the Saudi action in Bahrain and that of other Gulf monarchies to fund opposition Sunni groups in the Syrian civil war. The barren decade saw a demographic explosion, continued ascendance of autocrats, the fall of tourism and the absence of opportunities for gaining knowledge and jobs reviving the Arab revolutions in 2019 in Algeria, Libya and Sudan. Once again, there is no surety that it will bring about a democratic polity in these countries.

The Syrian Civil War

The brutal reaction in March 2011 in Dara'a can be explained by the existence of a network of security agencies, part of the Syrian shadow state, each outbidding the other in an effort to show loyalty to the regime. Hafez Assad's shadow state has ensured that governance institutions were subordinated to the security agencies. With their disunity, and incompetence in holding terrain, the opposing Islamic groups were unable to shield local populations from regime forces nor protect them from the misbehaviour of their own cadres. The inability of the rebel groups to create effective alliances was the need to kowtow to the often antagonistic and variable priorities of their foreign sponsors.

Throughout the ten years of the civil war, the regime has asserted its sovereignty on the distribution of UN humanitarian assistance placing itself in a controlling position vis-à-vis the groups and areas where the assistance was destined. It created an institutional framework for international relief that ensured that such assistance was distributed at the regime's wish and not according to the UN's needs assessment. It established the regime's sovereignty internationally and staved off any possibility of an attack based on 'responsibility to protect'.

The Syrian civil war has given a new meaning to borderlands in defining the stream of people-to-people contact and relationships with Turkey, Iraq, Jordan, Israel and Lebanon. It has thus redefined the human geography of the country, disrupting former economic ties and networks, making control of the border a vital resource in the war. It has seen borderlands becoming places for the congregation of refugees, trade and economic activity and of humanitarian organizations and NGO's. It encouraged the growth of an illicit economy based on oil, antiquities, trade, people, chemicals and pharmaceuticals.

The civil war spawned eco-sectarianism by using identity politics to gain the exclusivity for exploiting natural resources, particularly oil, gas and water. The resulting high cost of wheat and failure to subsidize agriculture accounted for a good number of environmental refugees. These mostly Sunni refugees were largely responsible for the alienation of the Alawite dominated government. The latter's inability to respond to the changed environmental, economic and social realities was an important cause for the spread of the civil war.

Interestingly, an important reason for the longevity of the civil war was also the regime's proclivity to tamp down, or ramp up, hostilities in particular areas and checkpoints to meet its economic needs. The business side of the civil war not only ensured survivability of the regime but of the opposition groups as well. The regime was not above using variegated war tactics against different opposing groups depending on the level of cooperation that they received.

Chemical Weapon Use

A running theme in the civil war has been the use of chemical weapons even after the Syrian government had been fully disarmed, and by January 2016, its stockpiles completely destroyed by the OPCW. Nevertheless, the use of chemical weapons by both sides has continued. As of January 18, 2019 OPCW assessed 336 incidents of the use of chemical weapons, mostly chlorine gas. In winning back territory from the rebel groups, the Assad regime pursued a strategy of collective punishment against populations supporting or hosting insurgents. Its aim in using chemical weapons, in its battle tactics, was to spread fear. It also pursued systematic annihilation of administrative institutions and public services, like bread-making facilities and hospitals, to break rebel attempts to create rival performance of statehood.

In the absence of a negotiated settlement, the conflict will continue though the focus is increasingly shifting to the rebuilding of the country. Only then, can the refugees and displaced return. Apart from between $200 billion and $350 billion needed for rebuilding the physical infrastructure, a political process is needed to establish governance in line with UN Security Council Resolution 2254(2015). Although Bashar Assad has started on reconstruction in the recaptured areas, yet at the national level the process has the danger of becoming flawed. Enabling legislations to tax civilians to contribute towards reconstruction, Decree 66 that allows government to designate and sell to developers' areas for housing colonies, and demanding title deeds from returning refugees has cast a pall on the impartiality of the process. Assad's challenge remains delivering an inclusive redevelopment process to his people.

Contrary to other countries that faced popular uprisings, Bashar Assad and his inner circle have kept their lock on power and survived ten years of chaos. He appears more secure and confident than at any time since 2011. The government dominates in the country and controls all major cities and seventy per cent of the population. Its alliances with Russia and Iran are secure. The overall trend is manifest and Bashar Assad will have a say in any future political dispensation in the country. International opinion has also veered round to accepting that a strong Assad-led Syria might be a reliable yet useful nuisance as it holds the keys to current challenges in the Middle East.

Assad's former foes, having failed to severe Damascus' link with Iran through military pressure, have changed tactics by building economic linkages of their own to prevent Syria completely falling in the Iranian basket. The US, Britain and Israel are no longer averse to Bashar Assad continuing in power. With the Western nations deprioritizing Assad's removal the need is for an agreed formula for governance incorporating a time frame for Bashar Assad to hand over power to a democratically elected government.

Foreign Interference

Throughout the eight years of the civil war and multiplying foreign participation, majority of the Syrian people, particularly the minorities have reposed confidence that Bashar Assad as the better alternative when compared to the numerous radical Islamic groups. The refugees in the camps in Jordan, Lebanon and Turkey want to return to a Syria free from foreign interference. The foreign countries actively involved are France, Iran, Qatar, Russia, Saudi Arabia, Turkey, United Kingdom and United States. Of these only Russia and Iran are at the invitation of the Syrian government. All others are in contravention of the fundamental UN principles of non-interference and preservation of national sovereignty. Further, neither do these countries have a common goal in Syria nor are they like-minded on the region's future.

Syria's Allies

Iran sees Syria as its fulcrum for influence in the Arab world especially after its close relations with the Iraqi government. Although one is an avowed secular regime and the other a theocratic state, they have been allies since the 1979 Iranian revolution. Since 2013 Iran's military intervention in Syria has grown manifold. It has allows Bashar Assad to survive the long civil war. Like Bashar, Iran has also avowed the civil war as a fight against terrorism. Iran's presence also meant that of the Lebanese Hezbollah who have joined the battle. In every sense, this is quid pro quo for Syrian assistance in providing a conduit for the flow of Iranian arms and munitions to the Hezbollah in Lebanon. Iran's goals are the preservation of this route and possibly establishing a permanent military presence on the Israeli border on the Golan. Israel has drawn a red line on any Iranian attempt to change the status quo on its border and continued aerial attacks on Iranian sites within Syria. In another dimension of the sectarian war underlying the Syrian civil war, Iran has together with Russia and Turkey marginalized both the Western and Gulf powers in the conflict.

Building on the Iranian presence, **Russia** entered the civil war in 2015 emboldened by the slack in United States and Western presence. Its goals have been to shore up its long-standing ally in Syria, to project its regional role in the Middle East and to divert attention from its forays in Crimea and Ukraine. Once again, in accepting the opposing groups as terrorists, Putin drew a parallel with the situation in Chechnya. Russia's discomfort in the use by the UN Security Council of R2P in the Libyan case was reflected in its vetoes to ensure against a repetition in the Syrian case. Thus, Russia gave Syria its support both in the UNSC and on the ground. In so doing, Russia sent a message of support to other countries going through the Arab revolutions. Russia's interventions altered the course of the civil war in Bashar Assad's favour, helped it to consolidate its only naval base on the Mediterranean at Tartous and build an air base at Hmeimim with sophisticated weaponry to deter US Prompt Global Strike (PGS) capability. Russia has also taken steps to lend its weight to the Syrian President in raising international finance for rebuilding the country. As a the initiator of the Astana process on building peace, Russia's presence has assured Bashar Assad, helped to rein in Iran, brake Turkey's pursuit of its Syrian goals vis-à-vis the Kurdish group PKK, and control

Israel's aerial forays into Syria. Russia has kept open channels to all the powers involved in the Syrian conflict.

Syria's Regional Foes

Recep Tayyip Erdogan sees **Turkey's** intervention as a revival of a neo-Ottoman sentiment articulating Turkey's intent to keep a hand in Syrian affairs following the civil war. Turkey has received advantages from its membership of the Astana peace process. It has enabled Turkey's 'territorial creep' in Syria at Afrin and Idlib. Its military invasion of Syria to create a *cordon sanitaire* within Syria is in blatant disregard for any UN principle including self-defence. Turkey aims to distance the Kurdish group, YPG and particularly its component, the PKK. It also aims to resettle at least 2 million Syria refugees, of the 3.2 million presently in Turkey, in its proposed buffer zone unmindful of fuelling new tensions. Turkey's pleadings with the United States got Erdogan an agreement to address Turkey's security concerns making the withdrawal of US troops from northeastern Syria an invitation for Turkey to invade. Turkey, Qatar and Saudi Arabia have been the leading regional states seeking overthrow of Assad. All three have seen the Syrian civil war as a key arena for their regional ambitions, yet all three needed the now withdrawn US involvement.

Saudi Arabia-Syria relations have fluctuated at the best of times. The intention to divert regional attention from the frailty of its own regime, in the face of Arab revolutions, has always been uppermost in Saudi calculations. It led to Saudi involvement in the Syrian civil war in support of radical Islamic groups, including the Islamic State. Yet during Hafez Assad's time, the relations were at a good level even though the fact that a Shia sect ruled over a majority Sunni population always rankled. The alliance between Syria and Iran, anathema to the Saudi king, deepened their rivalry. The implication of Bashar Assad in the killing Saudi protégé, Lebanese premier Rafik Hariri, made for an unbridgeable gap. The final straw was the Alawi domination over the Sunni majority spurring extreme Saudi animosity towards Syria. They saw the civil war as a battle that was domestic, between the Syrian Sunni and Shia, and regional, with the Gulf States fear of being overwhelmed by spreading Shia salience stretching from Iraq to Syria and Lebanon.

Interestingly, **Qatar's** involvement in the Syrian civil warin was provoked by the Qatari Emir Hamad's desire to secure his legacy.

Although once a close friend of the Assad family, Qatar responded to a political opportunity in Syria becoming a major source of external funding for the radical Islamic groups. Its financial muscle became a major source of its influence on these groups. Yet what it did not count on was the fickle loyalties of these groups that defeated its purpose of becoming the king-maker in the civil war. At the same time, Qatari funding of Sunni Islamic groups in Syria, were seen by Saudi Arabia and UAE as undermining their domestic stability and regional position. The resulting diplomatic tension led in 2017 to a continuing blockade of Qatar by Bahrain, Egypt, UAE and Saudi Arabia. With its vast oil and gas reserves, Qatar has emerged a winner with help from Iran and Turkey. Its hosting of a major US military base also got it acceptance from President Trump. It has continued to maintain good relations with both the United States and Russia as well.

During the ten years of the civil war, presidents Barak Obama and Donald Trump decided **US** strategy and military presence in Syria. Under neither president has the United States taken a leading role given the public fatigue after two long wars in Iraq and Afghanistan. Neither considered that the Syrian civil war directly endangered America's national security. While Obama had a keen sense of the limits of American power and rejected moralizing interventionism, Trump's outlook is that the Middle East's problems, including Syria, were not for America to fix and the fate of the region lies in the hands of its own people. The only issue on which both were united was the need to combat the use of chemical weapons. While Obama failed to act against his own 'red line', Trump executed two strikes against the Assad regime for using these weapons. While the war aim of defeating the Islamic state was common to both, Trump declared defeat of the entity in signalling a withdrawal from Syria. He gave up his earlier war aim of staying in Syria until Iran retreated. His preference to extricate America from the Syrian quagmire is manifest, yet his abandoning the Syrian Kurds YPG in the face of the Turkish invasion has come in for bipartisan opposition in US Congress. His vacillation on whether to reposition US troops has made for a fickle Middle East policy in contrast to strong support shown by earlier US presidents. In general, the United States' main interests in Syria have been advanced—weakening of the ISIS and reduction of use of chemical weapons by Bashar Assad. The United States, working with Russia and the UNSC P-5, must address the issue of providing Syrians humanitarian assistance and funding to rebuild the destroyed country. Their role in designing an acceptable political settlement in accordance with UN Security Council Resolution 2254(2015) will be crucial.

The **United Kingdom** has historically considered the Middle East as a region of its vital interest. Its policy has aimed at preserving stability and access to the region's resources. The refugee crisis building up on EU's borders and Russia's support to the Assad regime and ISIS-inspired terror attacks in London provided the *raison d'etre* for British involvement in the civil war. Britain also took a hard line against the use of chemical weapons by the Assad regime. It involved its air force in air attacks on Syria's chemical facilities and funding of so-called moderate opposition groups. At the same time, its open policy on Syria emphasized provision of humanitarian aid to the refugees and helping to end the civil war.

France's interventionist policy on Syria was to reinforce its self-perception as a great power and to provide an alternative to US policy. It also aimed to use its Syria policy to garner enhanced security cooperation with the Sunni Arab states and consolidate those markets for its armaments. The ISIS-inspired terrorist attacks in Paris provided additional reason for French involvement. French involvement included aerial attacks on ISIS locations and sending of covert agents to support selected opposing Islamic groups. It also insisted that only Assad's departure would enable military cooperation between France, Russia and Iran. At the same time, even France under presidents Hollandeand Macron gave up the goal of regime change in Syria. France has floated an 'International Partnership against Impunity for Use of Chemical Weapons'. It has announced substantial funding during 2018–2020 of over Euro One billion for emergency humanitarian assistance for Syria. France supports the establishment of an agreed political framework to end the Syrian civil war in terms of UNSC Resolution 2254(2015).

Each of the eight powers enmeshed in the Syrian civil war have pursued their own agenda, or that of their proxies, unmindful of the terrible tragedy they have forced on the Syrian people. This has resulted in the inability to secure even a lasting ceasefire. Yet the future of the country and its well-being depends on the powers involved there even more than on Bashar Assad. Now that Bashar Assad has won back most of his country, will they start the carnage again or work jointly to alleviate the suffering of the Syrian people and rebuilding the country?

The UN Security Council has worked through multiple and parallel fora in Geneva, Vienna and Astana has unanimously approved UNSC

Resolution 2254(2015) that provides a blueprint for a settlement. It lays down principles for a settlement based on a close linkage between a ceasefire and a parallel political process emphasizing a Syrian-led and Syrian-owned political transition. It calls for a credible, inclusive and non-sectarian governance based on a new constitution and open and free elections. It suggests the need for confidence-building measures to re-establish trust and accountability, ceasefire monitoring and prevention of terrorist acts by ISIS and related groups. The need to create conditions for safe return of the refugees and internally displaced by allowing a safe flow of humanitarian assistance throughout the country and cessation of attacks against hospitals and other public facilities.

A study of the long and tortuous negotiations on UNSC Resolution 2254(2015) from 2012 between parties with multiple interests has demonstrated that although agreement on particular issues was difficult at the best of times, yet it was productive when this transpired. The negotiations centred around writing a new constitution that guaranteed Syrian sovereignty and territorial integrity, the elements of a lasting ceasefire, humanitarian assistance, supervision forces and related issues, release of detainees and the missing, use of chemical weapons, terrorism, refugee return and facilities, the Syrian opposition and the future of Bashar Assad.

The political process in Syria anchored in UNSC Resolution 2254(2015) was pursued on multiple tracks contiguously coterminous with the long and increasingly complex civil war. It starkly differs from similar processes in Afghanistan and Iraq both marked by the absence of a unanimous UNSC Resolution and by primacy of the United States. Another contrast is that in Syria Bashar Assad is still in place whereas in Iraq and Afghanistan there have been multiple leaders dictated by tribal and religious linkages.

In Iraq, the majority Shia, while asserting their numerical superiority and political primacy have in place the accoutrements of democracy yet have undermined the minority Sunni, in a payback for their domination, for four decades, under Saddam Hussein—their version of 'victors' justice'. In Afghanistan, the evolution of the political process, over eighteen years of the war has primarily been in US hands with growing marginalization of the 'elected' government in the discussions on United States' exit with the Taliban.

A post-war scenario in Syria will require near simultaneous steps towards de-escalation including ushering an enduring ceasefire, return of the refugees and the internally displaced, rebuilding of hospitals, roads, schools, housing, conservancy services and water supply. It will also require deciding on a political structure for the country, rejuvenation of agriculture and industry and ensuring internal peacekeeping. A durable peace will only be possible when the four UNSC permanent members have no further interest in sponsoring various anti-Assad groups. In this respect, Russia can play a major role in culling out a minimum acceptable agreement aimed at promoting a durable ceasefire. A possible precedent can be the 1960 'Treaty of Guarantee on Cyprus' with Cyprus, Greece, United Kingdom and Turkey as guarantors. The same formula could be considered with all P-5 as guarantors of a peace and constitutional agreement on Syria.

The sectarian dimension makes it more difficult to secure the interest of regional powers—Iran, Turkey, Saudi Arabia and UAE—in a durable ceasefire. A solution may rest with the new constitution acknowledging, with guarantees from the major powers, the primacy of the Sunni majority. Similarly, despite the Assad regime having an agreement with the Kurdish groups in fighting the Turkish Army, a constitutional guarantee for their autonomy will be essential to secure their cooperation.

At the same time, the pervasive animosity between the majority Sunni and the minorities needs to be defused. The time has come for the Organization of Islamic Cooperation (OIC) to take a hand in ending the Syrian conflict. Given its sectarian underpinning, the OIC remains the only organization to tackle the roots of the internecine sectarian struggle within Islam and bring about an understanding within the Islamic fold.

The need to secure adequate resources for creating conditions for the return of the refugees and displaced will require a UNSC-sponsored bargain between the length of Bashar Assad's tenure beyond 2024 and imperative need to provide needed resources and the modalities for reconstructing the country.

The drafting of a new constitution will be based, inter alia, on the following guidelines:

1. The basic documents for reference will include the Syrian constitutions of 1950 & 2012, the Egyptian constitution of 2014 and the Turkish constitution of 1982;
2. Acceptance of Syrian Sunni as the majority community;
3. A multi-party system, including the Arab Ba'ath Socialist Party, avoiding de-Ba'athification;

4. Consociational democracy that would allow passions to cool before a more broad-based system is established;
5. General elections based on a proportional system like in Turkey prescribing a minimum percentage of votes for representation in parliament;
6. A prime ministerial system with limited powers for the president including inability to declare a national emergency;
7. Secularism as the organizing principle of the state with a division between the religious and political authority;
8. Reform of the legal system;
9. Constitutional guarantees for all minorities both Islamic and non-Islamic and recognition of the special status for the Alawites;
10. Guaranteed accountability and legal redress for all communities;
11. Catering to the security concerns of the people;
12. Confidence-building measures like location of detainees and missing and unhindered right of citizenship and return;
13. Reform of the police and intelligence services;

The constitutional negotiations will crucially depend on the dilemma of creating a political set-up that eventually sees the exit of Bashar Assad.

Much still hinges on the military dimension of the conflict with Turkey's invasion to create a buffer zone on the Syrian side of the border. With the Syrian Army joining the Kurdish YPG in this the confrontation would be long. The Russian troops are enforcing an agreement reached on October 22, 2019 under which Russian and Syrian border guards will remove the YPG from 30 kms (19 miles) from the Turkish border. From October 30, 2019, Russian and Turkish forces will patrol a narrower strip of land in the 'safe zone' that Ankara has long sought in northeast Syria. Turkey has secured its long-term demand by leveraging its strength with the United States and Russia. Bashar Assad visiting the front in Idlibhas called Erdogan 'a thief … now stealing our land' although Turkey is holding covert contacts with Damascus, partly via Russia, despite public hostility.

In the end, Syria's fate is no longer for Syria alone to decide. It will depend on the regional and international powers that have intervened. At the same time, with near control of the country's entire territory, Bashar Assad's government speaks like a victor. There is little incentive to change the systems that have served a useful purpose during the civil war.

Both Bashar Assad and Syria are caught in a double-edged dilemma. Only changes in the political, economic and social organization of the country, howsoever incremental, will assure that the civil war does not re-ignite, yet the very fact of these changes would reduce the longevity of the Assad regime. At the end of military operations by all parties, over almost a decade, a situation in which Assad remains in power, with restrictions on his presidential autonomy, will foster a process towards making Syria a more open and democratic state and preserving its system of secular government.

Mumbai
January 2020

Rajendra Abhyankar

Contents

CHAPTER 1

The Unending Syrian Conflict: Internal Fall-Out and External Impact

'The current situation led to a desperate feeling of no hope for the future', said Adel Toukan and his wife when I interviewed them on June 29, 2017 at the Zaatari camp in north Jordan, ten kilometres east of Mafraq, almost at the tri-junction between Syria, Jordan and Iraq. His wife added, 'if not the Syrian army, then one of the militant groups would have taken him away. If that happened, I was scared of rape! The country-side is extremely unsafe!'.

The camp, set up in 2012, has gradually evolved into a township, housing nearly 80,000 refugees, in this inhospitable area.[1] Adel and his wife fled with two little children from the Da'raa region in south-west Syria, where the anti-Assad rebellion, initially peaceful, started on March 15, 2011. They have spent four years in the camp already and have added two more children.

A family of four, comprising the *pater familias*, his wife, and two young adult sons echoed Adel's sentiment. They had fled from the Ghouta area near Damascus, when the father witnessed a third son killed by an aerial bomb. They sold their share of rich family agricultural land and left. They run a grocery shop in the camp and intend to do so until they can return. Over the years, they have brought appliances that help them to stock ice cream and other refrigerated goods. Rather unexpectedly, all

[1] Editors, 'Zaatari Refugee Camp- Factsheet- September 2019', reliefweb, September 30, 2019, https://reliefweb.int/report/jordan/zaatari-refugee-camp-factsheet-september-2019.

R. M. Abhyankar, *Syria*,
https://doi.org/10.1007/978-981-15-4562-7_1

of them with one voice said they would return home when conditions allowed the Syrian government to take charge of their future! None of them wanted to migrate to a third country. The old man was clear that outsiders must stop interfering in their country. 'For the time being we suffer the "unknown" state which prevails, nothing is certain in the political situation. Till Syria's days of crisis are resolved we live day-to-day' said the head of the family.[2,3] They refused to give their names fearful of the long reach of the Syrian government.

The Zaatari camp, on a barren sandy stretch is a township of small homes constructed of tin with thermocol sheets reinforcing the roofing. Some families have been in the camp ever since its inception. According to the Jordanian camp commandant, apart from those in the camp, Jordan had more than a million refugees outside, majority in Amman. Similarly during the Iraq war, a neighbourhood of Amman was conurbated by Iraqis, mostly well to do, who have become a permanent part of the city. No doubt, a good number of Syrian refugees will stay on even after a resolution in Syria. The UN High Commissioner (UNHCR) has done yeoman service in provisioning the camp and providing food, medical services and free electricity. The last has been a major draw in keeping the refugees within the camp and enabling them to pursue some trades. Echoing the sentiment of the refugee families, the Camp Commandant was hopeful that one day, at least those in the camps would return home.

As it enters the tenth year, there is no sign of an end to the continuing conflict in Syria. Its most visible impact is the huge refugee flow; the accompanying humanitarian crisis is comparable with that caused by the Second World War. Since March 2011, more than 465,000 Syrians, including 55,000 children, were killed in the fighting and over a million injured; over 12 million—half the country's pre-war population—are displaced[4] of whom almost 5 million are refugees in Jordan, Turkey and Lebanon. As the civil war has continued Turkey has used the situation to seek geopolitical advantage by seeking to control of the Syrian province of Idlib as a buffer often offering the spurious reason of wanting to settle the refugees there.

[2] Zataari Refugee Camp interviews by the author translated by Ms. Sameera al-Husseini, June 29, 2017, No. 1 of 2.

[3] Zataari Refugee Camp interviews by the author translated by Ms. Sameera al-Husseini, June 29, 2017, No. 2 of 2.

[4] Ibid. Alia Chughtai.

Syria in History

Traces of human civilization since the seventh millennium BC at Ugarit (1800 BCE–1300 BCE),[5] six miles north of Lattakia (then Latonia), on the Mediterranean coast, have yielded rich archaeological finds which attest to uninterrupted human habitation. Since millennia, 'Syria was always an enigma: being variously described as 'mysterious', 'puzzling' or 'strange' reflecting the many facets it has presented to the world. Starting with the Chaldeans, going through the Egyptian and Persian dynasties, with Macedonia and the emperors of Greece and Rome, and the European emperors, Syria has historically provided the ground for intellectual ferment and unending conflict that shaped the region.

Its geographical position coupled with Syria's history of nurturing three world religions, Judaism, Christianity and Islam, has endowed the country with a unique place in the march of human civilization. It sits at the civilizational confluence of four cultures: Arab, Persian, Turkish and Hebrew. The links of ethnicity, family and tribe, forged over generations, have continued to play an important role in the evolution of the country and its people. They provide the historic roots of tensions that have led to recent developments.

True to its history, Syria, once again, has provided a battleground for competing ideas and beliefs. 'Some countries seem destined from their origin to become the battlefields of contending nations which envision them. Into such regions, and to their cost, neighbouring peoples come from century to century to settle their quarrels and bring to an issue the question of supremacy which disturbs their little corner of the earth'.[6]

Throughout history, notwithstanding its relatively small size,[7] Syria, with its multifaceted character, became pivotal in influencing the direction of the region. Historically Syria has been the trigger, and the base, for forces determined to upset or destroy the existing order. It has held true from the Crusades coming down to the Islamic State(ISIL) which

[5] Heilbrunn, 'Timelines of History: Ugarit', The Met Museum, New York, https://www.metmuseum.org/toah/hd/ugar/hd_ugar.htm.

[6] G. Maspero, 'The Struggle of Nations: Egypt, Syria and Assyria', published by Society for Promoting Christian Knowledge, Northumberland Avenue, London (1896), Chapter 1, https://archive.org/stream/struggleofnations00maspuft/struggleofnations00maspuoft_djvu.txt.

[7] https://www.britannica.com/place/Syria.

launched a Jihad against its opponents, both Muslim and non-Muslim. Syria's neighbours—Jordan, Iraq, Turkey, Lebanon and Israel—continue to experience internal strife linked with the Syrian situation. It is beginning to resemble the nearly 16-year long civil war in Lebanon that had reverse effects in Syria, eventually degenerating into everyone fighting everyone else.

The consequent effects of the ongoing Syrian insurgency have radiated religious, societal and governmental instability in a devastating impact on all its neighbours, the region and on international peace and security. It reinforces the contention that Syria remains a 'pivotal' regional state.

A Pivotal State

Historically, Halford Mackinder saw a 'pivotal state' through an imperialist lens in his Heartland theory.[8] It was incumbent to control such a country in order to dominate a region.[9] During the Cold War, United States most often applied the epithet of a 'pivotal state' to countries susceptible to communism. In this definition, uppermost was the ability of a particular state to swing a country, and hence, a region, towards collapse leading to trans-border mayhem: migration, communal violence, pollution, disease and economic degradation.

While population and size are important determinants of the 'pivotal' nature of a state, they are not the only factors that determine its character. It is a function of the inward and outward linkages embedded in its national DNA. It comprises a mix of size, population, ethnic and religious diversity, linguistic affinity, economic strength and vitality, social structure and political organization. The proportions in which these various elements exercise their influence vary. Rather what is crucial is the potential impact of the interplay of these elements on a country's

[8] Francis P.Sempa, 'Halford Mackinder's Last View of the Round World', *The Diplomat*, March 23, 2015, https://thediplomat.com/2015/03/halford-mackinders-last-view-of-the-round-world/.

[9] Magaret Scott & Westenley Alcenat, 'The Geopolitical Paradigm of Halford Mackinder's "Heartland Theory," States That the Power That Controls Central Asia-the Great Pivot-Would Eventually Emerge as the Most Powerful State in International Politics', Revisiting the Pivot: The influence of Heartland Theory in Great Power Politics, www.creighton.edu/fileadmin/user/CCAS/departments/PoliticalScience/MVJ/docs/The_Pivot_-_Alcenat_and_Scott.pdf.

national temper.[10] Syria's mix of minorities, and its credo of a secular ethos inspired by the Arab Baath Socialist Party,[11] has made it unique in a region that has moved towards an Islamic character in its political organization.

Syria—together with Jordan—represents the modern-day Levantine crossroads that link Europe with Iraq/Iran, the Gulf and Northern Africa. Thus, control over Syria gives the ability to secure political advantage through control over the flow of goods, people and activities between several (sub) continents. Rule over Syria also provides the power to expand or reduce the Kurdish and the Palestinian conflicts through sanctuary, material support and diplomacy, to exercise significant influence on Lebanon until the Israeli—Lebanese conflict remains unresolved.

Syria's current situation is due to both internal and external pivots: internally, the most important factor has been the continuous contestation within Islam that has exposed hitherto latent sectarian divisions; and those between the Islamic and non-Islamic population of the country. With two-thirds of the population being Sunni Arab, the resurgence of an aggressive stand by them, against the long surviving Alawi-dominated power structure, was inevitable. More so, in the context of a similar transformation in political power, that took place in Iraq, in favour of the long-oppressed majority Shia. The authoritarian power structure ensured that a militant struggle would be the only way to provoke change.

Like this antique land, Syria's cities carry an enormous weight of human experience. Damascus, the longest continuously inhabited city in the world, has become an epitome of human tolerance. Nothing illustrates this better than the Umayyad Mosque[12] that for over two millennia has been hallowed ground for three religions, Judaism, Christianity and Islam. It has bred a culture that has welcomed minorities of every hue

[10] Robert Chase, Emily Hill & Paul Kennedy, 'Pivotal States and US Strategy', Foreign Affairs, January–February 1996, http://www.foreignaffairs.com/articles/Algeria/1996.01.01/.

[11] Paul Berman, 'Ba'athism: An Obituary', *The New Republic*, September 14, 2020, https://newrepublic.com/article/107238/baathism-obituary.

[12] Annie Lebatt, 'Great Mosque of Damascus', Metropolitan Museum, New York, May 9, 2012, https://www.metmuseum.org/exhibitions/listings/2012/byzantium-and-islam/blog/where-in-the-world/posts/damascus.

including Islamic minorities like the Yezidis,[13] Druze,[14] and Alawi,[15] and non-Islamic minorities like the Assyrian Christians, the Catholics and others to survive for generations peacefully and in a harmonious manner. Effectively Syria has been governed as a coalition of minorities with the Alawites, seen as a sect of the Shia, controlling the major levers of power including the command structure of the Ba'ath Party set up in a *coup d'etat* in 1963. It is in direct contrast to the stricter Islamic societies that have characterized the Arab and Islamic world.

The concept of a pivotal state gained further meaning in the twenty-first century. A pivotal state has a foreign policy independent from regional power centres because of globalization and the global world order. If successful, such a state can pave the way for a new understanding of global politics, particularly in a scenario of current world 'disorder' when the rules set after the Second World War are in a churn. A new international order is in the making and states like Syria,[16] located at the seam of the international system, become crucial to its security and stability.[17]

Syria's trajectory since March 2011, dominated by armed Islamic insurgency, supported by every major and regional power, has made it the pivot of the emerging international order. The Syrian insurgency continues to engage the world's capabilities and capacities while exposing its susceptibility to spreading the virus of intolerant, anti-pluralistic and violent tendencies far beyond its borders. These reactive tendencies found a fertile ground among Arab autocracies seeking to assure their survival in

[13] Yasmin Hafiz, 'Yazidi Religious Belief: History, Facts and Traditions of Iraq's Persecuted Minority', Huffpost, US, August 14, 2014, https://www.huffingtonpost.in/entry/yazidi-religious-beliefs_n_5671903?ri18n=true.

[14] Encyclopaedia Britannica, 'Druze, Religious Sect', February 13, 2020, https://www.britannica.com/topic/Druze.

[15] Devin Trivedi, 'Primer on the Alawites in Syria', Foreign Policy Research Institute, December 1, 2016, https://www.fpri.org/article/2016/12/primer-alawites-syria/.

[16] Mehmet Ozkan, 'A New Approach to Global Security: Pivotal Middle Powers and Global Polities', 2012, http://sam.gov.tr/wp-content/uploads/2012/02/Mehmet Ozkan1.pdf.

[17] Tim Sweijs, Willem Theo Oosterveld, Emily Knowles & Meno Schellekens, 'Why Are Pivotal States so pivotal? The Role of Pivotal States in Regional and Global Security', The Hague Centre for Strategic Studies, The Hague, Netherlands, 2014, https://hess.nl/sites/default/files/reports/Why_are_Pivotal_States_so_pivotal_The_Role_of_Pivot_States_in_Regional_and_Global_Security_C.pdf.

the face of the Arab popular revolutions. It frustrated the popular hopes and energies invested in the Arab revolutions that began from Tunisia.

The internecine revolution in the Arab world starting in December 2010, the misnamed Arab Spring,[18] was a wave of initially nonviolent, and later violent, demonstrations, protests, riots, coups and civil wars in North Africa, West Asia and the Gulf. The initial heat of the protests saw the overthrow of long-standing dictators, Tunisian President Zine El Abedine Ben Ali in January 2011[19] and Egyptian President Muhammad Hosni El Sayed Mubarak[20] in February 2011. It reached Syria, in March 2011 in Der'aa,[21] where the popular protests provoked a brutal and violent reaction.

The effect of the Tunisian Revolution starting on December 17, 2010 radiated to Libya, Egypt, Yemen, Syria and Iraq where either the regime was toppled or major uprisings or social violence occurred, including civil wars or insurgencies. Sustained street demonstrations took place in Morocco, Bahrain, Algeria, Iran, Lebanon, Jordan, Oman and Sudan. Minor protests occurred in Djibouti, Mauritania, the Palestinian National Authority, Saudi Arabia, Somalia and the Moroccan-controlled Western Sahara.

The wave of initial revolutions and protests to bring down the autocratic rulers in an assertion of 'people's power' had faded by mid-2012. The dislodging of long-standing dictators resulted in power vacuums that were seized by the regime forces or well-organized Islamic groups like the Muslim Brotherhood. Early hopes that these popular movements would end corruption, increase political participation and bring about greater economic equity foundered on the absence of leadership, an agreed agenda and direction for political change.

[18] Amanda Taub, ' The Unsexy Truth about Why the Arab Spring failed', Vox, February 27, 2016, https://www.vox.com/2016/1/27/10845114/arab-spring-failure.

[19] Editors, 'Zain al-Abidine Ben Ali, Tunisian Dictator president 1936–2019, *Financial Times*, September 20, 2019, https://www.ft.com/content/1411c86e-daf6-11e9-8f9b-77216ebe1f17.

[20] Natasha Turak, 'Ousted Egyptian President Hosni Mubarak Dies at 91', CNBC, February 25, 2020, https://www.cnbc.com/2020/02/25/egypts-ousted-president-hosni-mubarak-dies-state-tv-says.html.

[21] Joe Sterling, 'Dara'a: The Spark That Lit the Syrian Flame,' CNN, March 1, 2012, http://www.cnn.com/2012/03/01/world/meast/syria-crisis-beginnings/index.html.

Counter-revolutionary action by the 'deep state' in Egypt; by the Saudi-led Gulf Cooperation Council's military interventions in Bahrain and Yemen; and the terrible results of UN Security Council approved Western air attack in Libya created a fertile ground for hard counter-action by the Assad government in Syria. The contentious battle across the Arab world, between a mobilized people and recalcitrant regimes to assert and consolidate the power of a democratic polity, remained still-born. In many countries, like Syria, it went into an active yet quietest phase.

Only uprisings in Tunisia and Libya, and the near uprising in Morocco, resulted in transition to constitutional democratic governance with Islam at its centre. Yet in Libya,[22] the transition was unstable and saw dual authorities. Since March 2016 conflict between two rival governments, the Libyan House of Representatives and the General National Congress allied to the Government of National Accord has politically divided the country. The reaction by entrenched forces to these popular uprisings has varied depending on the motivation of the ruling powers.

In Morocco and Jordan, heightened perception by the monarch allowed elections leading to government by Islamic parties. In Egypt, despite the Muslim Brotherhood winning the first-ever free and fair elections, their haste to consolidate a stricter Islamic government led President Mohammad Mursi to jail where he died of heart attack in June 2019. By popular demand, once again, the army became, and remains, the arbiter of last resort.[23]

Both Saudi Arabia and Qatar, despite the former's boycott and unacceptable conditions to the latter, have continued to fund and arm radical Islamic groups fighting against the Assad dispensation, making Syria the battleground for a proxy sectarian war with Iran. At the same time,

[22] Editors, 'Libyan Government of National Accord Announces Moving from Defence to Attack Against Haftar's Forces', Middle East Monitor, March 4, 2020, https://www.cnbc.com/2020/02/25/egypts-ousted-president-hosni-mubarak-dies-state-tv-says.html.

[23] Peter Hessler, 'Egypt's Failed Revolution', *The New Yorker*, January 2, 2017, https://www.newyorker.com/magazine/2017/01/02/egypts-failed-revolution.

Saudi Arabia's unsuccessful role in the Yemen civil war[24,25] and its attack on the *Houthis*, or officially, *Ansar Allah*,[26] have created another massive humanitarian crisis putting the international spotlight on the Saudi kingdom itself.

Roots of the Syrian Civil War

The Syrian government's reaction to the initially spontaneous and peaceful uprising was an extreme use of state power. The brutal use of force in Dar'aa by the Syrian police and Army, sparked on March 15, 2011, the 'day of rage'. During the nine years since, the unending spiral of violence encompassed the country. The epithet used by Warren Christopher, former US Secretary of State for the 1990 Bosnian Civil War in describing it as 'a problem from Hell' equally applies to the Syrian Civil War.[27]

Its effects—national, regional and global—exposed the frailty of political will, the triumph of national and partisan concerns and disunity within the UN Security Council, coupled with the apathy of the international community to provide the massive humanitarian relief needed by the millions displaced within Syria, or rendered refugees. Syria, and its population, has become the septic focus for a proxy sectarian war endlessly playing out in the backdrop of a revived Cold War between Russia and the United States and its Western allies.

The Syrian economy is limping and its agriculture has been devastated. Within Syria, 95% of people lack adequate healthcare, and 70%

[24] Kathleen Schuster, 'Yemen's War Explained in 4 Key Points', DW, August 11, 2017, http://www.dw.com/en/yemens-war-explained-in-4-key-points/a-40056866.

[25] Sudarsan Raghavan, 'Six Reasons the Crisis in Yemen's South matters', *The Washington Post*, August 31, 2019, https://www.washingtonpost.com/world/six-reasons-the-crisis-in-yemens-south-matters/2019/08/30/f6ab0e22-ca7c-11e9-8067-196d9f17af68_story.html.

[26] Bethan McKernan, 'Who Are the Houthis and Why Are They Fighting the Saudi Coalition in Yemen?', *The Guardian*, November 21, 2018, https://www.theguardian.com/world/2018/nov/21/who-are-the-houthis-fighting-the-saudi-led-coalition-in-yemen.

[27] Bart Barnes, 'Former Secretary of State Warren Christopher, Who Negotiated Settlement to the Iran Hostage Crisis Dies at 85,' *The Washington Post*, March 19, 2011, https://www.washingtonpost.com/local/obituaries/former-secretary-of-state-warren-christopher-dies-at-85/2010/09/21/ABCPk6t_story.html?utm_term=.12b85267cbe1.

lack regular access to clean water. Half the children are out of school. The economy is shattered, and 80% of the population lives in poverty. In 2016, from an estimated pre-war population of 22 million, the UNHCR has identified 12.8 million Syrians requiring humanitarian assistance, of whom more than 6.1 million displaced internally and about 6.7 million are refugees outside of Syria.[28] Tragically, humanitarian assistance has become a negotiating counter in the ongoing civil war making it impossible to reach, in a sustained manner, the millions affected.

The ongoing conflict has had active military participation of four UNSC permanent members, US, UK, Russia and France and regional players, Israel, Iran, Jordan, Qatar, Saudi Arabia, Turkey, UAE and the Hezbollah, on either side of the conflict. It has defeated all efforts within, or linked to, the United Nations Security Council. The proxy sectarian war, between the Sunni and Shi'a that lies behind the conflict, makes it imperative to address a renewed understanding within Islam in parallel with ceasefire and peace. The breakdown of this understanding had led to the rise of the Islamic State of Iraq and the Levant (ISIL)[29] or its Arabic version, *Daesh*, on the embers of the militancy during the US occupation of Iraq. Its potential for disruption and terrorism beyond the region, particularly in Europe, will continue despite ISIL's virtual eviction from both Iraq and Syria although 6000 to 10,000 ISIS militants remain in Syria and Iraq.[30]

Consequences of the Civil War

Bereft a UN Security Council mandate, international military participation in the Syrian conflict has seen divided prioritizing of war aims based on the national interests of each country. Between the goals of defeating the ISIL, or removing Bashar al-Assad, each country has preferred to act in its own light. It has led to conflicting military action and a free

[28] https://www.unrefugees.org/news/syria-refugee-crisis-explained.

[29] Al-Jazeera, 'The Rise and Fall of ISIL Explained', June 20, 2017, https://www.aljazeera.com/indepth/features/2017/06/rise-fall-isil-explained-170607085701484.html.

[30] Sarah Al Mukhtar, Troy Griggs, K.K. Rebecca Lai & Tim Wallace, 'The Islamic State: From Insurgency to Rogue State and Back,' *The New York Times*, October 10, 2017, https://www.nytimes.com/interactive/2017/10/22/world/middleeast/isis-the-islamic-state-from-insurgency-to-rogue-stateandback.html?action=click&contentCollection=Middle%20East&module=RelatedCoverage&region=Marginalia&pgtype=article.

flow of armaments, communication equipment, and soldiers and military 'experts', to opposing sides. The destabilization of Europe, with a vast number of refugees aspiring entry, has made its own Muslim population susceptible to fear and vulnerability on issues of terrorism and human rights. In 2015 and 2016, Europe became a destination of choice for an estimated 650,000 Syrians, 5% of all those displaced worldwide by the conflict. Neither has the United States remained immune from these fears with the US Administration denying entry to nationals of Iran, Somalia, Sudan, Yemen, Syria and Libya.[31]

Enter Iran

The active involvement of world and regional powers in Syria shows no sign of abating with Iran, President Assad's staunchest supporter, coming under the US scanner after the latter withdrew, on May 8, 2018, from the Joint Comprehensive Plan of Action (JCPOA) popularly known as the Iran nuclear deal.[32] The United States' reintroduction of a sanctions regime on Iran, despite opposition of the European powers, aims to reduce Iran's footprint in the region. Following the killing of Major-General Qassem Suleimani, Iran announced in January 2020 that it will no longer observe the agreement's limitations on the number of centrifuges it is permitted to operate.[33]

With Syria once again, becoming the battlefield for foreign powers, any hope is lost for an early wind-down of the Syrian civil war. Syria has become a 'free-fire zone' for world and regional powers and the question becomes moot whether the country's present borders can remain intact. The poignancy of the question becomes more distressing considered in the context of the long-lasting effect on the country and its people. The centrifugal nature of the opposing forces within Syria ensures that

[31] Sabrina Siddiqui, Lauren Gambino & Oliver Laughland, 'Trump Travel Ban: New Order Targeting Six Muslim- Majority Countries Signed,' *The Guardian*, March 6, 2017, https://www.theguardian.com/us-news/2017/mar/06/new-trump-travel-ban-muslim-majority-countries-refugees.

[32] Mark Lander, 'Trump Abandons Nuclear Deal He Long Scorned', *New York Times*, May 8, 2018, https://www.nytimes.com/2018/05/08/world/middleeast/trump-iran-nuclear-deal.html.

[33] Ankit Panda, 'Iran Has Not Abandoned the Nuclear Deal', *The New Republic*, January 8, 2020, https://newrepublic.com/article/156140/iran-not-abandoned-nuclear-deal.

any breakdown of the current borders will directly impact its neighbour making it the only guarantee of Syria's longevity.

An appropriate moment for restarting the peace process was lost with the United States' determination to evict Iran from Syria where it is Assad's staunchest supporter. It introduced a dangerous new element into an already volatile region. The United Nations Security Council remained powerless with a divided P-5 and Western reluctance to convene it. UN Secretary General Antonio Gutierrez was provoked on April 13, 2018 to exhort the Security Council ' ...to overcome divisions and prevent dangerous situations from spinning out of control...'[34] given that the state of chaos in the Middle East, particularly the conflict in Syria, that had become a threat to international peace and security.

In contra-position to restarting the peace process, the United States, and Western powers have increased their military exposure in Syria. Israel, Saudi Arabia and UAE, ranged with the West, have their own motivations to reduce Iran's power in the region. For Israel, Iran represents its most significant threat; for Saudi Arabia, UAE and Qatar, it embodies the long-running ideological schism within Islam.

This development comes when President Bashar Assad, having withstood strong and multi-directional military and political pressure, is in control of most of the country. ISIL has been reduced to a sliver of territory, on the Iraq border, at Abu Kamal; the remnants of the insurgent Islamic groups evacuated to the north-western province of Idlib have coalesced under the Hayat Tahrir as Sham, the terrorist group that holds sway in the province.

Turkey has not observed its September 2018 agreement by which it had agreed with Moscow to establish a de-escalation zone in Idlib and signed the accompanying Sochi Memorandum of Understanding. It obliged Turkey to clear terrorist groups from Idlib and allow safe passage on the M4 and M5 highways, in exchange for a freeze in Syrian regime attacks on the opposition. The collapse of this agreement has meant active hostilities between the Turkish and Syrian forces the latter actively supported by Russia. In the neighbouring Syrian province of Afrin, the Turkish Army and supporting insurgent groups continue to oppose the Kurdish groups.

[34] UN Security Council document SC/13293 of April 13, 2018, https://www.un.org/press/en/2018/sc13293.doc.htm.

The Russian military is enforcing a de facto no-fly zone over Idlib, where the Syrian army, backed by Russian and Iranian units, has retaken the M5 highway, and appears poised to continue an offensive to capture the M4. The offensive has uprooted thousands forcing them to flee to the border with Turkey, where they are being kept in refugee camps, or into Turkish-controlled Afrin and northern Aleppo. Turkey finds itself in a cleft stick unable to escalate for fear of Russian air onslaught and not being able to rely on US support since it does not fall in NATO's mandate. The United States although Turkey's NATO ally has little interest in the Turkish armed forces being bogged down in an unwinnable war in Syria. Turkey appears to have bitten off more than it can chew. Its best option would appear to be to work towards a ceasefire using Russia's position of dominance in the situation.[35]

Thus, as Assad has regained control of the country, tensions between Iran and Israel have also ratcheted up, with Israeli officials warning they will not accept a permanent Iranian military presence in Syria.[36] Israel's major missile attack in April 2018, in response to the first-ever Iranian rocket attack on its troops in the Golan Heights, hit Iran's military sites in Syria targeting air defence positions, radar stations and a weapons warehouse. The early morning bombardment killed 23 people, the UK-based Syrian Observatory for Human Rights (SOHR) said. Israel has continued its attacks on Iran's assets in Syria with the aim of dislodging Iran's entrenched position in Syria. The latest in February 2020, a month after the US drone attack killing Qassem Suleimani who had worked to create Iran's sustainable presence in Syria.[37]

[35] Aaron Stein, 'Cleaning Up Turkey's Mess in Idlib and Ending the War', Warontherocks.com, February 25, 2020, https://warontherocks.com/2020/02/cleaning-up-turkeys-mess-in-idlib-and-ending-the-war/.

[36] Bethan McKernan, 'Israel and Iran on the Brink of War after Unprecedented Syria Bombardment', *The Independent*, May 10, 2018, https://www.independent.co.uk/news/world/middle-east/israel-iran-war-latest-syria-golan-heights-rocket-air-strikes-a8344291.html.

[37] Judah Ari Gross, '12 Pro-Iran Fighters Said Killed in Syria Strikes Attributed to Israel', Times of Israel, February 6, 2020, https://www.timesofisrael.com/12-pro-iran-fighters-said-killed-in-syria-strikes-attributed-to-israel/.

As Efraim Halevy, former head of Mossad,[38] has said, "You have all the players locked in battle in a very, very small area of land. We have a gradual escalation in the region and the question is who is going to blink first?'

Unending Civil Conflict

The situation continued to deteriorate with fighting between the official Syrian Armed Forces, and its allies, and the large number of opposition groups involved in the Syrian civil war.[39] The conflicting aims of their varied international backers have also provoked inter-rebel group conflict within the larger civil war. The groups are broadly the Syrian Arab Republic and its allies Russia, Iran and the Lebanese Hezbollah; Syrian armed opposition groups and their mainly foreign allies, Democratic Federation of Northern Syria and allies, and the Islamic State of Iraq and the Levant (ISIL) and allies.[40] In sum, they accounted for nearly a thousand separate and disparate groups.

They received armaments, technological and related assistance, and specialist forces from a variety of countries ranged on both sides of the divide including Russia, US, France, Iran, Iraq, China, North Korea, Czech Republic, Australia, Netherlands, Germany, Norway, Jordan, Qatar, Saudi Arabia, Turkey, Libya, Israel, Hezbollah and Iraqi Kurdish Forces (KDP Peshmerga, PUK Peshmerga). The variety, scale and deployment of the international forces in the Syrian civil war have resulted in constantly changing geographic holding patterns of the combatants. The success of any UN exhortation to international backers to cease such support becomes more difficult.

The Syrian-Russian relationship has two dimensions: first, arms transfers and active involvement of Russian forces on the side of the government, and second, its interest in holding on to port of Tartous, Russia's

[38] Mathew Kalman, 'Efraim Halevy Steps Out of the Shadows', The Times of Israel, February 16, 2017, https://www.timesofisrael.com/spotlight/tickets-on-sale-efraim-halevy-ex-mossad-chief-steps-out-of-the-shadows/.

[39] Lina Sinjab, 'Guide to Syrian Rebels', BBC, December 13, 2013, https://www.bbc.com/news/world-middle-east-24403003.

[40] Erwin van Veen, 'Syria: Foreign Interventions and the Revenge of Realpolitik', Clingendael Spectator, November 5, 2019, https://spectator.clingendael.org/en/publication/syria-foreign-interventions-and-revenge-realpolitik.

sole outlet on the Mediterranean. Arms transfers from the United States and other major powers continue to fuel the opposition groups in the bloody civil war. Regional players such as Iran, Qatar and Saudi Arabia continue to play a significant role.

The Syrian civil war has turned the country into a training ground for jihadists of European origin who have travelled to Syria to join the fight against the Assad government. These radicalized and traumatized jihadists endowed with skills honed in a deadly conflict, once they return, pose a serious security risk to their home countries. The spreading of the Syrian conflict to other countries of the Middle East, including Lebanon, Turkey, and Northern Iraq is a time-bomb threatening them.

The inability of these powers to find a mutually acceptable solution to the conflict in this pivotal state is one of the key factors prolonging the conflict. The complex situation means that any successful peace agreement will not automatically solve the country's problems. What comes later is just as crucial for ensuring the safety, security, stability and future happiness of the Syrian population. With a twenty-one per cent decrease in the population, there will be fewer people to rebuild the country.

The Military Situation

Raqqa, in the north-west of Syria, the first big city captured in early 2014, became ISIL's capital. The group went on takeover large parts of the country towards Aleppo in the north, and along the Turkish border. However, by the end of 2017, they had lost control of most of this land. An alliance of Syrian Kurdish and Arab fighters backed by US forces retook Raqqa on October 17, 2017 ending three years of ISIL rule.[41]

The Syrian army after weeks of fighting also retook the city of Deir al-Zor on November 3, 2017,[42] the largest city in eastern Syria and ISIL's last major stronghold. The city was important because of its proximity to the Iraqi border. Opinion remains divided whether ISIL retains any presence in the area. Similarly, other reports state that the city is

[41] Robin Wright, 'The Ignominious End of the ISIS Caliphate,' *The New Yorker*, October 17, 2017, https://www.newyorker.com/news/news-desk/the-ignominious-end-of-the-isis-caliphate.

[42] AFP, Beirut, 'Isis Dealt Twin Blows with Loss of Deir ez-Zor,' *The Guardian*, November 3, 2017, https://www.theguardian.com/world/2017/nov/02/deir-ez-zor-cleared-of-last-islamic-state-fighters-isis.

now completely free from terrorism, while the Syrian army and its allies clear the last pockets of ISIL resistance. Around 350,000 civilians in the province have fled from their homes.

Yet the fight to liberate Syria from other insurgent groups continues. After clearing the area around Deir ez Zor, the Syrian Army with Russian troops, negotiated deals to evacuate the rebel groups to Idlib. The east Ghouta, outside of Damascus, was recaptured in April 2018, and the long-held rebel town of Douma. Most opposition groups, in similar deals involving surrender of heavy weapons, were allowed to relocate themselves in Idlib.[43] Bashar al-Assad is now in control of almost all of Syria although since September 2018 the battle to retake Idlib and Afrin has been continuing. The entry of Turkey and its control over Afrin has introduced an unwanted dimension into the long-running insurgency.

The divided aims and international and regional participation in the Syrian civil war on both sides has added complexity to the civil war and made its resolution impossible. The most devastating impact has been on the Syrian population displacing them within their own country and rendering others refugees. The resultant humanitarian crisis was aggravated by its impact on Syria's economy and agriculture. The last nine years, have seen the breach of virtually every international law and practice. Repeated efforts by the UN Security Council and other interested countries like Russia and Turkey have failed to bring an uninterrupted ceasefire.

Displaced and Refugees

Up to end of 2016 of the pre-war population of 22 million, 13.5 million were in need of humanitarian access of which more than 6 million internally displaced according to SCPR.[44] Until December 2017, a little more than 5.44 million were refugees outside Syria.[45] Turkey has the largest number, about 3.6 million followed by Lebanon (2.2 million), Jordan (1.26 million), Germany (600,000), Saudi Arabia (0.5–2.5 million), UAE

[43] Al- Jazzera, 'Syria: Rebels Evacuate Last Opposition-Held Enclaves', May 8, 2018, https://www.aljazeera.com/news/2018/05/syria-rebels-evacuate-opposition-held-enclave-180508181950653.html.

[44] SCPR, Syrian Centre for Policy Research, Damascus, http://scpr-syria.org/.

[45] Editors, 'The Syrian Refugee Crisis Explained', UNHCR, February 24, 2020, https://www.unrefugees.org/news/syria-refugee-crisis-explained/.

(242,000) and Iraq (230,000). Smaller numbers went to forty-one other countries in the Middle East, Europe, Asia and South America. Thus, the Syrian civil war has had an impact on every major country in each continent.

Mike Noyes, head of humanitarian response at Action Aid[46] stated, 'in the last five years, half of Syria's pre-war population — more than 11 million people — have been killed or forced to flee their homes. At the current rate in five years' time Syria will be all but annihilated…An entire generation of young people have been exposed to the horrors of war and denied access to basic services such as education and healthcare.' An estimated 400,000 people are living in besieged areas where humanitarian access is limited, and where some are dying of starvation.

The war has left families destroyed, flattened towns and cities, and left generations in a state of despair. According to SCPR, with 1.9 million, representing a tenth of the Syrian population, are injured and 470,000 people killed almost double the UN estimate of 250,000. The UN tally does not represent the latest picture since it stopped counting those killed since 2016 due to paucity of accurate figures.

UNICEF warned of child soldiers as a 'particular concern', saying an increasing number are recruited to fight. Children report being actively encouraged to join the war by parties to the conflict offering gifts and 'salaries' of up to $400 a month.[47] Some 2.6 million Syrian children are living as refugees or on the run in search of safety, helping to fuel a global migrant crisis. Many children have spent several bitter winters living in makeshift shelters. More than 1 million Syrian refugee children—over 40%—are missing education.[48]

The Syrian refugees are in double jeopardy: as refugees, they are worried about their property left behind and concerned about the fate of those left behind. Their greatest agony, as represented by those in the camps in Jordan, Turkey and elsewhere, is when they could return. Yet

[46] Razia Akkoc, 'What Has Been the Real Cost of Syria's Civil War?' *The Telegraph*, March 15, 2016, http://www.telegraph.co.uk/news/worldnews/middleeast/syria/12146082/What-has-been-the-real-cost-of-Syrias-civil-war.html.

[47] John Davison, 'Syrian War Creates Child Refugees and Child Soldiers', Reuters, March 14, 2016, https://www.reuters.com/article/us-mideast-crisis-syria-children/syrian-war-creates-child-refugees-and-child-soldiers-report-idUSKCN0WG0R0.

[48] UNICEFUSA, 'Syrian Crisis, Child Refugee Crisis', February 23, 2018, https://www.unicefusa.org/mission/emergencies/child-refugees/syria-crisis.

even more, they confront a host of problems in the country of refugee. In one way or another, their presence impinges on both the domestic and foreign policy of the country of refuge and needs to be contextualized within the political framework of the host country.

In Turkey, for example, with the large number in camps, there is a rise of anti-Arab and anti-migrant feeling among the local population. In Lebanon, they are over twenty-five per cent of the country's population. The refugees also suffer from a wide range of mental health problems, either the exacerbation of existing disorder, or new problems caused by the conflict including the process of adaptation to a refugee status. The high proportion of children among the refugees, nearly 2.3–2.5 million, has meant an increase in the practice of child marriage.

International experience on the return of refugees, as seen in the Palestinian case, has been dismal and the receiving states will need to work on a plan for their eventual incorporation into the host societies. This is particularly important for those who have received large number like Turkey, Jordan and Lebanon and others in the Arab world.

Economy and Life Expectancy

From its wealth to infrastructure and population to economy, Syria has 'almost all been obliterated', the authors of the SCPR report noted. The World Bank, in its January 2016 analysis of the economic impact of war, stated that 2015 saw an increase in attacks on medical facilities. Citing research from the World Health Organization (WHO) and International Federation of Red Cross and Red Crescent Societies, it stated that the attacks have destroyed, either partially or completely, more than 50% of hospitals. The intentional destruction of hospitals is an important factor fuelling the largest global migrant crisis since World War II.[49] 'More than half of hospitals and health care facilities in Syria are closed or functioning only partially, and there are severe shortages of staff, equipment and supplies. Over half the country's health care personnel have left the

[49] Bethany Allen Ebrahimian, 'Hospitals Become the Front Line in the Syrian Civil War, Foreign Policy', May 31, 2017, http://foreignpolicy.com/2017/05/31/syria-hospitals-assad-civil-war-russia-usaid/.

country since the crisis began'.[50] 'Each doctor used to look after the needs of around 600 people-now its up to 4000' according to UNICEF.

It then comes as no surprise that life expectancy has dropped from 70.5 years in 2010 to an estimated 55.4 years. The country's economy and infrastructure are falling apart. Boasting one of the highest literacy rates in the Middle East before the war, 2016 figures showed more than 45% of children were no longer attending school. The report's authors warned this would have a 'dramatic impact' on Syria's future.

International Law Implications

The consistent theme in the long-running Syrian civil war is the regular and systematic breach of international law and long-held United Nations principles. Its follow-on effect will have a profound effect on the future conduct of international relations. Among these, are non-interference in the internal affairs of sovereign states; use of force for collective security only upon UN Security Council authorization; ensuring civilian populations do not become tools of the warring sides; and the primacy of providing humanitarian assistance.

International laws, treaty obligations, and international institutions force nations to weigh the enormous costs and consequences of war, seek the consent and participation of stakeholders, and consider the broader principles and precedent at stake before embarking upon war. Rather than provoking such assessments, the Syrian situation, given the involvement of world and regional powers, has seen a chaotic situation unmindful of its effects on the cohesiveness of the country or the continued agony of its people.

Syria is still a sovereign state that has maintained relative control over its borders, economy, and population. Notwithstanding its disregard for international law, including the use of chemical weapons and attacks on civilians, the Syrian government has not abdicated its sovereignty in a way that invites attack by external powers. Further, under international law, the conflict within Syria is an internal conflict. 'Two basic legal principles animate our current international system: states are sovereign, and they shall not, generally speaking, attack each other. The United Nations charter reflects these two principles, and recognizes just two

[50]WHO, 'Syrian Arab Republic Annual Report 2016', World Health Organization, Geneva, http://who.int/hac/crises/syr/sitreps/syria_annual-report-2016.pdf?ua=1.

exceptions in its text: action taken pursuant to a UN Security Council resolution, and individual or collective self-defense'.[51]

In the former case, action is permitted only pursuant to a unanimous UN Security Council resolution for example, the first Gulf War in Iraq (1991) or Libya (2013) and similar action in Afghanistan and Somalia. In the Syrian case, veto by Russia and China has ensured there will be no sanction for any UNSC-authorized military action in Syria. With regard to self-defence, possibly Turkey, Jordan, Israel, Iraq, or Lebanon could respond directly to Syrian belligerent acts, as could their allies like NATO and the United States. Despite the Syrian Civil War's spillover effect, and the occasional skirmish on the Turkish or Israeli borders, the Syrian war has arguably not yet created any cause for individual or collective self-defence.

The military presence of Turkey in Afrin does not fall under UNSC norms. Its presence infringes UN norms on sovereignty of states; neither does it fall under the, the much-abused, international practice on pre-emptive self-defence. The Syrian government has not indicated, by words or deed, it planned an imminent attack that *could* justify Turkish armed intervention. Legally, this argument also suffers due its heavy reliance on proof of imminence and intent that are hard to demonstrate.

Similarly, the controversial justification provided by the norm of 'responsibility to protect', used in the Libyan case, could be stitched together in the Syrian case emphasizing the need to enforce the Chemical Weapons Convention and the adverse regional security impact of the Syrian Civil War, including refugee flows, weapons movements, and border instability. Yet even in this case, UNSC approval is mandatory, and even if available, would lead to, arguably, an unlawful war justifiable only on political grounds.

The Syrian Peace Process

The ensemble of international initiatives to resolve the Syrian civil war started in 2011 with two attempts by the Arab League. Interestingly, as the years passed in a fruitless search for peace, the ground situation became increasingly complex. With a multiplicity of opposing radical

[51] Phillip Carter, 'International Law Constrains US Action in Syria', Truman National Security Project, http://umanproject.org/home/doctrine-blog/international-law-constrains-u-s-action-in-syria/.

Islamic groups, it saw the military involvement of four permanent UN Security Council members, France, UK, US and Russia, and of regional powers Saudi Arabia, Qatar, Turkey and UAE.

Starting with the first Geneva Conference convened by Kofi Annan and the Arab League (March–May 2012) and Geneva II convened by Lakhdar Brahimi,[52] eight rounds of Geneva conferences were unsuccessful in even ushering a lasting ceasefire.[53] The Geneva Conferences on Syria so far have not achieved the direly needed outcome: a permanent ceasefire to allow international action on ameliorating the massive humanitarian tragedy. The UN Security Council, attesting the enduring division within the P-5, passed only nineteen unanimous resolutions in seven years. While the rest remained stillborn, they exposed the deep division within the P-5 with Russia, somewhat paradoxically, championing Syria's sovereignty, in a sure sign of a revived Cold War. The UNSC's singular, perhaps only, success was the phased removal of the Syrian regime's stockpile of chemical weapons and securing Syria's adherence to the Chemical Weapons Convention.[54]

President Assad's acquiescence, due to Russian pressure, to surrender his chemical weapons was a trade-off with his own longevity. Without Assad in control, it was unlikely that the chemical weapons stockpile could be destroyed. Yet in agreeing to it, Assad gave up his only counter to Israel's nuclear weapon. Following UN Security Council Resolution (UNSCR) 2118(2013) the OPCW[55] completed its task by January 4, 2016.[56] Nevertheless, the scourge of the use of chemical weapons, mainly chlorine, by both sides has not abated. The latest was allegedly on February 6 and 7, 2018 in the Damascus suburb of Douma. While the United States has bombed Syrian facilities in retaliation, Russia has stated

[52] Raymond Hinnebusch & I. William Zartman, 'UN Mediation in Syrian Crisis: From Kofi Annan to Lakhdar Brahimi', International Peace Institute, March 2016, https://www.ipinst.org/wp-content/uploads/2016/03/IPI-Rpt-Syrian-Crisis2.pdf.

[53] Al-Jazeera.com, 'Syria Blame Game Continues after Failed Geneva Talks', https://www.aljazeera.com/news/2017/12/syria-blame-game-continues-failed-geneva-talks-171216063721465.html.

[54] Arms Control Association, 'The Chemical Weapons Convention (CWC) at a Glance', https://www.armscontrol.org/factsheets/cwcglance.

[55] OPCW, 'Organisation for Prohibition of Chemical Weapons', https://www.opcw.org/about-opcw/.

[56] OPCW, Organisation for Prohibition of Chemical Weapons', https://www.opcw.org/special-sections/syria-and-the-opcw/.

that the UK was involved in the chemical weapons attack.[57] The CWC team's has been reduced to a bystander with Russia stating that only the Security Council can make a determination of the source of the attack.

In parallel, talks were convened to give added impetus to encourage a dialogue between the Syrian government and the opposing Islamic groups in Vienna (October 2015), Lausanne (October 2016) and multiple rounds in Astana (December 2016–March 2018).

During the talks, while the opposition has insisted on discussing a political transition, the Syrian government has insisted on discussing terrorism—a broad label it applies to any group opposed to its rule. Meanwhile, the opposition has consistently struggled to reconcile the competing interests of its various patrons and to assemble a unified delegation that could credibly represent the interests of the more than a thousand armed groups operating in Syria.[58]

No lasting peace agreement is possible without involving a wide range of Syrian voices in any political process to determine their shared future.[59] Furthermore, unless the UNSC can impose a 'cease-and desist' injunction on the external players deeply involved in the conflict, an over-arching understanding becomes difficult to reach. A parallel discussion between major Islamic countries, possibly under the OIC, is a *sine qua non* to address the sectarian issue that undergirds the conflict. Only then will an intra-Syrian political process be feasible. Whether Russia and the United States as allies of the opposing camps, can still lead such a two-track process remains moot.

This introduction has sought to delineate the manifold dimensions of the unending Syrian civil war. A legally sovereign country was laid waste with immediate and long-term consequences for the country's beleaguered and dispersed population. The involvement of all major and regional powers attests to Syria's pivotal nature in the continuation of the

[57] BBC News, 'Syria War: What We Know about Douma 'Chemical Attack', April 16, 2018, http://www.bbc.com/news/world-middle-east-43697084.

[58] Lisa Roman & Alexander Bick, 'It's Time for a New Syria Peace Process', FP, September 15, 2017, http://foreignpolicy.com/2017/09/15/its-time-for-a-new-syria-peace-process/.

[59] Ravali Yendala, 'Why the United Nations Has Repeatedly Failed to Bring Peace and Stability to Syria', YKA, YouthkiAwaz, May 1, 2018, https://www.youthkiawaaz.com/2018/05/in-light-of-the-ongoing-syria-crisis-un-failure/.

conflict. It calls into question the sanctity of long-held United Nations principles, and thus, the continuation of that organization. As the civil war has become increasingly complex every country, particularly the P-5, have set aside every United Nations principle. An entire country has become a 'free-fire zone'[60] with devastating consequences to the land and its people. The following chapters will elaborate issues raised in the introduction.

Chapter 2: Why Syria Matters: The Tragedy of a Pivotal State

Syria's pivotal nature stems from its enduring history and civilization, and its susceptibility to engender and synthesize diverse, and often contradictory, streams in civilization, religion, and politics. In nurturing three great religions—Judaism, Christianity and Islam—Syria's contribution to world civilization is incomparable. At the same time, in a repetition of history, the civil war has made Syria the *septic focus* of a failing international system. The outcome of the civil war will determine the future contours of the system. This chapter focuses on Syria's multiple dimensions, alluded to in the introduction, highlighting its contribution to regional and international stability. An understanding of the unique character of the country and its people becomes crucial to visualizing outcome of the civil war.

Chapter 3: The Syrian Conflict and Its Aftermath

The failure of the Syrian revolution was the violent culmination of the popular revolutions that thrust themselves in 2010 upon the Arab world, known popularly as the 'Arab Spring'. Bashar al-Assad's uncompromising reaction was the culmination of a reactionary trend aimed at defeating the upsurge of the popular Arab desire for a democratic polity. The extreme and violent reaction by Syrian government forces, while driving the popular will underground, opened the field for organized radical Islamic groups. The chapter looks at the reasons that motivated the Syrian government in persisting with its violent reaction and whether another road was possible. In the context of the US occupation of Iraq, the Syrian reaction created a rationale for the entry of regional and world powers

[60] A term used during the Vietnam War, https://thevietnamwar.info/free-fire-zone/.

into the civil war. The motivation for their entry, unmindful of international law prescriptions, is elaborated. An examination of the contrary forces that halted the Arab spring is equally crucial to understanding the endless nature of the conflict in Syria. The chapter will consider the impact on Syria of the revival of the popular democracy wave.

Chapter 4: The Assad Presidency: Should Longevity Trump Acceptability?

A number of factors favoured the ascendency to presidency in 1972 of Hafez Assad: Syria's revolving door governments since independence in 1948; the Arab defeat in 1968 against Israel; the burning Arab desire for unity and solidarity; and the ideology of Arab Ba'ath Socialism whose secular ethos favoured Assad's community, the minority Alawites. Each of these played a major part in his acquisition, retention and consolidation of power. Hafez Assad positioned Syria as a hard-line state projected as the 'bleeding heart of the Arab world'. By the time of his death in 2000, the Assad family was in absolute control of Syria's future. Bashar Assad, his son and successor, promised a more open economy and polity to the Syrian people. Yet this was short-lived due to domestic imperatives of consolidating power and external constraints imposed by developments in Iraq. The chapter analyses the rise and consolidation by the Assad family of the country's governance to highlight factors that led to increasing polarization of public opinion. It will also elucidate the reasons for the rapid loss of their credibility and the options now available. At a time when Assad is in control of most of his country, he remains a potent force in any negotiations for a post-civil war political dispensation. In this context, the chapter will raise possible options for Bashar Assad, his government and his community.

Chapter 5: Role of Regional and International Powers

The unending Syrian civil war has involved every major and regional power against the Assad government. Except for Russia and Iran, their active military involvement against a sovereign country, with a legally constituted government, has overthrown the cardinal UN principle of non-interference in internal affairs of states. Russian and Iranian participation on the side of the government has helped Assad to regain the country. It has divided the UN Security Council, and the General Assembly, making Syria the *septic focus* of a world order in change. Both camps have thrown to the wind the founding UN Security Council principles and international law that these very powers have applied, during the last seven decades, to international crises. It has demonstrated the increasing self-serving use, by its permanent members, of the Security Council. The chapter delves deeper into the motivations and role of the countries actively involved: France, Iran, Qatar, Russia, Saudi Arabia, Turkey, United Kingdom and United States. It will also examine whether reasons for the multinational civil war not spilling beyond Syria's borders will prevail.

Chapter 6: International Efforts Towards Peace: Agency and Results

Since 2012, the UN Security Council has tried, with limited success, to bring in a ceasefire moving towards peace in Syria. With the failure of the Kofi Annan and Lakhdar Brahimi missions and following eight Geneva conferences, the peace-making effort has passed to the Astana Process run by Russia, Turkey and Iran. After eight rounds in Astana, the participants have agreed to provide forces to police and keep the peace in contiguous provinces of Syria. The Syrian government's view appears to look into the agendas, which some participants may pursue, to Syria's detriment. Meanwhile, the Astana track continues to buttress the Geneva track as do the dialogues in Vienna and elsewhere. This chapter will examine the reasons for lack of success that stem from both the inability of the UNSC to act unitedly and the fact of the participation of four of the P-5 in the Syrian conflict. It will also suggest the need to establish a parallel process, composed of all Islamic countries, to find a viable way out of the festering sectarian conflict, led by Iran and Saudi Arabia, within Islam. Without such an understanding, all efforts at peace making will remain truncated and incomplete.

Chapter 7: Future Evolution

In the light of the foregoing, this chapter will postulate on the possible future scenarios for Syria in terms of viability and regional peace. The Syrian situation has made the transition from disruptive, yet centripetal, internal forces becoming centrifugal and affecting its neighbours. Before the Syrian civil war, conflicts in the region remained confined within national borders because of cross-border linkages of family, tribe and sect. For the first time, the Syrian civil war has had a fall-out on the military engagements between ISIL and the Iraqi Army in Mosul, and between the Saudi multinational force and the *Houtis* in Sanaa. It has the potential to spread through West Asia and the Gulf. With the impact of the vast refugee outflow towards Europe, the internationalization of the Syrian conflict, exacerbated by ISIL-inspired terrorism in France, UK, US and other countries in Europe. Should Bashar al-Assad continue to retain control over the country the chances for Syria retaining its present geographical borders are stronger. The concluding chapter will examine the possible alternative scenarios for Syria until the civil war continues and thereafter. Much depends on a determination whether, with Assad's virtually complete control over the country, the political end game has started. It will also elaborate future options for Bashar Assad and the Alawite community as a whole. At the minimum, the possibility remains of his continuing as a participant in the process of government formation as part of a revived peace process.

CHAPTER 2

Why Syria Matters

Possessing a unique geography, Syria is at the crossroads of major world religions, empires and economic and mercantile networks. Its timelessness and antiquity have made it a pivotal state in the region. Its enduring proclivity to engender and synthesize diverse, often contradictory streams in civilization, religion and politics have made it the battleground for opposing ideas, practices and beliefs. Syria's ingrained cultural pluralism resulted in the presence of a multiplicity of minority groups, both ethnic and religious.

Syria's Secularism

Syria's view of itself rests on the fact that it lies astride the civilizational confluence of four cultures: Arab, Persian, Turkish and Hebrew.[1] The list of Syria's conquerors includes 'the Hebrews, the Babylonians, the Assyrians, the Hittites, the Egyptians, the Greeks, the Romans, the Byzantines, the Arabs, the Crusaders, the Mongols, the Mamelukes, the Ottomans, the British and the French'.[2]

[1] Joshua J. Mark, 'Ancient Syria', Ancient History Encyclopedia, June 17, 2014, https://www.ancient.eu/syria/.

[2] Nadav Morag, 'Syria: Why Its Future Matters to More Than the Middle East', Colorado Technical University, June 2012, https://www.coloradotech.edu/Media/Default/CTU/documents/resources/ctu-syria-backgrounder.pdf.

R. M. Abhyankar, *Syria*,
https://doi.org/10.1007/978-981-15-4562-7_2

It was natural that Syria has nurtured three great religions—Judaism, Christianity and Islam—marking it as the cradle of religious plurality. Its present population between eighteen and twenty-three million is a mosaic of ethnically, culturally, and religiously distinct communities. It continues to profess a secular polity—the only one in the Middle East. Yet, despite restrictions on political activity, the country's people can claim to be one of the most secular in the region. The presence of diverse people of minority faiths, both within Islam and outside, attests to its effectiveness in allowing these minorities a role in the governance of the country. The members of all minorities feel safe and free to meet and worship without discrimination.[3] The constitution, and related laws and policies, protect religious freedom; yet the government does impose restrictions on this right, particularly against those groups it considers extremist in nature.[4] Ninety per cent of the Syrians adhere to an Arab identity; roughly nine per cent are Kurdish, Armenian, Circassian and Turkoman filling out the mix reinforcing Syria's unique character in the region. Sunni Muslims make up seventy-four per cent of Syria's overall population providing the central symbolic and cultural orientation. Of these, a minority are of the Yazidi faith, reducing the core Sunni Arab majority to roughly two-thirds of the populace, while about 16% of the population, while Arab in ethnicity, consists of Twelver Shi'a, and other offshoots of Shi'a Islam—Alawi are 11% of the population, Druze, and Isma'ilis. Christians, of various Eastern Orthodox and Uniate traditions and the Latin Rite, along with a smattering of Protestants, make up 10% of the population. Syria's Arab Jewish community has, largely disappeared since the early 1990's because of emigration and the civil war. In 2012 reportedly there were only 20 Jews left in Syria. The last Jew left Aleppo in September 2016.

Going ahead from the first constitution of 1974 promulgated under Hafez Assad, the 2012 constitution reiterates the old bargain in stating that the President must be a Muslim and that the majority of laws will

[3] Andrew England, 'Syria's Religious Tolerance Belies Critics', *Financial Times*, September 15, 2018, https://www.ft.com/content/3b50f052-8333-11dd-907e-000077b07658.

[4] US Department of State, Bureau of Democracy, Human Rights and Labor, 'International Religious Freedom Report for 2018', https://www.state.gov/j/drl/rls/irf/religiousfreedom/index.htm?dlid=168276 &year= http://www.state.gov/j/drl/rls/irf/2010_5/168276.htm.

'based on Islam'. This injunction accords with the fact that Islam, in its different interpretations, is a legacy of the Syrian people as a whole and its redistributive tenets with a centralized enforcement authority has had an affinity for the Syrians with their Levantine ancestry.[5]

With ten years of the ongoing civil war, the Syrian crisis has evolved into struggle for power coloured by an underlay of sectarian contestation that bodes ill for a long accepted ethos of tolerance in the country. Thus the Syrian constitution of 2012 guarantees religious freedom in Article 3 and Article 33. Article 3 stipulates that 'the State shall respect all religions, and ensure the freedom to perform all the rituals that do not prejudice public order; the personal status of religious communities shall be protected and respected'. It remains the only country that professes to a secular credo in West Asia.

The need to juggle relationship of land, kinship and politics between them has greatly influenced the evolution of the country and its people, and their relationship with those across its borders. As evidenced by the country's history, the eclectic mix of different cultures has influenced Syria throughout the centuries. Syria's cultural markers like cuisine, music and festivals attest to multiple influences like Turkish, Persian, Mediterranean, Arab or French.

Archaeological Historicity

An ancient land, since the seventh millennium BC, Syria has hosted diverse civilizations that now rank it as the universal heritage of humankind. The archaeological site of Ugarit (1800 BCE–1300 BCE),[6] also known as *Ras Shamra* is at the headland, six miles north of Lattakia (then Latonia) on the Mediterranean coast. The civilization accidentally discovered in 1928, was at its height from c.1450 BCE until its destruction in c.1200 BCE, possibly by the mysterious Sea Peoples.[7] It had a

[5] Stelios Michaelopolous, Alireza Naghavi & Giovanni Parolo, 'Trade, Geography and the Unifying force of Islam', VOX CEPR Policy Portal, December 8, 2012, https://voxeu.org/article/trade-geography-and-unifying-force-islam-0.

[6] Heilbrunn, 'Timelines of History: Ugarit', The Met Museum, New York, https://www.metmuseum.org/toah/hd/ugar/hd_ugar.htm.

[7] Evan Andrews, 'Who Were the Sea Peoples?' History.com, June 2, 2017, https://www.history.com/news/who-were-the-sea-peoples. During the second millennium B.C, a mysterious band of maritime warriors known as the "Sea Peoples" wreaked havoc on the

script, attested by the ancient Ugaritic texts and a language by archaeological evidence. It has yielded rich archaeological finds that tell us about uninterrupted human habitation. Syria, lying within the Fertile Crescent, played host to a large number of diverse civilizations over nearly five millennia leaving behind major and enduring centres of belief, politics and commerce like Damascus, Aleppo and Palmyra. Unlike elsewhere, the sites of these ancient civilizations continue to provide the nucleus of living spaces for the people of the city and the country. Today they define the modern nation's hybrid identity forged over millennia among numerous ethnic and religious groups. This unique feature distinguishes Syria from other ancient river valley civilizations along the Indus, Nile and the Huang He and Chang Jiang in China.

'The country, at the crossroads of Europe, Africa and Asia, boasts tens of thousands of sites of archaeological interest, from the ruins of the earliest civilizations to Crusader-era fortifications to the wonders of Islamic worship and art. Syria's enchantment comes from its antiquities that are part of the living, breathing texture of everyday life',[8] not fenced off as in European and other countries. Syria has six World Heritage sites: the ancient cities of Aleppo, Bosra, Damascus, Palmyra as those in northern Syria, and Crac des Chevaliers and Qal'at Salah El-Din. Ebla, now Idlib, virtually the last bastion of opposition left in Syria, was founded around 3000 B.C.E. and flourished through trade with Egypt, Sumer and Akkad until around 240 B.C.E.

Analysis through satellite imagery indicates that five of the six World Heritage sites exhibit significant damage except for Damascus. The excavations at *Tell Ramad*, on the outskirts of Damascus, confirm that the city was inhabited as early as 8000–10,000 BC.[9] Recognized by UNESCO in 2008 as the Arab capital of culture, Damascus lays claim to the oldest continuously inhabited city in the world. Arabs traditionally referred to

Mediterranean. "They came from the sea in their warships," reads one ancient inscription, "and none could stand against them." There are accounts of the Sea Peoples attacking Egypt, Turkey, Syria and Palestine. Despite the indelible mark they left on history, scholars know almost nothing about their culture or nationality.

[8] James Harkins, The Race to Save Syria's Archeological Treasures', Smithsonian.com, March 2016, https://www.smithsonianmag.com/history/race-save-syrias-archaeological-treasures-180958097/.

[9] Al Jazeera, 'Damascus: The Arab Cultural Capital', February 2, 2008, al-jazeera.com, https://www.aljazeera.com/focus/arabunity/2008/01/200852517261995 8297.html.

present-day Syria and a large, vaguely defined surrounding area as *Bilad as-Sham,* which translates as 'the northern region', 'the north', 'Syria', or 'Damascus' or 'the green land'. The last comes from the time when most Haj caravans from the north and the east passed through Damascus on their way to, and back, from Mecca. On their return, having crossed the Nafud desert,[10] Damascus was the first sight of green that they saw thanks to the river *Barada* that provides water to Damascus. By AD 661, Damascus was the seat of the powerful Omayyad caliphs and has remained one of the most important and impressive cities in the Muslim world. The Omayyad mosque, at the heart of old Damascus, has been hallowed ground, continuously for two millennia, for the Greek and Roman religions, Judaism, Christianity and finally, Islam. It uncommonly displays the traces of all its earlier incarnations with no attempt over the ages to obliterate what had gone before.

Aleppo, often portrayed as second to Damascus, and a bastion of Islamist resistance to the Ba'athist government, has been a vital node of commerce and trade connecting routes across Asia, including with Moscow, and Yiwu and Guangzhou in China. The historical networks connecting the Levant, Egypt, Anatolia, South Europe and South East Europe into a single Mediterranean arena of exchange, puts Aleppo in a broader frame than of the nation state or a putative cultural area defined by Arabness or Islam.[11] Until beginning of the insurgency, shifting mercantile networks always secured Aleppo's status as a regional commercial and manufacturing hub supplying markets in Turkey, the Caucasus and the Arab world. These trans-regional connections shaped the city's social and economic dynamics.

The ancient city of Palmyra, in a desert oasis,[12] evokes a vision of Syria, transcending the region's modern-day strife, of a crossroad of

[10] Al Nafud, Encyclopedia, https://www.britannica.com/place/al-Nafud. The al Nafud desert in northern Saudi Arabia, is a portion of the larger Arab Desert. It lies at an average elevation of 3000 feet (900 metres) and covers about 25,000 sq. miles (65,000 sq.mts).

[11] Paul Anderson, 'Aleppo in Asia: Mercantile Networks Between Syria, China and Post-Soviet Eurasia since 1970', *Journal of History and Anthropology*, Vol. 29, 2018, Taylor Francis Online, August 30, 2018, https://www.tandfonline.com/doi/full/10.1080/02757206.2018.1513930.

[12] Brigit Katz, 'Ancient City of Palmyra, Gravely Damaged by ISIS, May Reopen Next Year', Smithsonian.com, August 29, 2018, https://www.smithsonianmag.com/smart-news/ancient-city-palmyra-gravely-damaged-isis-may-reopen-next-year-1-180970160/.

Greek, Roman, Persian and Islamic cultures.[13] The monumental ruins of Palmyra, located in the middle of the Syrian Desert, approximately 146 miles (235 km) northeast of Damascus and 130 miles (210 km) southwest of Deir ez-Zor, date primarily to the city's heyday between the first and third centuries CE. During this period, Palmyra was an economic powerhouse with privileged access to goods flowing along an east–west trade route that linked the Mediterranean to India and China. It was also a cultural centre where influences from the Greco-Roman world to the west met and merged with Persian and Parthian influences from the east. During the second half of the third century CE, the long-distance trading system went into decline and ushered in a period of intense political manoeuvrings.[14] Under the leadership of its famous queen Zenobia, efforts to establish Palmyra's independence from Rome led ultimately to an aggressive campaign of expansion into Egypt and Asia Minor. She was forced to surrender by the Roman emperor Aurelian and taken captive, according to legend, 'in chains of gold to Rome' to retire in one of the villas in the Tivoli gardens.

In the aftermath, the city found itself more firmly under the control of Rome and never attained its former glory. The city remained a shadow of its former self during the Byzantine and Islamic periods. In recognition of its historical importance and universal cultural value, Palmyra was inscribed in 1980 on the UNESCO World Heritage List. With escalation of the Syrian civil war, it is since 2013 on UNESCO's List of World Heritage sites in danger. More recently, the site, and the adjacent modern town of *Tadmor* with its high security prison, became a focal point in the conflict between Syrian government forces and ISIL, both intent on controlling this strategic location and associated infrastructure (including weapons depots, oil fields, a military airbase and a prison).

The continuation of the large-scale destruction of these antiquities by the Islamic State not only negated traces of human civilization but also

[13] Anne Barnard, 'Syria's War Takes Heavy Toll at a Crossroad of Culture', *New York Times*, April 16, 2014, https://www.nytimes.com/2014/04/17/world/middleeast/syrian-war-takes-heavy-toll-at-a-crossroad-of-cultures.html.

[14] Michael Danti, Michael, Tate Paulette, LeAnn Barnes Gordon, Abdalrazzaq Moaz, Cheikhmous Ali, Kathryn Franklin & David Elitzer, 'Special Report on the Importance of Palmyra', ASOR Cultural Heritage Initiatives, June 2, 2015, http://www.asor-syrianheritage.org/special-report-on-the-importance-of-palmyra/.

sought to deny Syria's ancient historicity and its importance to the adherents of the major western religions. Some of the most valuable sites were collateral damage in the shelling and crossfire between government forces and various rebel factions; others were sold by the ISIL, bit by valuable bit, to buy guns or, just as likely, food or a way to escape the chaos. Satellite images of treasured historical sites show the soil so completely pockmarked by holes, the result of thousands of illicit excavations, that it 'resembles the surface of the moon—destruction and looting on an industrial scale' according to UNESCO director general Irina Bokova.

Despite contrasting political allegiances, Syria's archaeologists have worked together for the preservation of these masterpieces. Ma'amoun Abdulkarim, Director of Antiquities and Museums told me that Palmyra's most important artefacts and statues were removed to Damascus as ISIS approached. The last rescue operation was completed three hours before Palmyra fell; three of his employees were wounded in the clashes. Another recent collaboration with opposition-friendly archaeologists in the northern Syrian province of Idlib, yielded an agreement by all the armed parties and the local community to put valuable objects, including engraved tablets from the Babylonian era, behind a thick layer of concrete in the provincial museum in Idlib city. 'You cannot open it easily', Abdulkarim assures me, of the improvised security arrangement. 'You need an electric machine'. All the same, he worries that Islamist extremist groups might not respect the agreement. 'No one has taken it until now, because of the local community', he says. 'But all the groups know where it is'.[15] ISIL's depredations of Syria's archaeological treasures were evocatively brought out by 'the public execution on August 18, 2015 of Khaled al-Asaad,[16] 82-year-old head, for more than forty years of Palmyra's antiquities and a beloved archaeologist. 'ISIS beheaded al-Asaad and hung his body from a column in the city, condemning him as a 'director of idolatry'. But according to some reports, the Islamists killed him because he

[15] James Harkin, 'The Race to Save Syria's Archeological Treasures,' *The Smithsonian Magazine*, March 2016, https://www.smithsonianmag.com/history/race-save-syrias-archaeological-treasures-180958097/.

[16] Kareem Shaheen & Ian Black, 'Beheaded Syrian Scholar Refused to Lead Isis to Hidden Palmyra Antiquities', *The Guardian*, August 19, 2015, https://www.theguardian.com/world/2015/aug/18/isis-beheads-archaeologist-syria.

had refused, during more than a month of captivity and interrogation, to reveal the location of antiquities that his staff had hidden away'.[17]

Sites and items of archaeological interest have always been collateral damage in times of conflict most recently during World War II. Yet the targeted destruction of millennia-old antiquities in the birthplace of human civilization, home to ancient centres of power has been an unprecedented threat to humankind's shared heritage. The widespread looting of antiquities that accompanied Syria's slide into chaos was primarily due to western interest and globalized markets. The destruction of Syria's archaeological heritage is a blow to the modern nation's hybrid identity, forged among numerous ethnic and religious groups. 'If we lose the Syrian heritage, we lose the Syrian common memory. And then we lose the Syrian identity', said Ma'amoun Abdulkarim'.[18]

ISIS's wanton destruction of the archaeological treasures in Iraq and Syria aimed to deprive the people of their cultural identity and history and deprive the Syrian people of the history of their cultural diversity. It amounts to 'cultural cleansing' that is yet to be recognized in international law protecting cultural heritage. 'The 1954 Hague Convention, the Second Protocols, the World Heritage Convention and the Rome Statute provide for the protection of cultural heritage but none are sufficient, neither do they address the destruction of cultural heritage as a specific means of persecution'. It is imperative that the international community codify such acts as a crime under the International Criminal Court[19] and recognize the importance of cultural heritage and its value to all humanity.[20]

[17] Ibid. James Harkin.

[18] Ibid.

[19] Ella Weiner, 'Can the International Criminal Court Help Protect Cultural Heritage,' *CSIS*, Vol 13, https://www.csis.org/npfp/can-international-criminal-court-help-protect-cultural-heritage.

[20] Caitlin V. Hill, 'Killing a Culture: The Intentional Destruction of Cultural Heritage in Iraq and Syria under International Law', *Georgia Journal of International and Comparative Law*, May 17, 2017, https://digitalcommons.law.uga.edu/cgi/viewcontent.cgi?referer=https://www.google.com/&httpsredir=1&article=2378&context=gjicl.

Syria's Human Geography

'Syria lying at the junction of three continents has made it the transit ground for conquering armies and commercial caravans from time immemorial. It has been called the bridge to Africa and the key to Asia'.[21] Syria borders Turkey to the north, Iraq to the east, Israel and Jordan to the south, and Lebanon and the Mediterranean Sea to the west. Its 71,000 square miles (183,900 square kilometres) area has inevitably led to linkages of its ethnic and religious communities and tribes stretching across national borders.

Prior to the conflict, borderlands represented marginal and less-developed areas within their own states between Syria and its neighbouring states.[22] At the local level, this peripheral position helped to sustain family or tribal cross-border ties as well as smuggler networks and other illegal activities (with the exception of the Syria–Israel border). There were no cross-border transnational spaces per se in the region. Since the civil war, these borderlands are part of the nexus of military strife, an object of competition for control, as well as sites of massive demographic transformation and sustained—albeit asymmetric—trans-border legal and (mostly) illegal activity. Notwithstanding the destructions and ruptures due to the conflict, these areas have increasingly turned into interconnected relational spaces—albeit because of a booming war economy and the forced displacement of millions of Syrians within and outside Syria.

At the same time, the new transnational spaces no longer ensure the historical, political, legal or territorial continuity of the border. They replicate its segmentation as they connect spaces on either side of a crossing point. As a result, the different types of cross-border flows of goods and people depend heavily not only on the tide of military successes and defeats, but also on the quality of the relationships between the authorities

[21] Basie L. Ashton, 'The Geography of Syria', *The Journal of Geography Macomb*, Illinois, Vol. 27, August 1, 1928, https://search.proquest.com/docview/1290492691/fulltextPDF/515EFD262FA349C9PQ/1?accountid=11620.

[22] Leila Vignal, 'The Changing Borders and Borderlands of Syria in a Time of Conflict', International Affairs, July 2017, Vol. 93, No. 4, pp. 809–27, https://www.chathamhouse.org/sites/default/files/publications/ia/INTA93_4_03_Vignal.pdf.

in control on either side of the border. For instance, owing to disagreements between the PYD[23] and the KRG,[24] the *Simalka* crossing was closed from March to July 2016, leading to serious disruptions in the local economy and in the circulation of people in northeastern Syria; it was reopened by the KRG in August 2016, but only for trade. With the emergence of these spaces of transnational circulation, the position of previously marginal borderlands has changed, not only in the general territorial and political economy of Syria, but also in that of its neighbouring states. In Syria, the border is undoubtedly a vital resource for the war. In the borderlands of neighbouring countries, the conflict has translated into a massive refugee presence, the circulation of combatants and traders, the relocation of Syrian economic activity (especially in Turkey), and an increasingly visible presence of international humanitarian organizations and NGOs.

The conflict has led to the disruption of former economic ties and networks, but also, at the local level, to the emergence of new economies linked to the war and to the flows of refugees. Moreover, the partial or total closure of trade routes that previously went through Syria led to the use of alternate ones. Thus the borderlands have extended themselves geographically—for example in Turkey, the borderland along Syria has extended all the way to Istanbul, a city in which in 2016 an estimated 400,000 Syrians lived. The salience of borderlands in the general dynamics of the Syrian conflict explains why in Jordan, Turkey and Lebanon these former marginal areas are now more connected to the core, and paradoxically receive more political attention and funding, than ever before in their history. While neighbouring states do not necessarily have the means, capacity or political will to support their weakened borderlands, their security aspect has undoubtedly gained new prominence.[25]

[23] Carnegie Middle East Center, Kurdish Democratic Union Party (PYD), March 1, 2012, https://carnegie-mec.org/diwan/48526?lang=en.

[24] KRG, Kurdistan Regional Government, Gov.KRG, March 14, 2020, https://gov.krd/english/government/the-prime-minister/activities/posts/2020/march/pm-masrour-barzani-speech-on-the-coronavirus/.

[25] Ibid. Bessie L. Ashton.

Religion and Ethnic Populations

Over thousands of years, Syria was exposed to, and occupied by, the great cultures and empires of the region and witnessed a flow of diverse religious ideas and theologies and cultural exchanges. It is noticeable that many sects grew up through a melding of ideas from different faiths, and in particular an interest in mystical strands such as Christian Gnosticism and Islamic Sufism with a focus on hidden beliefs.[26] Damascus had been a Roman and Christian city, but in 706 C.E., the Omayyad Mosque was built under Caliph Ibn al-Walid. Indeed, before the Great Mosque was built, the Cathedral of St. John in Damascus was used by both Muslims and Christians for worship in toleration of the other.[27]

Modern Syria remains a melting pot of many religious sects. The Christians themselves, numbering 2.5 million, consisted of varied sects like the Chalcedonian Antiocans, Melkites, Armenians, Syriac Catholics, Chaldean Catholics, Roman Catholics, Maronites, the Armenian Apostolic Church, the Syrian Orthodox Church and others. When the French took control of Syria, the territory already had a cohesive identity as well as a deeply rooted tradition of religious pluralism.[28]

Since ancient times, the contemporary states of Syria, Lebanon, Jordan and Israel were referred as Syrian lands. Syria's religious fabric grew even richer during the next few hundred years. First, Muslim separatists established Shi'ism in opposition to the Sunni, or orthodox, version of Islam. Over time, Shi'a Islam also split into multiple belief systems. In Syria, most Shi'ites are members of the Alawi sect. The eleventh century witnessed the birth of the Druze faith, which grew out of Islam but became a distinct religion incorporating elements of Christianity, Islam and mysticism. Prior to the French occupation, these groups lived side by side in relative peace.

From 1925 to 1927, Syrians of multiple faiths, ethnicities and political ideals united against French rule, in what was known as the Great

[26] The Review of Religions, 'Syria's Religious Heritage', November 13, 2013, http://www.reviewofreligions.org/9983/syrias-religious-heritage/.

[27] Dr. Mustafa Siba'i, 'The Islamic Civilization', 2002, Awakening Publications, Swansea, UK, pp 82–83.

[28] Andrea Williams, 'Syria's Forgotten Pluralism and Why It Matters Today', The Conversation, April 15, 2017, http://theconversation.com/syrias-forgotten-pluralism-and-why-it-matters-today-76206.

Syrian Revolt. Although the rebellion was ultimately crushed, it showed the French that their colonial subjects could put their differences aside to face a common enemy. In order to prevent the development of nationalist sentiment and opposition, the French deliberately pitted Syria's ethnic and religious groups against one another. The French also promoted sectarianism by periodically shifting borders and redistributing political support. The war engaged multiple factions organized along religious lines.

The historical flow of religions through Syria over many millennia have led to interesting sects including the Alawi who revere Imam Hazrat Ali and follow the Twelver Shi'a tradition, although some sources suggest that they assign divine attributes to Hazrat Ali possibly even corresponding to the Christian Trinity.[29] Many of their beliefs are secret from outsiders, perhaps due to centuries of isolation from mainstream society, and their beliefs are said to include reincarnation. They were greatly influenced by Ismailis and may have been absorbed in Syria from the Qarmatians[30] and the Order of the Assasins, formally known as Nizari Ismaili or as *Hashishim* in Syria.[31] They have a holy book called the *Kitab al-Majmu* that is said to include writings from Aristotle. There are differing accounts about their beliefs including claims that they believe women do not have souls, that they permit the drinking of alcohol, and celebrate other festivals such as Christmas and the Zoroastrian New Year. Due to the ongoing secrecy, it is hard to confirm their precise beliefs.

The other notable sect is the Druze Community, which exists in Syria, Lebanon, Israel and Jordan and who class themselves as Monotheistic (*al-Muwahhidun*). Their name is said to derive from an early preacher Ad-Darazi from 1016 C.E. who had promoted the idea that Khalifah

[29] "Alawite (Shi'ite Sect)', *Encyclopaedia Britannica*, October 20, 2013, http://www.britannica.com/EBchecked/topic/12399/Alawite.

[30] Mohanned Rahman, 'The Qamartians: The World's First Enduring Communistic Society', World Bulletin, March 22, 2014, https://www.worldbulletin.net/history/the-qarmatians-the-worlds-first-enduring-communistic-society-h127416.html.

[31] Vincente Millan Torres, 'The Original Warriors of Alamut, National Geographic', November 21, 2018, https://www.worldbulletin.net/history/the-qarmatians-the-worlds-first-enduring-communistic-society-h127416.html.

Al-Hakim in Cairo was divine.[32] The Druze began as an Ismaili Shi'a tradition, influenced by Greek and various mystic tendencies including the Gnostics and Jewish mysticism. There have been theological disputes among the Druze over whether God was incarnated into humans, especially HazratAli[ra] and his descendants. The Druze often conceal their beliefs just as the Alawites do in a custom known as *Taqiyya*, although they do have a text called *Rasa'il Al-Hakim*. The Druze believe that Al-Hakim will return as the *Mahdi* (Guided One). The Druze maintain their secrecy through the purity of their community. They do not allow conversion or intermarriage.[33]

'The Sunni Arabs range from the highly pious to the very secular and are divided between an urban elite and the rural masses that traditionally have had diverging political loyalties. Like many countries in the Middle East, the sharpest divide may not so much be religious or ethnic as ideological and existential, pitting Muslims who want to align politics with religion against those who wish to keep them apart. Of all the groups, the Kurds and the Sunni Islamists are the greatest threats to the Syrian state because their political movements have the cohesion, established agendas, outside support, and sense of grievance to drive them to challenge central authority'.[34](Fig. 2.1)

The Syrian conflict is multidimensional including socio-economic grievances and sectarian strife. It is a class conflict between a wealthy ruling elite and marginalized communities and was mostly confined within the Sunni Arab community.[35] The Syrian government was able to incorporate to its side the non-Sunni ethno-sectarian groups such as the Christians, the Druze, the Alawites or the Kurds, given the failure of the opposing radical Islamic groups. It basically gave Damascus a stronger

[32] Cyrill Glassé, 'The Concise Encyclopaedia of Islam', 1991, Harper San Francisco Second Edition, London, UK, p. 103, https://www.google.com/search?q=cyril+glasse+new+encyclopedia+of+islam&rlz=1C1GCEJ_enUS844US844&oq=Cyril+Glasse+&aqs=chrome.2.69i57j0l4.12084j0j7&sourceid=chrome&ie=UTF-8s.

[33] "Druze (religion)." *Encyclopaedia Britannica*, October 22, 2013. http://www.britannica.com/EBchecked/topic/172195/Druze.

[34] Seth Kaplan, 'Syria's Ethnic and Religious Divisions,' Fragile States, February 2012, https://www.fragilestates.org/2012/02/20/syrias-ethnic-and-religious-divides/.

[35] Hashem Osseiran, 'How Sectarianism Can Help Explain the Syrian War,' newsdeeply.com, March 6, 2018, https://www.newsdeeply.com/syria/articles/2018/03/06/how-sectarianism-can-help-explain-the-syrian-war.

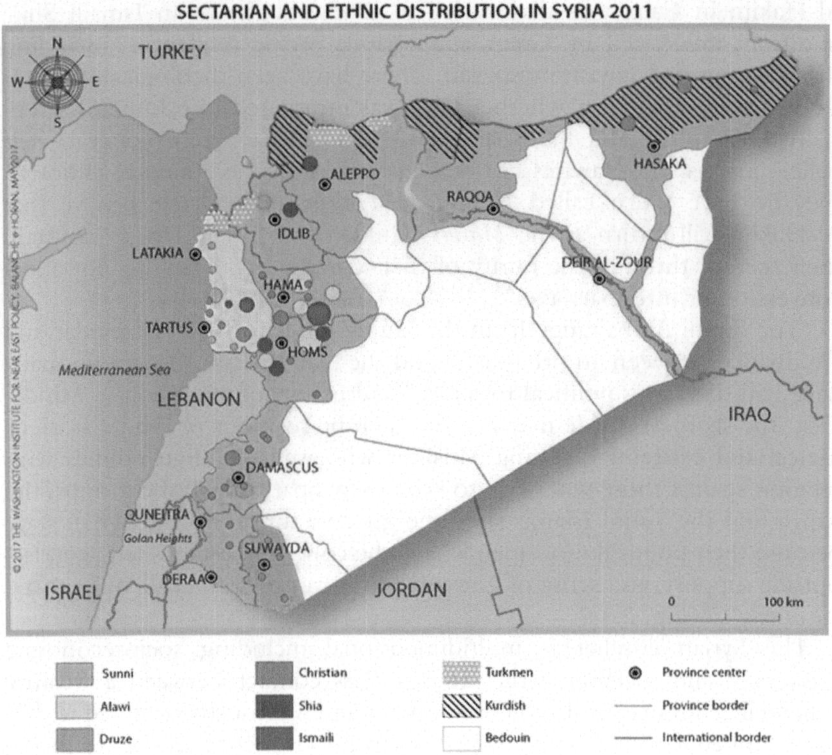

Fig. 2.1 Sectarian and ethnic distribution in Syria 2011 (*Source* Used with permission, The Washington Institute for Near East Policy, copyright 2018)

mobilization capacity. The government could reach out to these minorities and tell them the state will protect them from the 'terrorists' or the 'Islamists'. Even though the Baathist system of governance is avowedly secular, administrative appointments and the distribution of administrative districts often privilege certain sections over others. The ongoing conflict has created and reinforced the proliferation of sectarian militias across the country e.g. Christian militias in places like Wadi al-Nasara between Homs and Tartus and Ismaili militias in places like Salamiyah.

The Ottomans through the *millet* system established religious belief as the primary identity marker for the people. It has continued throughout the Syrian conflict as well. Undoubtedly, it has influenced similar inter-sectarian tension in Lebanon transforming popular mobilization from interest-based and political into identity-based and religious modes.

The Syrian civil war has already reawakened longstanding issues related to sect and community that were repressed due to the adherence to the national imperative. These issues involving sectarian diversity and national unity are back in discussion encompassing the confessional democracy in practice in Iraq, to the question of the Alawi factor in a post-conflict Syria and the Kurdish resurgence reaching across Syria and Iraq into Turkey. The putting in place of a consociational democratic architecture appears to provide a way forward.[36]

It reflects on the need to preserve today the feeling of brotherhood between people of all faiths extant in Syria at its zenith as written records show, such as Ibn Jubayr's from his visits to Damascus around 1184 C.E. This goodwill in society was possible because people were attuned to their spirituality, whatever their faith or sect. Syria needs to reflect on this today to preserve its heritage and ingrained pluralism when people of the same faith are at war with each other and innocent women and children are losing their lives.

Eco-Sectarianism and Civil War

Against the backdrop of climate change, the phenomena of eco-sectarianism, explains the relationship between sectarian violence and environmental pressures in fragmented and unequal societies with a weak sense of national consciousness and languishing nation-building projects.[37]

The combination of cultural divisions and resources scarcity due to ecological problems creates a fertile ground for escalation of conflict. The seemingly sectarian reason for identity politics in such societies provides a cover for asserting rights to the exploitation and revenues from natural

[36] Adam Akerfeldt, 'Consociational Democracy in Theory and Practice', Research Gate, April, 8, 2016, https://www.researchgate.net/publication/306101234_Consociational_Democracy_in_Theory_and_Practice/.

[37] Afshin Shahi & Maya Vachkova, 'Eco-sectarianism: From Ecological Disasters to Sectarian Violence in Syria', *Asian Affairs*, July 16, 2018, Vol. 49, No. 3, pp. 449–467, https://www.tandfonline.com/doi/abs/10.1080/03068374.2018.1487697.

resources particularly oil, gas and water. In turn, it breeds sectarian radicalization as has happened in Chechnya, Dagestan and Sudan and Syria.[38] Thus the polarizing characteristics used for group mobilization and the competition over vital resources feed on each other. The unending civil strife in Syria leading to the loss of the peoples' trust in the government was responsible for engendering over one thousand radical Islamic groups opposing Bashar Assad.

Considerable research exists to prove that while the long drought from 2006 to 2010 may have been due to the over-use of water in intensive cultivation the subsequent shortages were badly handled by the government leading to growing dissatisfaction with the regime. It may nevertheless have been only a peripheral cause for the start of the civil war. The humanitarian crisis that followed the drought, a culmination of fifty years of mismanagement of water and land resources marked the failure of the Syrian government's water and agricultural policies.

During the drought the pattern of poor rainfall was marked in the northeastern governorates of Deir ez-Zor, Hassakeh and Raqqa while other regions had largely recovered by 2008–2009. Nevertheless, before 2011 Syria's agricultural sector underwent intensive development, particularly in the northeast of the country. The country's irrigated area doubled over the past 20 years from 651,000 hectares in 1985 to 1.35 million hectares in 2010. Sixty per cent of this surface area was irrigated with groundwater being extracted at an unsustainable rate. Ninety per cent of the country's water went to agriculture, by far the highest percentage in the region, with very low irrigation efficiency. Over 80% of the land was still irrigated through traditional flooding methods and losses in the open concrete government constructed irrigation canals ranging from 10 to 60%. Growing demand and the continued drive to expand the irrigated area created a water deficit. Syria's total available water resources for use were estimated at 15.6 billion cubic metres in 2007. Total average annual water withdrawal in the same year was 19.2 billion cubic metres. The resulting 3.59 billion cubic metres deficit was compensated with water from dam reservoirs and groundwater reserves. Syria's annual per capita water availability dropped to 882 cubic metres in 2007, classifying it as a water-scarce country.[39]

[38] Ibid.

[39] Ibid. De Chantal.

This was coupled with the growth in Syria's population from 3.3 million in 1950 to approximately 21.4 million before the refugee outflow. It also increased the population living in urban centres. This explosive growth was the result of a strong pro-birth policy launched in the 1950s that led to an official ban in the sale and use of contraceptives in the 1970s. Syria's annual average population growth rate remains among the highest in the region at 2.94%; down from around 3.75% in the 1970s. This growing population taken with the government's inability to implement water conservation policy progressively exacerbated the situation.

The long drought in Syria from 2004 to 2010 saw a flagging of the Syrian government's response to the need for providing relief expenditure to the farmers to ensure that they did not leave the land. 'Attracted by the high prices of wheat in 2006, the government sold its strategic reserves. Consequently, it was unable to provide adequate relief to the deprived agricultural areas'.[40] It was not the drought per se, but rather the government's failure to respond to the ensuing humanitarian crisis that formed one of the triggers of the uprising, feeding a discontent simmering in rural areas. It saw large-scale migration of populations to the cities and widespread malnutrition. The government shifted responsibility for water mismanagement blaming environmental pressures stemming from global warming.[41] Subsidies to peasants were rescinded and investment was channelled into other sectors.

Indeed, the government's reluctance to deal with the pressing crisis contributed to the feeling of inequality and generated narratives of victimhood among the Sunni majority. Many Sunni farming communities believed that their Alawi counterparts received state support and compensation that neglected the Sunni communities. The small-scale and subsistence farmers suffered worst, between 2007 and 2010, reportedly herders in eastern Syria lost 80 per cent of their livestock.[42] The drought

[40] Ibid. Afshin Shahi & Maya Vachcova.

[41] Francesca De Chatel, 'The Role of Drought and Climate Change in the Syrian Uprising: Untangling the Triggers of Revolution', Middle Eastern Studies, May 7, 2014, https://blogs.commons.georgetown.edu/rochelledavis/files/francesca-de-chatel-drought-in-syria.pdf.

[42] Mahmoud Solh, 'Tackling the Drought in Syria', Nature Middle East, September 27, 2010, http://www.natureasia.com/en/nmiddleeast/article/10.1038/nmiddleeast.2010.206.

triggered a wave of migration to the major cities particularly Homs, Hama, Dara'a and Damascus making these mostly Sunni farmers environmental refugees. Migration statistics reveal that between 40,000 and 60,000 families sold their belongings and moved to cities.[43] The government set up temporary camps, failing, however, to provide required services for the displaced. The city of Dara'a, where the Syrian Uprising started, received numerous refugees, at a time when there was already a strain on public services with the recently arrived 1.5 million Iraqi refugees. The government's failure to address the pressing humanitarian crisis added to public dissent followed by heavy-handed response by the governor.

For the majority Sunni agricultural class in Syria water as a productive resource is vital to the livelihood of a quarter of its population. The loss of income and the mass urban migration contributed to resentment due to the unequal distribution of social rights pushing them to the margins. The mostly Sunni environmental refugees were largely responsible for the alienation of the Alawi-dominated government that mounted strong action against the opposing groups. The resulting humanitarian crisis aggravated dormant grievances. 'The feeling of abandonment and powerlessness and of being betrayed by the government easily transformed itself into hatred and vindictiveness'.[44]

Most importantly, Syria's large agricultural communities were acutely affected by drought that implicitly influenced the public attitude towards the political status quo, and thus contributed to the instigation of protest movements that sparked the civil war.[45] It is clear that bad environmental conditions and non-existent management by the Syrian government had a negative effect on communal harmony.

Areas of conflict were a boon to the illicit economy with the erosion of territorial borders and the internationalization of non-state actors with its focus on the smuggling of oil, antiquities, and people, and illicit trade from human trafficking to drug smuggling. Yet narcotics trade is often omitted though in Syria 'this trade centers around one of the most favored

[43] Ibid.

[44] Ibid.

[45] Caitlin E. Werrell & Francesco Femia (Eds.), 'The Arab Spring and Climate Change: A Climate and Security Correlations Series', Centre for American Progress 2013, https://climateandsecurity.files.wordpress.com/2012/04/climatechangearabspring-ccs-cap-stimson.pdf.

drugs in the Middle East, albeit one relatively unknown outside the region: Captagon, an illegal amphetamine stimulant sometimes referred to in Arabic as *Abu Hilalain*. It is in high demand in the wealthy Gulf states like Saudi Arabia, the UAE, and Qatar, where its inexpensive yet powerful high overshadows its highly addictive quality, for which it is banned in most of the world. It is the drug of choice among young Saudi partygoers, more so than hashish, cocaine, heroin or ecstasy. Abuse of fenethylline, brand name Captagon, and its counterfeit versions continue to be available despite its illegality.[46] 'Historically, hubs of Captagon production have been located in Eastern Europe, Turkey, and Lebanon. As of now, Captagon is produced almost exclusively in Syria'.[47] Syria's centrality to the Captagon trade for a number of years has meant that the transit routes out of Syria have kept changing depending on changes in the control of insurgent groups along its borders. It is an unintended consequence of the long-running civil war.

Syria's Geostrategic Importance

Syria's geostrategic position, often referred to cover a wider region, has provided the roots of tensions that have determined regional developments. It has always been seen as the lightning rod as much for intellectual ferment as for unending conflict. Throughout history, notwithstanding its relatively small size,[48] Syria, with its multidimensional projection, became pivotal in influencing the direction of the region. Repeatedly, Syria has been the trigger, and the base, for forces determined to upset or destroy the existing order. Syria's neighbours —Jordan, Iraq, Turkey, Lebanon and Israel—continue to experience internal strife and external conflict traced to, or linked with, Syria. It recalls the nearly 16-year long Lebanese civil war that eventually degenerated into everyone fighting everyone else. The Syrian civil war, now in its tenth year, is a war with global implications since all the participants—including four of the five permanent

[46] Mirren Gidda, 'Drug's in War: What Is Captagon, the 'Jihad Pill' Used by Islamic State Militants', *Newsweek*, December, 5, 2017, https://www.newsweek.com/drugs-captagon-islamic-state-jihad-war-amphetamines-saudi-arabia-608233.

[47] Mark Krantz & Will Nichols, 'A Bitter Pill to Swallow: Connections Between Captagon, Syria and the Gulf', SIPA, *Columbia Journal of International Affairs*, May 18, 2016, https://jia.sipa.columbia.edu/bitter-pill-swallow-connections-captagon-syria-gulf.

[48] https://www.britannica.com/place/Syria.

members of the UN Security Council have sought to interpret, in their own interest, the cardinal principles enshrined in the United Nations Charter. It is also a dimension of the 'proxy religious war' in the region between Iran and Saudi Arabia raging also in Yemen and Iraq.

In bringing all major world powers on the same battlefield its outcome could provoke the eclipse of the United Nations itself.[49]

Assad's Staying Power

Bashar Assad's survivability in Syria's long-running civil war has been remarkable. The ability of his state to outplay its regional and international enemies has been a surprise. 'Rather than just the Russians and Iranians being responsible for this, there was a coherent strategy to win back not just the territory but also the alliances that it temporarily lost during the course of this war. And unlike Saddam after the first gulf war, Bashar al-Assad is already remerging fast as a regional player again'.[50] His success owes greatly to the exploitation of the ethnic fault lines in Lebanon, Iraq, Turkey and Palestine and support from other stakeholders like Lebanon's Shia and Christian communities, the Palestinian factions, the Alevi and Arabs of Turkey and the Iraqi Shi'a. His ability to divide opponents on both the battlefield and diplomatic table was an important factor to turn the tide in his favour with unparalleled military and political support from Russia and Iran and by key Arab states like Egypt and Algeria.

Bashar al-Assad's re-emergence in 2018 as a pivotal Arab leader avowed to promote stability in the region is an ironic twist of fate. Seven years after the Arab League, Saudi Arabia, and UAE shunned the Syrian Arab Republic, Bahrain and Egypt are leading the push for Assad and Syria to be reinstated into the Arab League. Furthermore, Assad's success is also attributable to Syria's unique geography and history during the cold war. It led Damascus, during the Arab Spring, to a fate vastly different to that of Baghdad, Tripoli, Cairo or Tunis.

[49] Seth Frantzen, 'Syria: The Largest (and Most Important) Conflict of the 21st Century', *The National Interest*, April 16, 2018, https://nationalinterest.org/feature/syria-the-largest-most-important-conflict-the-21st-century-25406?page=0%2C1.

[50] Kamal Alam, 'Pax Syriana: The Staying Power of Bashar Assad,' *Asian Affairs*, January 30, 2019, Vol. 50, No. 1, pp. 1–17, https://www.tandfonline.com/doi/full/10.1080/03068374.2019.1567099?scroll=top&needAccess=true.

For most Syrians, the widespread pluralistic nature of governance, albeit a one-party system, had kept stability in an otherwise unruly part of the Middle East. Similarly, despite corruption and a lack of economic mobility the state had the best public services in the Arab world. Before the war, Syria also had the most robust state education system in the Arab world. Assad's survival is due to the loyalty of the Syrian military with no major defections. It remains one of the only armies in the Arab world, where Greek Orthodox, Maronite Catholics, Sunni, Druze and Alawite can all rise to the top without prejudice based on sect or religion.

Since March 1949, Syria has experienced sixteen army coups, nine of which were successful in overthrowing the incumbent rulers. The army had never really gone back to barracks before the arrival of Hafez al-Assad. The Army-Ba'ath faction that has ruled Syria for the last four decades was not an all-out dictatorship but a balance of communities 'between rural and urban Syria, mercantile and tribal Syria, and the political families that have urged the army to intervene one way or another from Syria's inception, whether these families were leftists, Nasserites, pan-Arabists or business-focused'.[51] The divergent business interests and feudal family politics converged on the armed forces, with the aim of ensuring that a strong stable Syria had some leverage over Iraq, Lebanon and Jordan. The system made each of these a co-parcenary in building the state.

Hafez al-Assad and Mustafa Tlass[52] decided that given the external threats, the army above all must have a nationalist agenda and be an institution devoid of politics.[53] The ideological agreement between Tlass and Assad led to the complete purging of politics from the military and a separation of powers not seen before in Syria. By the time Bashar al-Assad took office the Syrian Army had firmly erased its French colonial legacy of sectarian beginnings. The education system, run along on party lines, evened out relations between rural and urban, tribal and religious sects. Rather than mainstream politics, the family structure was co-opted into the Party keeping the army stable and neutral.

[51] Ibid. Kamal Alam.

[52] Kirill Semenov, 'Who Controls Syria? The Al Assad family, the Inner Circle and the Tycoons', Russian International Affairs Council, February 12, 2018, https://russiancouncil.ru/en/analytics-and-comments/analytics/who-controls-syria-the-al-assad-family-the-inner-circle-and-the-tycoons/.

[53] N. Van Dam, 'The Struggle for Power in Syria: Politics and Society under Assad and the Ba'th Party', 2011, I.B. Tauris, London, p. 63.

One by one its enemies have redeveloped diplomatic ties, and even the Israelis concluded in 2018 that they could see diplomatic links with Syria open up again. The UAE, Bahrain and Kuwait under Saudi approval have all reopened their embassies and have gone against the conventional wisdom that Syria will only have Iran as a wealthy backer. Syria proved time and again that it was 'the bleeding heart of the Arab world' a back-handed tribute to Syria's consistently hard line against Israel and its critical geographical position which made it always triumph against its bigger enemies such as Israel, Turkey and Iraq. Syria has once again reiterated its role after President Trump's unilateral declaration on Israel's sovereignty over the Golan Heights.[54] Bashar al-Assad has survived the fall-out of the Hariri assassination in Lebanon, the fall of Saddam Hussein and the early losses in the civil war. His return into the Arab fraternity will mark the defeat of major Arab countries and Turkey through their proxies against Assad.

Bashar al-Assad has had support from key elements of Syrian society while his army and intelligence remains one of the most diverse in the Arab world: Christians, Druze, Sunnis are all at key decision-making positions, a legacy he inherited from his father. It is well said that in Syria the best of all possible worlds is to be an Alawi, in the Army, yet high positions are not excluded to members of other communities' that have been co-opted into the system. Bashar has enjoyed support from Egypt and Algeria with the two largest Arab Sunni armies. The pluralistic state was the defining factor in his staying power.

The Assad regime, in power for nearly 40 years, has survived a tough neighbourhood—bordered by Iraq, Israel, Jordan, Lebanon and Turkey—by a combination of guile and cozying up to more powerful countries, first the Soviet Union and now Iran. In a state of war with Israel since 1948, Syria provides material support to the Islamist groups of Hezbollah and Hamas; it is also determined to reclaim the Golan Heights captured by Israel in 1967 with Mount Hermon that dominates the area.

'Relations with the United States, rarely good, turned particularly dire after the 2003 U.S. invasion of Iraq, when George W. Bush, citing Syria's opposition to the war and support for Iraqi insurgents, threatened regime change in Damascus and demonized Syria's young president as a Middle

[54] Mathew Lee & Deb Reichmann, 'Trump Signs Declaration Reversing US Policy on Golan Heights', AP, March 25, 2019, https://www.apnews.com/da3b37642ce648658d1e6a8de2d43846.

Eastern prince of darkness'.[55] Yet Syria marked in 1947 the first attempt by the United States to enter the Middle East that may end with President Trump's decision to withdraw his troops from the country. As early as 1947 United States was interested in an oil pipeline, running through Syria to the Mediterranean. Syria's location once again became crucial as it had in history to the Crusaders. The machinations with the Syrian political leadership by two CIA agents to filibuster a British attempt to run an oil pipeline from Saudi Arabia through Syria and to enable the construction of an ARAMCO pipeline failed after a few years due to change of Syrian leadership and ARAMCO's takeover by the Saudi government. When US ally Adib Shishakli was overthrown in 1954 the USSR provided arms deals and warded off three counter-coup attempts. The pipeline was shut down in 1976 reducing US interest in the region.[56]

It's been two decades since Bashar took office, as Syria appears poised to re-emerge to a pivotal role in regional affairs. The road to Middle East peace runs through Damascus though after eight years of civil conflict 'it will be hard for Syria to move forward without tending to its crippling internal disrepair'.[57]

Syria's Political Culture

Syrian political culture is marked by the predominance of Arab Ba'athist thinking in particular[58]:

- It has an allergy to accepting foreign aid and suspicion of the West, particularly the United States, in view of Syria's hypersensitivity

[55] Don Belt, 'Shadowland: Poised to Play a Pivotal New Role in the Middle East, Syria Struggles to Escape Its Dark Past', Fault lines and Field-Notes, *National Geographic*, Vol. 216, No. 5, pp. 52–75, http://donbelt.org/wp-content/uploads/2015/01/Fault-Lines-and-Field-Notes-PDF-7812.pdf.

[56] James Barr, 'Once Upon a Time, America needed Syria', Foreign Policy, September 18, 2018, https://foreignpolicy.com/2018/09/18/once-upon-a-time-america-needed-syria/.

[57] Ibid. Don Belt.

[58] Yassin al-Haj Saleh, 'The Political Culture of Modern Syria: Its Formation, Structure and Interactions', Political Case Studies: Conflict Research Centre, March 2013, http://www.mafhoum.com/press7/225P9.pdf.

to all that is external and the constant and heavy presence of an inside/outside dichotomy.

- In a parody of the enemy being constantly at the gates, the distinct mobilizationary aspect of all speeches and political ideologies in the country, regardless of the political constituency of the speakers or leaders. It reflects the internationalized and unstable character of the Middle East, and Syria in particular, that suited the ruling elite allowing it to maintain the state of emergency. In operation since 1963 when the Ba'ath Party assumed power, it was rescinded on April 21, 2011 by Bashar Assad.
- Another constant of Syrian political culture is the treatment of homogeneity as a high and quintessential virtue, while difference and plurality are dismissed as occasional and ephemeral phenomena. It exhorts the populace to show greater solidarity and homogeneity.
- 'Syrian political culture is distinguished by its strong "statist" character with the leader and the coterie surrounding him the real decision-makers. The concept of state thus becomes synonymous with that of politics and social and public life. It reflects the total presence of the state in all aspects of life. The result is the exclusion of civil society from engagement in the political and intellectual life of the country'. It was an important reason for the onset of the civil war in the country particularly the lifting of the state of emergency and martial law and demands for the release of all political prisoners.
- The reiteration of a patriotic discourse to stress strengthening of the national fibre has in effect weakened the stand of the democratic opposition, imposing the oppression of the Ba'ath that monopolizes patriotism and negates the calls—both internal and external—to democratise.
- Both the mobilizationary and revolutionary factors with the statism and collectivism they inspire have jointly contributed to the weakening of the chances for growth of liberal elements within the Syrian and Arab political culture. While the need for a powerful internally interventionist state in the Middle East is seen as necessary and perpetuates dictatorship, the Syrian conflict attests to the need for a measure of popular participation anchored to a democratic social contract that guarantees of pluralism and individual liberties.

As a result, Syrian political culture has remained moribund further consolidated by the endless civil war with the participation of major and regional powers. All the changes witnessed since March 2011 were within the ranks of a narrow and elitist framework. Bashar Assad's staying power and the resilience of the Ba'athist state is due largely to the fact that there were no major defections—specifically from the inner circle—despite financial compensation offered by the Gulf States and the West. In a complete reversal of previous expectations, the Kurds and Erdogan again grudgingly look to Damascus, the Arabs—despite an Iranian presence—march back to Damascus, and Lebanon and Israel again reverts back to dealing with Assad as the arbiter.[59]

Military units of sixty-five states were active at the height of the Syrian conflict, some like Turkey with their own troops, and others like the United States also sub-contracting the war to their secret services or military contractors. The US-led anti-ISIS coalition alone comprised 67 states along with Russia and Iran. Each phase of the conflict drew in new actors, empowered others and weakened yet other. Syria thus evokes the fragmentation of the Thirty Years War, the failed goal of Woodrow Wilson at the Versailles Conference after the First World War and the sabre rattling of the Cold War. It is the most important conflict of the twenty-first century and its legacy will carry forward long into the future. It has, for the first time since WW I, symbolically redrawn the map of the region. The effects of the ongoing Syrian conflict have reinforced Syria's position as a 'pivotal state' in radiating religious, societal and governmental instability in a devastating impact on all its neighbours in the region and on international peace and security.

Syria's strategic importance in the region arises from its borders with five countries: Iraq, Israel, Jordan, Lebanon and Turkey. Conflict, sectarian division and the co-mingling of cultures and families have marked Syria's history with each of them. Yet this is not all. The various religious groups in the country are equally reflected in their adherence to the various ethnic and religious minorities. The Free Syrian Army, the main rebel force, is 90 per cent Sunni, evocative of the sectarian element that underlies the civil war. The Syrian Kurds have their own groups and fight for a different goal.

[59] Kamal Alam, 'Kissinger's Prophecy Fulfilled in Syria', War on The Rocks.com, January 23, 2019, https://warontherocks.com/2019/01/kissingers-prophecy-fulfilled-in-syria/.

The unending Syrian civil war is equally about mind-numbing and endless rivalries at multiple levels: the covert confrontation between the United States and Russia for assertion of primacy in the Middle East; between NATO[60] members, United States and Turkey, given their divided and nationalistic goals; and between Israel and Iran with their exacerbating hostility. 'There is something different about this', said Faysal Itani, an expert on the Syrian conflict at the Atlantic Council.[61] 'It's never been as much of an international war as it has now become' transforming into an international contest fought over Syrian territory. Syria's neighbours have aligned themselves along religious lines: majority Shia Iran supporting Assad, while Sunni majorities in Qatar and Saudi Arabia back the rebels.

'The Syrian war has now been outsourced', said Christopher Phillips, a Syria scholar at Queen Mary University of London. 'The decision-makers are now not really Syrians, perhaps with the exception of Assad'. Foreign involvement in the civil war first took the form of 'diplomatic support, then it was economic support, then it was material support for fighters, then it was fighting them directly. … And I don't see why that shouldn't continue'.[62] For a mix of reasons—historical, religious, geographic and geopolitical—Syria now represents one of the world's thorniest challenges with its refugee crisis and puts Russia and Iran on a possible collision course with the United States and its allies.

For Assad, the next issues, apart from clearing the country of the remnants of the opposing Islamic groups in Idlib and elsewhere, is to work out a mutually beneficial relationship with Russia and Iran that leave him free to exercise his writ. In this context, it will be appropriate to briefly analyze Iran, Turkey and Saudi Arabia's role since the onset of the Syrian civil war.

[60] North Atlantic Treaty Organization, 'What Is NATO', https://www.nato.int/nato-welcome/index.html.

[61] Uri Friedman, 'Syria's War Has Never Been More International', *The Atlantic*, February 14, 2018, https://www.theatlantic.com/international/archive/2018/02/syria-civil-war-next/553232/.

[62] Ibid. Friedman.

Iran, Turkey and Saudi Arabia

Syria and Iran's shared strategic concerns regarding Israel, Iraq, and the United States bring them together. Washington has little leverage with either regime. Their resilience against internal foes has been marked by a common understanding, even if Syria's minority-dominated dictatorship portrays itself as a champion of secular Arab nationalism, while Iran flies the banner of revolutionary Islam although as a Persian country it is often at odds with the Arab world.[63]

Their endurance is due largely to the geopolitical factors and shared threat perceptions. Iran and Syria are drawn together by their opposition to the US-led regional security order, and this alliance reflects the desire of 'middle powers' to 'defend their autonomy against intensive Western penetration of the Middle East'. These shared concerns explain how Syria and Iran were able to transcend their ideological differences to work towards shared visions of regional autonomy and reduced foreign penetration of the Middle East. In recent years, especially since 2011, Iran has demonstrated its strong commitment to its ally and has been a major player in the Syrian conflict. Iran has consistently supported the Syrian government by sending military advisers to the country, establishing transnational militias there and providing political support in the international arena.[64]

Since the Lausanne Treaty of 1923 confirmed Turkish annexation of the border province of Hatay (*Arabic* al-Iskenderun) it has formed the backdrop to vexed, often friendly, relations between Turkey and Syria. These treaties and agreements' provisions, particularly the entry in 1938 of Turkish troops in the province, not only strengthened Turkey's presence but also paved the way for its unification under its domination in 1939 following a favourable vote of the National Assembly of Hatay. The Allied powers acquiesced in it to keep Turkey neutral rather than joining the Axis powers. On the Syrian side al-Iskenderun has been, over the decades, memorialized in song and folk tales. Syria's putative and popular

[63] Daniel L. Byman, 'Syria and Iran: What's Behind Their Enduring Alliance,' Brookings, July 19, 2006, https://www.brookings.edu/opinions/syria-and-iran-whats-behind-the-enduring-alliance/.

[64] Hassan Ahmadian & Payam Mohseni, 'Iran's Syria Strategy: The Evolution of Deterrence,' International Affairs, Chatham House, February 4, 2019, https://www.belfercenter.org/publication/irans-syria-strategy-evolution-deterrence.

sense of ownership and of the Ba'athist government has not been dented by Turkish efforts to promote strong economic relations.[65]

For decades, Turkey was a rarity: a secular democracy with a Muslim majority, a liberal economy, and a solid alliance with the West. It was NATO's only Muslim-majority country and, for a brief while, the likeliest candidate to carry the same distinction as a member of the European Union (EU). Against this current, there has always been an opposing camp vying for a more activist foreign policy. The Islamists were particularly strong in this camp. When they came to power in 2002, under the leadership of President Erdogan and his Justice and Development Party (AKP), Turkish foreign policy underwent a complete overhaul. As Europe grew wary of Turkey's prospective membership, Turkey's political consensus on EU membership unravelled.

With the civil war in Syria, Turkey's foreign policy finally faced the fate its critics long feared. Ankara sank deep into the morass it had been expected to change by its example. Turkey became caught in a three-way fight with two groups that it considers terrorists—the Kurdish-separatist Kurdistan Workers' Party (PKK) and the radical jihadist Islamic State.[66] Turkey entered the war in 2011, backing and training rebels bent on bringing down Bashar al-Assad. As the conflict shifted from an uprising against his dynastic rule to a bloody war drawing in several world powers, the country has become increasingly marginalized. Turkey, Russia and Iran agreed to uphold de-confliction zones in 2018 aiming to reduce violence. For Turkey, 'strategically, the goal is to keep a toe in the Syrian waters and the peace process', said Joost Hiltermann, program director for International Crisis Group. Yet in Idlib, part of the de-confliction area, Russian planes are now helping the Assad regime bomb rebels, some of whom continue to be supported by Turkey. Furthermore, Turkish

[65] Shaimaa Magued, 'Turkey's Economic Rapprochement Towards Syria and the Territorial Conflict over Hatay', *Journal of Mediterranean Politics*, 2019, Vol. 24, No. 1, (online 20 July 2017), https://www.tandfonline.com/doi/full/10.1080/13629395.2017.1353583?scroll=top&needAccess=true.

[66] Selim Can Sazak & CaglarKurc, 'From Zero Problems to Zero Friends? The Past. Present and Future of Turkey's Role in Regional Security', The Century Foundation, https://tcf.org/content/report/zero-problems-zero-friends/?session=1.

troops are already in Afrin and engaged in active hostilities with the Syrian Army.[67]

Saudi Arabia's relations with Syria have always been tense albeit with periods of mutual support. Saudi Arabia has always viewed its relations with Syria on two pillars in the backdrop of the Syria's majority Sunni population and the fall-out of any instability on the Kingdom, and the need to check Iran particularly its aspiration to acquire the nuclear weapon. The assassination of Prime Minister Rafik Hariri, close to the Saudi Royal family, closed off bilateral relations for some time. As Syria started in March 2011 its version of the Arab revolution, initially Saudi Arabia supported the Assad regime believing that any alternative would be dangerous to itself. It was only after Syrian government's rejection of the Annan Peace Plan and its strong action against opposing radical Sunni Islamic groups that Saudi Arabia entered a period supporting them, including the Islamic State,[68] by providing funding and other military wherewithal to topple Assad.

'The root of the Saudi involvement in the Syrian civil war lies in what…[is] referred to above as the intra-Islamic "cold war"; the Shiite camp led by Iran, with its allies Syria and Hezbollah, is facing off against the Sunni camp led by Saudi Arabia and the other Gulf monarchies, as well as Jordan, Egypt and even Turkey. Riyadh's intervention in Syria stemmed from concern for its Sunni brothers being massacred by Assad'.[69]

Saudi Arabia, to assert its leadership, was equally interested to bolster its humanitarian assistance program for Syrian refugees, mainly Sunni, in camps in Jordan and in Syria itself. 'It allocated $2.7 million a month to programs through the International Islamic Relief Organization of Saudi Arabia and the Saudi embassy in Lebanon. King Abdullah launched a national fundraising drive on behalf of Syrian citizens; the money

[67] Sue Engles Rasmussen, 'Behind Turkey's Actions in Syria: A Fear of Waning Influence,' *The Wall Street Journal*, February 16, 2018, https://www.wsj.com/articles/behind-turkeys-actions-in-syria-a-fear-of-waning-influence-1518810799.

[68] Editorial Board, 'Fighting While Funding, Extremism', *The New York Times*, June 19, 2017, https://www.nytimes.com/2017/06/19/opinion/saudi-arabia-qatar-isis-terrorism.html.

[69] Yehuda U. Blanga, 'Saudi Arabia's Motives in the Syrian Civil War,' Middle East Policy Council, Winter 2017, Vol. XXIV, No. 4, https://www.mepc.org/journal/saudi-arabias-motives-syrian-civil-war.

collected was used to send dozens of trucks to Syrian refugee camps in Jordan. The humanitarian campaign was strongly branded, including the logo printed on shirts and caps: 'Saudi Kingdom of Humanity."

In fact, the Saudi assistance to its neighbours and the refugees living there went beyond humanitarian aid'.[70] The third explanation behind Saudi involvement in Syria relates to the spread of radical Islam in Iraq and Syria. As the fighting continued, and the Islamic State's halo shone brighter, so did the Saudis' strong desire to bring down Bashar al-Assad. Saudi Arabia was also fearful of indoctrinated Saudi young men returning after being part of the Syrian rebel groups with battlefield experience and a radical religious doctrine they would ultimately direct against the regime. Saudi Arabia, leader of the Sunni world, largely failed to stymie Iran's growing strength in the Middle East and undermining Tehran by eliminating its ally in Damascus. At the same time, the Arab League's invitation for Bashar Assad to re-join could not have come without Saudi approval.

Conclusion

This chapter has tried to draw out the characteristics that make Syria a unique power in the Middle East. Syria stands alone in its archaeological significance for humankind and its pivotal situation in the region as well as the historicity of its long-inhabited towns and cities. Its human geography, including the tolerance of its ethnic and religiously diversity, is exceptional in the region. Syria's Ba'athist political culture has burnished Bashar al-Assad's staying power, coupled with exploiting all the available opportunities for playing off different powers. The fact that his Army overcame a variety of threats, including to itself, is a notable feature of the civil war.

Syria's continued survival is remarkable although the endless civil war has enmeshed four of the five UN Security Council members and all major regional powers. The failure of the United Nations Security Council to bring in a countrywide and lasting ceasefire asserts the UNSC's partisanship in addressing the issue. In the process, Syria faces a massive

[70] Ibid. Blanga.

number of refugees and internally displaced that has ruined its social and economic framework and affected Jordan, Lebanon and Turkey. UN Security Council Resolution 2254(2015) still remains the only unanimous framework to usher stability and an acceptable political framework to the country.

CHAPTER 3

The Syrian Insurgency and Its Aftermath

For many Syrians, the civil war began in the town of Dara'a,[1] an agricultural town on the border with Jordan hitherto known for having provided the staging point for Lawrence of Arabia's rallying of the Arabs against the Ottoman Army.[2] In March 2011, 15 teenage boys were arrested because of graffiti spray-painted on a high school wall. The images of Arab strongmen like Egypt's Hosni Mubarak and Tunisia's Ben Ali abdicating power prompted someone to scrawl on the wall: 'It's your turn now Doctor', referring to Bashar Assad, the ophthalmologist. Town officials could not find the perpetrator. The boys were held, beaten, had fingernails removed, and were tortured for weeks to extract a confession. While they were captive, their town revolted, protesting daily and calling on Assad to pressure the town's police chief to release them.[3] It was an irresistible force colliding with an immovable object.

[1] Jamie Tarabay, 'For Many Syrians the Story of the War Began with Graffiti in Dara'a', CNN, March 15, 2018, https://edition.cnn.com/2018/03/15/middleeast/daraa-syria-seven-years-on-intl/index.html.

[2] Scott Anderson, 'The True Story of Lawrence of Arabia', *Simthsonian Magazine*, July 2014, https://www.smithsonianmag.com/history/true-story-lawrence-arabia-180951857/?page=3.

[3] The Associated Press, 'Syria Government Forces Plant Flag in Dara'a, the Cradle of the Uprising', CBC, July 12, 2018, https://www.cbc.ca/news/world/syria-daraa-recapture-1.4744308.

R. M. Abhyankar, *Syria*,
https://doi.org/10.1007/978-981-15-4562-7_3

Arab Revolutions Revive, an Overview

The reaction from entrenched forces in the Arab countries—the Muslim Brotherhood and 'king's' political parties—had started well before that in Dara'a. The Arab revolutions, misnamed the 'Arab Spring', starting in Tunisia in December 2010 spread like wild fire across the northern African seaboard through every country until it reached Egypt. It was an assertion of the popular will for a voice in the governance of these countries. Seeing the back of long-standing dictators, President Ben Ali of Tunisia and Egypt's President Mubarak, the popular Arab revolution cascaded in 2011 across the Arab Peninsula to Bahrain where a series of Shi'a-dominated anti-government protests escalated to daily clashes. The Bahrain government repressed the revolt with the support of Gulf Cooperation Council and its Peninsula Shield Force.[4] Before being halted by the reactionary forces, the revolutions failed to achieve their avowed goal of creating a democratic polity in these countries. The high hopes for a new, free and democratic Arab world turned into civil wars in Syria, Libya, Yemen and Iraq. While 'on the surface, the political upheavals look like failed revolts against dictatorships, dig a bit deeper into the societies of these Arab countries and there are reasons to believe what we see is an epochal revolution'.[5] Instead of democracies Egypt, Bahrain and even Morocco, became dictatorships that are more repressive. Then is the Islamic State (ISIL), the most barbaric outcome of the chaos after the United States invasion of Iraq.

The re-emergence of the Arab revolutions in the future was inevitable given the demographic situation with the doubling of Arab populations since 1980. It was coupled with the economic collapse due to the fall in tourism, fluctuating oil prices and inflation increasing the cost of necessities. There was even stronger repression, arrest and torture of innocent citizens by state intelligence agencies and an increasing threat to minorities. Finally, to marginalize the intra-sectarian conflict in religion dictated the imperative need, despite the allergy of religious institutions, for a debate on the future of Islam and its role in governance. The revival of the Arab revolutions in 2019, after eight years, has taken many forms.

[4] Julian Reder, 'The Peninsula Shield Force: The Gulf Cooperation Council's Vestigial Organ', International Policy Digest, May 8, 2017, https://intpolicydigest.org/2017/05/08/peninsula-shield-force-gulf-cooperation-council-s-vestigial-organ/.

[5] Ibid. Koert Debeuf.

The revival has once again given hopes to the Arab masses increasingly accustomed to seeing dictators assuming power. Yet in many countries that had witnessed the Arab Spring of 2010 the outlook remains bleak.

In Yemen, the mass protest that forced President Ali Abdullah Saleh to flee after 30 years did not bring in democracy. Foreign military intervention led by Saudi Arabia, and other like-minded Arab countries, spawned armed opposition leading to another brutal, often forgotten, civil war. The Yemeni people have endured the worst cholera outbreak in the world while famine looms and tens of thousands of civilians have been killed or maimed.[6] An UN-brokered ceasefire for the vital city of Hodeida, and two other ports, is barely holding. Once again, the sectarian dimension of the war rules the day with the 'Saudi Crown Prince Mohammed bin Salman or MBS, the architect of international action in the war, unwilling to make concessions to the Iranian-backed Houthis,[7] and an end to hostilities seems a long way off'.[8] In Egypt's 'military republic', the military budget accounts for 4.6% of government expenditures and, once again, the Army plays a major role in the country's economy. Due to shortage of foreign and private investment, Egypt had to make a Faustian deal with Saudi Arabia, accepting its divisive support and influence. The interim military regimes in these countries are loath to make the needed changes by introducing more dynamism in the economy, de-centralize delivery of social services and introduce reform of the judiciary and media. The protestors in Algeria and Sudan still hold a veto power that could force the Army to make concessions, yet it remains moot. Their resolve to reduce the role of the Army in the country's life is their strong point. Cutting the size and influence of the bloated institutions and paramilitary forces of the Army could enable the military to emerge as the sole guardian of national security.[9]

In the meanwhile, following Gaddafi's demise, two governments rule the country kept in place by European countries that crucially depend

[6] Emma Graham-Harrison, 'Beyond Syria: The Arab Spring's Aftermath,' *The Guardian*, December 30, 2018, https://www.theguardian.com/world/2018/dec/30/arab-spring-aftermath-syria-tunisia-egypt-yemen-libya.

[7] Bruce Riedel, 'Who Are the Houthis and Why Are We at War with Them', Brookings, December 18, 2017, https://www.brookings.edu/blog/markaz/2017/12/18/who-are-the-houthis-and-why-are-we-at-war-with-them/.

[8] Ibid.

[9] Ibid. Ishac Diwan.

on the uninterrupted flow of the country's oil. A second ongoing civil war involves the troops of General Khalifa Haftar, the leader of eastern Libyan militias, who bids to capture the capital Tripoli and the UN-backed Government of National Accord led by Prime Minister Fayez al-Sarraj. An UN-brokered international conference held in mid-April 2019 to lay the groundwork for elections urged opposing Libyan factions to come together. By ordering his forces towards Tripoli, when U.N. Secretary General Antonio Guterres was in the city, to help organize the national conference, General Haftar has made his disdain for the peace efforts clear'.[10] Haftar, backed by the United Arab Emirates, France, Egypt, Russia and Saudi Arabia, was aiming to scuttle the conference in a brazen bid for power. Despite United Nations, appeals for stronger American diplomatic engagement General Haftar's backers in Abu Dhabi and Riyadh have ensured a warming from President Trump that aligns with the latter's preference for authoritarian leaders. A subsequent conference in Berlin in January 2020 once again has not led to the expected breakthrough in bringing about a ceasefire. In the meanwhile, with Turkey extending military support to the UN-backed government, and France backing General Haftar. It has split NATO with no resolution in sight. The two sides have announced a ceasefire and the GNA has announced elections in March 2021.[11]

Yet the conditions in Libya continue to worsen. The conflict has been dragging on for almost two years and the dynamics of international involvement has been shifting rapidly with significant external factors coming into play. 'Criminality and human trafficking is so rampant that gangs hold public slave auctions, and every year thousands of desperate migrants from sub-Saharan Africa are forced onto decrepit boats for the risky trip to Europe; many have met their deaths in the Mediterranean. The European Union has been accused of fuelling conflict by paying Libyan militias to crack down on trafficking routes. The number of people

[10] Frederic Wehrey & Jeffrey Feltman, 'Libya Is Entering Another Civil War America Can Stop It', *The New York Times*, April 5, 2019, https://www.nytimes.com/2019/04/05/opinion/libya-civil-war-.html.

[11] Guma al-Gumaty, 'Turkey, Syria and the Libyan Conundrum', AJImpat, January 18, 2020, https://www.aljazeera.com/indepth/opinion/turkey-russia-libyan-conundrum-200118144000930.html.

making the sea crossing has fallen but thousands are trapped and suffering in makeshift prisons inside the country'.[12]

Monarchies from Bahrain to Jordan and Morocco fared better than dictators, although all were forced to make concessions and are still grappling with the Arab Spring fall-out. The cradle of the Arab Spring, Tunisia, is its single success story. Within a month of Bouazizi's death, and the flight to Saudi Arabia of the autocratic president Zine al-Abidine Ben Ali, 'the democracy that came in its place, while facing terror attacks and economic troubles, is serving as a beacon of hope to progressive intellectuals and activists around the region. Yet ISIS assaults on the crucial tourism industry have dealt a heavy blow while the country struggles to control extremism and bolster a weak economy.' [13]

The conditions are no better in countries that have seen a revival of popular contestation. Mass protests in Algeria and Sudan have removed two ageing autocrats ending, 20 and 30 years, respectively, of absolutist rule. In both countries, the insurgents are in continuing negotiations with the army, yet again, the de facto manager of the transition to a new political order. 'The outcome of these power struggles will help to determine whether Algeria and Sudan become more democratic and prosperous or instead add to a decade-long chain of disappointed hopes in the region'.[14]

The protesters in both countries are aware of the 'Egyptian trap' where a general who takes interim charge becomes president for life. In both these countries, more so in Algeria, the army is a 'state within a state' not subject to civil laws, and an economic actor in the country. The tendency to protect itself is ingrained. The oil boom since 2000 protected the autocrats in these countries though it led to a distorted allocation of oil revenues. In Sudan, oil revenues decreased sharply from 2007 to 2017 due to the loss of oilfields to South Sudan after its separation. The fall from 16% of GDP to 1% meant a drastic fall in provision of social services and subsidies from 21 to 10% over the same period. Yet the share of military remained at thirty-one per cent in 2017. In Algeria too, oil revenues fell by fifty per cent from 2007 to 2017 yet the defence budget doubled to one-third of oil revenues.

[12] Ibid. EmmaGraham-Harrison.

[13] Ibid.

[14] Ishac Diwan, 'The Arab Spring's Second Chance', Project Syndicate, April 23, 2019, https://www.project-syndicate.org/commentary/algeria-sudan-army-power-struggle-by-ishac-diwan-2019-04.

Following the Saudi lead in Yemen, the absolute rulers of the Gulf States, particularly Qatar and UAE, have exploited to the hilt their newly acquired power to intervene in the neighbourhood through funds and armaments and religion unmindful of the little internal dissent. Yet, it has also increased tension between them, particularly Qatar and Saudi Arabia, complicating their relations with the United States and other western allies.

In contrast, the resistance model that Bashar al-Assad adopted in Syria in 2011 was in keeping with the state of Arab revolutions in other countries 'experiencing a period of political confusion, such as security vacuums, economic difficulties and social protests in Egypt, Tunisia and Libya, as well as Yemen. It also represented the failure of negotiations between the conflicting political forces to agree on the rules of the democratic political game. The revolutionary forces no longer had a plan that they could execute or social backing that would defend such a plan. The best description for this stage is the revolutionary forces' decline and the rise of the concept of a civil war as the only option, as happened in Syria and Yemen'.[15]

It was only by 2014 that in Syria the systematic formalization of the so-called counterrevolution or 'deep state' took place. The resistance consolidated with Abdel Fattah Al-Sisi's rise to power in Egypt, return of the old guard in Tunisia, the Nidaa Tounes Party, and fragmentation of the Gulf Cooperation Council on the weight given to political Islam. The emergence in Libya of a potential military dictator Khalifa Haftar is another twist in the fortunes of that country. He 'became a symbol of the complete decline and collapse of the revolutionary forces. As for Syria, Bashar al-Assad 'was a blatant example of the regime forces' rawness in killing, torture and annihilation. Militias outside the scope of the state began to emerge, such as Daesh in Syria, Iraq and Libya, Al Qaeda in Yemen and Syria, and the Houthis in Yemen'.[16]

In this background, the Syrian case becomes unique in that Bashar Assad has stayed the course overcoming relentless opposition from the countries involved and the numerous Islamic opposition groups. Syria dispelled the intoxicating sense of an Arab public coming together to

[15] Radwan Ziyada, 'The Arab Spring's Failure in Democratic Transition', Middle East Monitor, May 2, 2018, https://www.middleeastmonitor.com/20180502-the-arab-springs-failure-in-democratic-transition/.

[16] Ibid. Radwan Ziyada.

confront its despotic leaders instead spurring resistance by entrenched groups and interests. 'The focus on international military intervention that hangs over the Syria debate also differed sharply from the other revolts. Tunisian and Egyptian protesters were not calling for the United States to intervene on their behalf — but almost from the start, some parts of the Syrian opposition abroad sought to emulate the Libyan model and attract Western military intervention. The centrality of the question of military intervention shaped both opposition and regime strategies. It also helped to turn Syria into a battlefield for great-power politics, with Western diplomacy frustrated by Russia's cynical obstruction at the Security Council and refusal to pressure Assad for meaningful political change'.[17]

The Syrian Case

When the protests erupted in March 2011 in Dara'a, Syrian administration's brutal reaction was a foregone conclusion given the network of security agencies competing to prove loyalty to the government. Hafez Assad had built a state in which governance institutions were always subordinate to the security apparatus. Hafez Assad conceived the multiplicity of security agencies as an important source of control even though they competed with each other and monitored not only the public but also each other. By keeping the ultimate control in the hands of the president, the reaction in Dara'a was inevitable.

Lebanon's civil war lasted 15 years perhaps a precedent that points to another five for Syria. In Lebanon, the conflict evolved into a hydra headed monster to become, 'in Hobbes's famous phrase, a war of all against all: right against left, Syrians against Muslims, Christians against Syrians, Israelis against Palestinians, Palestinians against one another, Druze against Maronites, Israelis against Shiites, and Shiites and Druze against Americans, ad infinitum'.[18] The fighting ended with a foreign-brokered agreement in 1989 in Taif, Saudi Arabia. Along the way,

[17] Lynch, Marc, 'How Syria Ruined the Arab Spring', Foreign Policy, May 3, 2013, https://foreignpolicy.com/2013/05/03/how-syria-ruined-the-arab-spring/.

[18] Charles Glass, 'Syria Burning: Out Thirty Year's War?' *Nation*, Vol. 360, No. 10, pp. 24–26, https://eds.b.ebscohost.com/eds/detail/detail?vid=0&sid=54732fa3-fc46-46cc-ac72-b04ab7ec0af9%40pdc-v-sessmgr04&bdata=JnNpdGU9ZWRzLWxpdmUmc2NvcGU9c2l0ZQ%3d%3d#AN=128477723&db=ulh.

150,000 out of 3 million Lebanese died; many more suffered physical and psychological wounds; and perhaps a quarter of the population fled.

Lebanon then, like Syria now, confirmed Nuremberg prosecutor Hartley Shawcross's observation: 'It is the crime of war which is at once the object and the parent of the other crimes: the crimes against humanity, the war crimes, the common murders'.[19] Most of Syria's populated areas—the Mediterranean coast and the spine from Damascus north through Homs and Hama to Aleppo—are now in government hands. The government is working on two axes, first, building up the areas it has taken back by providing electricity, water, schools and other public services. Second, it is taking back the areas it can. The remaining area that the Syrian Army—aided by its Russian, Iranian, and Lebanese allies—is determined to take is Idlib province, which has rebels groups like Hayat Tahrir as Sham that having lost elsewhere is now backed by the Turkish Army. Syria's fate has fallen into the hands of foreign interests. Russia, Iran, Turkey and US, and to a lesser extent, Saudi Arabia and Qatar, are determining the course of events. Syria, mimicking the past, again provides the battleground for opposing interests to settle their quarrels, Israel and Hezbollah, Iran and Israel, United States and Iran and the United States and Russia.

After nine years of relentless conflict, it is undeniable that the regime is winning the war. It owes its ascendancy as much to its opponents' disunity and incompetence as to its own effectiveness and the on-the ground military support of Russia, Iran and the Hezbollah. Contrary to the tenets of guerrilla warfare, Syrian rebel groups have opted to seize and hold terrain for as long as possible. Welcomed initially by the local population and tolerated elsewhere, their failure to shield the population, from government's retaliatory action and the misbehaviour of their own rogue elements, in the end alienated them. 'They ended up occupying land they could not hold, populations they could not govern and risked the lives of those they could not defend.'[20]

Furthermore, the inability of the rebel groups to create effective alliances among the nearly one thousand opposing groups was due to their reliance on rival foreign powers, particularly Turkey, Saudi Arabia, and Qatar. United States, Britain, and France were equally involved,

[19] Ibid. Charles Glass.

[20] Ibid.

though without boots on the ground. As a result, the opposing groups had to kowtow to the often antagonistic and variable priorities of their sponsors. On the other hand, the government had the advantage that, with minimal haemorrhaging of its soldiers to opposition groups, the Army continued to hold major population centres, like central Damascus, most of Aleppo, and the coastal cities of Tartous and Latakia, the heartland of the Alawi region.

An interesting feature of the conflict has been the assertion from the beginning, by the Syrian government, of its sovereignty on distribution of UN's humanitarian assistance. 'Syrian regime's injection of its claims of state sovereignty into the humanitarian aid effort gave it access to critical benefits and resources produced by the "humanitarian space" built by UN agencies and international nongovernmental organizations (INGOs). At times of steep challenges against it, these benefits and resources were critical to the regime's resilience'.[21] The Syrian government, to assert access and control the modalities for the distribution to the population, cited UNSC Resolution 46/182 of December 1991. The resolution became a standard reference point for Syrian officials and diplomats insisting that the Syrian government was fully in charge of international humanitarian aid and the relief effort premised on unconditional respect for Syrian state sovereignty.

In so doing, the Syrian government regulated countrywide and unconditional access, delayed agreement on the modalities of UN-led operations, and imposed mounting conditions on UN agencies and INGOs working with them. 'The regime's ultimate control over the UN-led aid effort allowed it to consistently prevail and turn humanitarian assistance to its own advantage. These measures erected a suffocating institutional framework for international relief, imposed on local partners, infiltrated UN agencies, interfered with the UN's needs assessments'.[22]

Even UNSC Resolution 2165, authorizing UN agencies to 'use routes across conflict lines' and four border crossings, 'with notification to the Syrian authorities' could not improve matter since the United Nations

[21] Reinoud Leenders & Mansour Kholoud, 'Humanitarianism, State Sovereignty and Authoritarian Regime Maintenance in the Syrian War', *Political Science Quarterly*, Summer 2018, Vol. 133, No. 2, pp 225–257, https://eds.a.ebscohost.com/eds/detail/detail?vid=0&sid=9503ee87-3e77-48ce-bdc6-e116863931a7%40sdc-v-sessmgr03&bdata=JnNpdGU9ZWRzLWxpdmUmc2NvcGU9c2l0ZQ%3d%3d#AN=130267262&db=crh.

[22] Ibid.

Office for Coordination of Humanitarian Affairs (UNOCHA) and INGO were crucially dependent on the Syrian government. The actual mobilization of resources allowed the Syrian regime to siphon aid contributions, especially cash, channel aid away from opposition-held areas and affirm that aid was with the blessings of a sovereign state. It also enabled the Syrian government to reclaim its sovereignty internationally and so to stave off any likelihood of a Libya-type attack based on the doctrine of 'responsibility to protect'. International organizations are only able to work with the blessing of the Assad government in areas it controls—with a shrinking of the space still outside government's control.

The Syrian government was helped in its aim to assert its sovereignty by Russia emphatically framing, from August 2015, its operation of Russian warplanes, through a formal bilateral agreement between two sovereign states, from the government air base at Hmeimim, near Lattakia.[23] Iran too provided significant material and military support, through 'sovereign loans' in excess of US$5 billion and sending its Revolutionary Guards at the behest of the Syrian state. Thus, significant material, military, and diplomatic support was available to enable the government to assert its sovereignty.

Another interesting feature of the long-running civil war has been the proclivity of the government and the opposition groups to tamp down, or ramp up, hostilities depending on requirements of either side- whether strategic, military or economic. This also dictated, for the regime, the military strategy of regaining the country province-by-province through a salami tactic allowing the defeated opposition group to move out mostly to the northwestern Idlib province. Thus, 'wherever the warring sides want peace, there is peace. Where they contest territory, as they did until recently in the eastern quarters of Aleppo, there is war. Where they want profits, they collaborate'.[24] An example is the 'million dollar checkpoint' about ten miles from the centre of Damascus where on a suburban road between government and opposition zones of control in Damascus, both the Syrian army and their rebel enemies inspect cars, vans and pedestrians. 'Their shared objective is extortion, exacting tolls on medicine, food, water, and cigarettes, as well as people, that are moving in and out

[23] Maria Tsvetkova, 'Syrian Militants Rocket Russian Airbase in Syria- Russian Military', Reuters, May 6, 2019, https://www.reuters.com/article/us-russia-syria-military/syrian-militants-rocket-russian-airbase-in-syria-russian-military-idUSKCN1SC1SD.

[24] Ibid. Charles Glass.

of the besieged orchards and homesteads'.[25] Thus, the civil war is not without its business dimension explaining both the survivability of the opposition groups and the length of the conflict.

The government's tactic was a variegated strategy against different opposing groups with some of the latter offered a deal, while others faced heavy firepower. In some neighbourhoods, the government allowed the wounded out and medicine in. In others, it tightened the siege. The means varied, but regardless of the time taken, 'the objective was pacification and restoration of control by the government'.

Government negotiators used army and intelligence officers and its vast store of files on virtually every group and its members. It also enlisted pro-regime residents of contested areas, militiamen from a variety of groups and sympathetic clergy, local mayors, and community leaders. To obtain food, water, electricity and a respite from bombardment, the local people opted to put pressure on their self-proclaimed defenders to leave. The process of trial and error that the government called 'reconciliation' ended up meeting the government's goal if not winning the hearts and minds of the populace.

Chemical Weapon Use

Bashar Assad's use of sarin gas in the civil war, especially in the Ghouta, is cited repeatedly even after he gave up his chemical weapons stock in 2013 under a UN Security Council injunction. Syria acceded to the Chemical Weapons Convention (CWC) on October 14, 2013 and by August 18, 2014 the CWC confirmed that all declared stockpiles of Syrian chemical weapons material were destroyed offshore. On January 6, 2016, the Organization for Prohibition of Chemical Weapons (OPCW) officially confirmed the disarmament of Syria.

While he had access to these weapons, it was inevitable that he would use them in his bid to get back territories captured by the rebel groups. In doing this, Assad did not feel cowed down by President Obama having declared it a 'red line'. For example, in August 2013, the alleged use by the Syrian army of sarin gas fit its military strategy. The pattern for government forces has been to soften the target and flushing out the opposition with conventional artillery or from the air, occasionally adding

[25] Ibid.

chemicals to that assault. After which government forces go in with tanks and infantry to secure the areas and return them to government control. Ghouta had become a particularly stubborn target in an area crucial for its access to the capital and communications with other government-held areas. Chemical weapons not only work to flush out rebels from their position, they also serve the sinister purpose of spreading fear among the population, killing civilians—to send a message to fighters and civilians alike.[26]

The Syrian military's chemical warfare campaign is intertwined—logistically, operationally and strategically—with its campaign of conventional warfare. 'As of 18 January 2019, we were able to assess 336 incidents as either "credibly substantiated", "confirmed", or comprehensively confirmed'.[27] The designs of the Assad regime's improvised chlorine munitions have accounted for at least 89% of all chemical attacks throughout the war through the use the conventional 'barrel' or 'lob' bombs. The Syrian military formations employ both types mostly delivered by its helicopter fleet. In its war fighting strategy, 'the Syrian military has consistently prioritized striking population centers over rebel positions on the frontlines, even in the face of defeat on the ground. Indeed, the Syrian regime's persistent and widespread use of chemical weapons is best seen as part of its overall war strategy of collective punishment of populations in opposition-held areas'.[28]

The government has pursued a military strategy of collective punishment against populations supporting or hosting insurgents given its shortage of manpower and resources. In the background of sectarianism and rentierism that characterizes the conflict, this approach to counterinsurgency aims to inflict such unbearable pain that locals are forced to either withdraw their support from insurgent groups, or flee to areas outside regime control undermining rebel governance and facilitating government population control through provision of aid.[29]

Another aspect of the need to undermine rebel governance is the systematic annihilation of the administrative institutions and public

[26] Ibid. Ghitis Frida.

[27] Tobias Schneider & Theresa Lutkefend, 'Nowhere to Hide: The Logic of Chemical Weapon Use in Syria', The Global Public Policy Institute, February 17, 2019, https://www.gppi.net/media/GPPi_Schneider_Luetkefend_2019_Nowhere_to_Hide_Web.pdf.

[28] Ibid.

[29] Ibid.

services that shape rebel-civilian relations. The government has delegitimized its competitors and prevented the emergence of coherent alternatives through targeted aerial bombardment of rebel-held areas. It inflicted not only military, financial and psychological damage, but also interrupted and undermined diurnal practices through which rebels have tried to generate local support and consolidate their rule.[30] For the rebel groups, the establishment of administrative institutions and provision of public services has been crucial in their bid for legitimacy and ability to challenge state power. 'When armed actors regulate different aspects of civilian life successfully, they gain access to economic resources, civilian cooperation and recruits...They do so not simply through material inducements but also by way of symbolic efforts that give social meaning to their actions'.[31] Yet the military, and practical constraints during conflict, places limits on their ability and willingness to pursue these possibilities. Inevitably, they are in a cleft stick, whether to build permanent governance structures—making themselves clones of existing the state apparatus—and loose the flexibility needed to combat shifts on and off the battlefield. In fact, an important reason for the fall of ISIS was the debilitation that came from this contradictory choice.

Throughout the Syrian civil war, rebel attempts to 'perform the state' have been frequent, deliberate and purposeful. One of the most important of these everyday practices has been the provision of welfare, defined as the 'direct or indirect facilitation of services and programs that promote well-being and security'.[32] Given the Ba'athist interventionist legacy strongly associated provision of welfare, the rebel groups had no option but to imitate. The destruction of these efforts added another motive for the government's military attacks on rebel-held areas. In this context, the government's military operations against rebel groups have targeted bread-making facilities and hospitals to deprive these rebel groups of the two most important functions of the state. The aim was to destroy their capacity to provide a minimal level of subsistence and to ensure physical security and health.

[30] Jose Ciro Martinez & Eng Brent, 'Stifling Stateness: The Assad Regime's Campaign Against Rebel Governance', *Security Dialogue*, 2018, Vol. 49, No. 4, pp. 235–253, https://journals.sagepub.com/doi/pdf/10.1177/0967010618768622.

[31] Ibid.

[32] Ibid. Jose Ciro Martinez & Eng Brent.

Bombings in the opposition-held areas of Homs, Aleppo and Dara'a concluded that 'the denial of medical care as a weapon of war is a distinct and chilling reality of the war in Syria' (United Nations Human Rights Office of the High Commissioner, 2013). Despite international condemnation, as of October 2016, the Syrian government and its allies had reportedly conducted approximately 90% of all attacks against medical facilities. Government's aerial bombardment also intended to push local civilians to pressure the fighters in their midst to surrender rather than continuing resistance.

Assad's Success

Taken together, the military and diplomatic developments of the recent past leave no room for doubt: Assad has decisively won the conflict. The rebels' former backers have not only given up on challenging the government, they now actively want to embrace it—whether in public or in private. Unlike the geopolitical winds that buffeted Saddam Hussein in the 1990s after the first Gulf war, everything is blowing strongly in Assad's favour.[33] Bashar al-Assad's battle to retain power is on its final leg, but putting back the country as it was before the war will take time and the international willingness to provide assistance. Hundreds of thousands are dead, millions will remain displaced, Syria has been balkanized at the whim of external powers, and rebuilding may not begin for many years in some areas.

In the absence of a negotiated settlement, there is unlikely to be a clear stopping point to the conflict. There is nevertheless an increasing focus domestically, and internationally, on how to pick up the pieces. Rebuilding could make daily life livable and enable refugees to return. 'The challenge is that reconstruction is not just about roads and bridges. It enables the Assad government to assert its power through a deeply political process. United States and other Western governments that had hoped to see Assad leave have few options, except possibly economic assistance to retain advantage. Eight years after government repression transformed nonviolent demonstrations into civil war, Syria's physical

[33] Hassan Hassan, 'Assad Has Decisively Won His Brutal Battle', *The Guardian*, December 30, 2018, https://www.theguardian.com/world/2018/dec/30/syria-year-cemented-assad-victory-trump-us-troops.

infrastructure has been devastated. Cost of reconstruction is estimated between $200 and $350 billion.

Syria seems unlikely to enter a post-conflict phase anytime soon although Assad has already started on reconstruction, symbolically launching the process in August 2017 with the reopening of the Damascus International Fair. 'Assad's version of reconstruction is [however] very different from supporting a broader process of post-conflict transformation. Instead, it is entrenching power dynamics and enabling the victors to consolidate their gains'.[34] The war was fought and won at the local level, the so-called peace is being built locality-by-locality. The government has recaptured one city at a time, cutting surrender deals with local rebel groups. They have paved the way for the government to launch reconstruction in these recaptured areas.[35]

At the national level, the Assad government is strengthening its grip on post-war Syria through enabling legislation. The legislature has approved a 10% tax on civilians to contribute to reconstruction. The government is attempting to rein in loyalist militias and incorporate rebels into its forces from recaptured territories. It has also strengthened the authority of the Ministry of Awqaf to crack down on religious expression, circumscribing space for future political mobilization. 'Assad is also creating a legal architecture to reconstruct the country in his own vision, benefiting his allies and displacing his adversaries. Decree 66, passed in 2012, allows the government to redesign informal housing areas by selling them to developers, who can evict owners or residents without recourse after a 30-day notice period'.[36]

It will permanently dispossess many refugees and internally displaced people, just nine per cent of whom possess adequate property title deeds. The government has selectively applied Decree 66 to destroy and resettle former opposition strongholds in accordance with urban plans that predated the civil war. The flagship of the Decree 66 project in Damascus is in Basateen al-Razi, a site of anti-government protest that the government is transforming into a gleaming new development based on

[34] Anna Mysliwiec, 'When the Dictator Wins: How Assad Is Using Reconstruction to Strengthen His Grip on Syria', *Harvard Kennedy School Review*, 1 January 2019, Vol. 19, pp. 30–36, https://eds.a.ebscohost.com/eds/pdfviewer/pdfviewer?vid=1&sid=7222c5a9-7eb3-490a-9cf8-51939dbd4f1c%40sessionmgr4008.

[35] Ibid.

[36] Ibid.

2007 plans. Homs and Aleppo will similarly use Decree 66 as a blueprint to destroy and redevelop opposition-held parts of their cities, often with the guidance of pre-2011 plans as well. If Syrians from opposition areas are losing in the reconstruction process thus far, friends of the regime are winning. In this process often, Christian villages have been favoured rather than rather Sunni areas 'as if to punish all Sunnis for the anti-government stance of the many', wrote Marwa al-Sabouni in her book The Battle for Home: The Vision of a Young Architect in Syria. This reconstruction process could without doubt exacerbate divisions along class and sectarian lines.

While maintaining firm control through the Ministry of Local Self Government, reconstruction authority has been devolved to the local level, granting every state administrative unit the right to form investment companies. During the ongoing Geneva talks, there has been broad support for some form of decentralization based on Decree 107, which devolved power to local councils early in the conflict. These holding companies enable investors to make a profit and the state to gain access to reconstruction funds while sidestepping local communities. A web of connections ties these firms back to the regime, which is rewarding its allies with reconstruction tenders.

While the United States continues to condition reconstruction assistance on Assad's departure, the EU eventually could agree to stem the tide of Syrian refugees across its borders. Any future efforts should focus on making Syria a safe home for all Syrians. After years of exile Syrian refugees are ready to return, but many are reluctant out of the fear of mandatory military conscription, strict vetting procedures by security agencies, a high risk of detention, and uncertainty over whether they will be able to return to areas where they previously lived.

In the last eight years, the Syrian civil war has become increasingly complex with six major and continuing axes of conflict. The Kurdish-dominated SDF and United States still ranged against the Islamic State and the Assad government; Turkey fights the SDF and its allied Kurdish YPG militia while militarily opposing the government and its external allies—Russia, Iran and Hezbollah- in Afrin and together with the Syrian opposition groups sequestered in Idlib. Israel militarily opposes Iran across Syria particularly in the Golan Heights.

Conclusion

The Syrian conflict that has decimated the country for ten years, provoking a regional humanitarian crisis and drawing in actors ranging from the United States to Russia, appears to be drawing to a conclusion. President Bashar al-Assad, with the backing of Iran and Russia, seems to have emerged militarily victorious from the conflict. The nine years since 2011 saw the armed insurgency transform into a conflict of regional and international dimensions. At the height of the fighting, it saw radical Islamist groups, particularly the ISIS seize control over vast swathes of the country, only to lose it in the face of sustained counter-offensives by government forces and its foreign allies as well as a US-led coalition of Western militaries.[37]

In Syria, as well as in neighbouring Iraq, the war against the Islamic State is almost over, at least to the extent that the group's self-styled caliphate, has been largely overcome. The civilian population and the original parties to the wider conflict have suffered enormous losses. The government of President Bashar al-Assad has re-established control over two-thirds of the country. Yet it is much weaker today given its ongoing reliance on the intensive support of Russia, Iran and Iranian-sponsored forces to regain and hold territory.[38]

Assad now faces the challenge of rebuilding the country, including areas where he allegedly deployed chemical weapons against his own citizens. The question of who will foot the bill is still an open one. President Donald Trump's administration has been eager to distance itself from the situation in Syria, and Assad's allies in Moscow are unlikely to take on the heavy costs of reconstruction.

Meanwhile, the fighting is still not over, with the northwestern Idlib region remaining the flashpoint. It is the last major area outside of government control, and the lives of nearly 3 million civilians remain at risk as clashes heat up between Russian-backed government forces and

[37] The Editors, 'The Syrian Civil War Might Be Ending,but the Crisis Will Live On', World Politics Review (WPR), July 17, 2019, https://www.worldpoliticsreview.com/insights/28041/the-syrian-civil-war-might-be-ending-but-the-crisis-will-live-on.

[38] Volker Perthes, 'Conflict and Realignment in the Middle East', *Survival: Global Politics and Strategy*, 1 June 2018, Vol. 60, No. 3, pp. 95–104, https://www.tandfonline.com/doi/full/10.1080/00396338.2018.1470760.

the remaining Islamist militias in the province under the tacit protection of Turkish forces. Active hostilities since May 2019 between the Turkish and Syrian armies have led to a refugee outflow of nearly 300,000 to Turkey and the Aleppo area. The United Nations Refugee Agency (UNHCR) estimates that 6.7 million Syrians have fled the country since the fighting started, putting a significant strain on neighbouring countries and Europe. Even as the conflict winds down, it is unclear when or if they will be able to return.

The experience of the last nine years has demonstrated that future conflicts will be extremely complex with multiple interconnected conflicts occupying the same space and time. They will involve conflict-specific configurations of participants rather than based on existing alliances and there will be no expectation of international humanitarian intervention. Finally, the United Nations will be a nonfactor with veto-wielding UNSC members involved on the ground.[39]

[39] Steven Metz, 'What Syria Reveals about the Future of War', World Politics Review, February 16, 2018, https://www.worldpoliticsreview.com/articles/24205/what-syria-reveals-about-the-future-of-war.

CHAPTER 4

The Assad Presidency: Should Longevity Trump Acceptability?

Syria's independence from French rule on April 17, 1947[1] till the complete assumption of power in 1970 by Hafez Assad was a period marked by abortive attempts at democracy interspersed by coups d'état by military dictators, General Husni al-Zaim and Colonel Adib al-Shishkali. 'They brushed aside Syria's traditional political elite' and initiated sweeping legal, constitutional, bureaucratic, economic, social and political reforms designed to accelerate Syria's development'.[2] Despite continuous political change, 1954–1958 are evoked as the 'democratic years' in the life of the country. It expressed the 'widely held revulsion for the periods of war, oppression, and occupation that preceded 1954, as well as equally intense disappointment with the increasingly brutal and repressive regimes that followed'.[3] Yet the post-independence optimism soon evaporated in a welter of corruption and incompetence of Syria's civilian governments and the abortive experiment of the brief merger of Syria and Egypt into the United Arab Republic. The resulting series of coups, counter-coups, mass arrests, bloody street battles and increasingly

[1] Jessica Kwong, 'Syrian Independence Day facts: Syria Celebrates Freedom from France Days After Airstrikes,' *Newsweek*, April 17, 2018, https://www.newsweek.com/syrian-independence-day-facts-syria-celebrates-freedom-france-days-after-888257.

[2] Kevin W. Martin, 'Syria's Democratic Years: Citizens, Experts, and Media in the 1950', IU Press, November 24, 2015, http://www.iupress.indiana.edu/product_info.php?cPath=1037_1116&products_id=807725.

[3] Ibid. Kevin W. Martin.

R. M. Abhyankar, *Syria*,
https://doi.org/10.1007/978-981-15-4562-7_4

repressive governments led to the populist-authoritarian dictatorship of Hafez al-Assad.[4]

Until Syria's independence the idea of nationalism did not represent a project of nation building, but aimed more or less at the maintenance of the existing balance of forces between metropolitan and local ruling classes used to influence the balance of power between local notables and the French administration.[5] Thus the National Bloc—Syria's main political party until independence—was a vehicle for the defence and consolidation of their class interest. It had no mobilizing power outside the personal networks of its leaders. Nationalism was not a project of nation building. Despite the growth of an industrial class, the centrality of political power remained largely unchanged. For families who could not rely on property alone, state employment became a privileged strategy for advancement. The fact that military careers were considered beneath the social status of dominant families, officer positions were more readily accessible for the individuals that stood outside of the dominant networks of privileges.

Hafez al-Assad (1970–2000)

For Hafez al Wahash, belonging to an under-privileged community, joining the Syrian air force was the only guarantee of opportunity for further advancement.[6] He was born in 1930 in an Alawi family near Lattakia. The family lived a life of low status, an Alawi, a despised rural community, whom the dominant Sunnis considered religious heretics. 'Trained as a fighter pilot and sporting a new name, al-Assad (the lion vs. Wahash, 'beast'), the young cadet entered the conspiracy and coup-ridden politics of the new state. He survived the tumultuous United Arab Republic experiment with Nasser's Egypt (1958–1962) to become a key figure in the 1966 coup that brought the Alawi to supreme power. Assad then methodically eliminated his rivals. Neither the loss of the Golan Heights to Israel in June 1967 (he was Defence Minister), nor Syria's

[4] Ibid.

[5] Jonathan Viger, 'Class, Political Power, and Nationalism in Syria: A Historical Sociology of State-Society Relations', *Dialectical Anthropology* 42, No. April 2, 2018, https://www.researchgate.net/publication/324757638_Class_political_power_and_nationalism_in_Syria_a_historical_sociology_of_state-society_relations.

[6] Ibid. Jonathan Viger.

failed intervention into the Jordanian war with the PLO in September 1970 prevented his ascent. Two months later, he became master of Damascus. Hafez al-Assad had thus emerged from the hothouse of Syrian politics. Assad's own rise to power came to symbolize the rapid change in the old order. He overcame poverty and prejudice to become Syria's first Alawi President in the aftermath of the eighth military coup that the country had witnessed in 21 years.

Hafez al-Assad became the architect of modern Syria. His assumption of power on 17 November 1970 is marked as the anniversary of the 'Correctionist Movement' that ended Syria's chronic political instability since the first decades of its independence. He used the network he had built as Commander of the Syrian air force and Minister of Defence to seize power in 1970. To maintain his position, Hafez al-Assad created a system of divide and rule and personalised his power to such an extent that it was he alone who held the state together'.[7] He preached the ideology of Arab Baath Socialism,[8] advocating secular Arab unity across the Middle East under the direction of a small vanguard, itself controlled by a supreme leader. The Ba'ath ideology was instrumental to the justification of a secular polity that enabled Alawi domination over the Sunni majority. It also helped to pursue the claim to 'Greater Syria', an area encompassing Israel, Lebanon, Jordan, and parts of Turkey. In the beginning, the Ba'ath represented the urban middle class in Damascus and their efforts to gain a leading position in Syrian political life. Subsequently, the party proved to be a conduit for the social mobility of the rural population and minority sects. Its success in overcoming domestic rivals in the struggle for the control of Syria was due to its ability to mould the Syrian identity as a blend of Arabism, 'Syrianism' and elements of Islam.[9]

In this effort, the Assad regime made constructive use of the glory of the past. 'Archaeological finds at Ebla, south of Aleppo, capital of a

[7] Neil Quilliam, 'Syria: The Rise of the Assad's' Chatham House, November 4, 2015, https://www.bbc.com/news/world-middle-east-34709235.

[8] Paul Berman, 'Ba'athism: An Obituary', *The New Republic*, September 14, 2012, https://newrepublic.com/article/107238/baathism-obituary. The Arab Socialist Ba'ath Party (*Ḥizb Al–Ba'ath Al-'Arabī Al-Ishtirākī*) was a political party founded in Syria by Michel Aflaq, Salah al-Din al-Bitar, and associates of Zaki al-Arsuzi.

[9] Eyal Zisser, 'Who's Afraid of Syrian Nationalism? National and State Identity in Syria', *Middle Eastern Studies*, Vol. 42, No. 2, August 11, 2006, pp. 179–198, https://doi.org/10.1080/00263200500417512.

trading and military state 2500 years BC, and at Mari on the Euphrates, seat of a Sumerian kingdom of the same millennium, gave a great boost to Syrian national pride. The 15,000 tablets of the Ebla royal archive discovered in 1974–1975 were found to be written in a Semitic tongue, which Syrian scholars claimed located the origins of the Arabic language and monotheism itself in their country. Together with the 25,000 tablets of the Mari archive and the 300-room palace itself of the city, with its heated bathrooms, plumbing and kitchen utensils, the Ebla finds provide Syrians with evidence of their ancient superiority over the Hebrews to the south and their equality with the great civilizations of Egypt and Mesopotamia'.[10]

'This development lent considerable weight to attempts to portray modern Syria as the heir to *Bilad al-Sham*, even though certain parts of those historic lands were not under Syrian sovereignty. The regime adopted a narrative of glorification of Syria's past, moulding an Arab Islamic, and an even more ancient pre-Islamic and pre-Arab past, into a historical ethos for the Syrian state once it stabilized and entrenched itself. At the core of this ethos lay the claim that *Bilad al-Sham* was the cradle of world civilization and, simultaneously, the cradle of Arabism. Thus, the frustration, disappointment and self-doubt of the Syrian public in their state during the early decades was replaced by pride in the accomplishments of the modern Syrian state, bolstered by pride in a reworked or reconstructed past. This sense of national belonging was... enhanced by yet another element—the increasingly central role played by the state during Hafiz al-Assad's thirty year rule in the lives of the people, especially in the socio-economic sphere'.[11] This Syrian identity was constantly reinforced by the media, the educational system and the Ba'ath Party apparatus to mould a national consciousness and identity.

Assad reorganized the state along totalitarian lines that would not hesitate to employ strong measures at home and abroad. 'He joined Nasser's Egypt and Ba'athist Iraq in seeking Soviet aid but would never become Moscow's supplicant'.[12] Hafez Assad's seemingly tough negotiating tactics after Anwar Sadat has signed a separate peace with Israel

[10] Patrick Seale, Assad of Syria, pp. 446–447 quoted by Eyal Zisser.

[11] Ibid. Eyal Zisser.

[12] Harvey Sicherman, 'Hafez al-Assad: The Man Who Waited Too long', Foreign Policy Research Institute, July 7, 2000, https://www.fpri.org/article/2000/07/hafez-al-assad-man-waited-long/.

in 1978, PLO's Yasser Arafat in 1993 and Jordan's King Hussein in 1994, was intended to uphold the dignity of Arab unity without compromise. He had seen his dream of a comprehensive peace between the Arab countries and Israel evaporate. In stating that comprehensiveness was also vertical, Hafez Assad meant negotiating of all aspects of the peace with Israel. For Assad, Israeli Prime Minister Yehud Barak's inability to reiterate his promise to commit to the 1967 borders spelt the death knell of Assad's interest to go ahead with the possibility of an agreement lest his true intentions be questioned.[13]

It is impressive that he managed, in a turbulent period, to keep power for over thirty years. The rule of Hafiz al-Assad lasted until his death in 2000; that is, it was longer than the period that had elapsed between the country's independence and his taking office. For this reason, the state media always focuses on the political stability that marked Hafiz al-Assad's rule, contrasting it with the days of continuous coups and instability.[14] Although the world powers, and the stronger of the regional governments, often trifled with his predecessors, Assad made Syria a force to be reckoned with in the region.[15]

The dramatic turn in Syria's status, from a weak and unstable country to a regional power, setting its sights on influence and hegemony over the countries surrounding it, was the result of Hafez al-Assad's rule. His lifelong interest was power. With ruthless determination backed by indefatigable negotiating ability, he was able to eke out a major role for his small country amidst the large number of political changes that took place in his neighbourhood. It made Syria pivotal to the resolution of every challenge in the Middle East. 'Hafez Assad had always been ready to regroup in the face of superior force and ever ready to switch partners if the dance lost its purpose. Yet he was slow in coming to a decision primarily because he was … always hoping to revert to his original objectives. He was slow in 1974, and Sadat got to Washington first. He was

[13] Henry Seigman, 'Being Hafez al-Assad', *Foreign Affairs*, Vol. 79, No. 3, pp. 2–7, May-June 2000, https://www.jstor.org/stable/20049723.

[14] Yasin Al-Haj Saleh, 'The Political Culture of Modern Syria: Its formation, Structure & Interactions', Political Culture Case Studies: Conflict Studies Research Centre, March 2003, http://www.syriawide.com/modernsyria.pdf.

[15] Stanley Reed, 'Syria's Assad: His Power and His Plan', *The New York Times*, February 19, 1984, https://www.nytimes.com/1984/02/19/magazine/syria-s-assad-his-power-and-his-plan.html.

slow again in 1978, and Sadat got to Jerusalem first. He was slow yet again in 1993, and Arafat got to Oslo first. Finally, he was slow in 2000, and death got there first'.[16]

With the unexpected death of his elder son Basil in 1993, it was remarkable that in 2000 the transfer of power to Bashar al-Assad was smoothly engineered by Hafez al-Assad's inner coterie, all of whom were Sunni. There was no opposition from the highest echelons of the system. Bashar's years in power, especially from 2011, have seen even greater turbulence verging on his possible loss of power. Hafez Assad left Bashar 'an elaborate structure of parliament, party groupings, a constitution, and 99% voting victories, a facade for the Alawi generals and the army—all instruments of the maximum leader'.[17]

Bashar al-Assad (2000–)

Not having been schooled for power, unlike his older brother Basil, Bashar al-Assad's assumption of power was neither easy nor his path clear. Trained as an ophthalmologist and living in UK, Bashar seemed initially to rather be doing something other than governing Syria. Yet he proved that it would have been a 'mistake to assume that power reluctantly assumed will be power tentatively exercised. Genes, national and international expectations, and the imperative of survival proved a lot more important than temperamental tendencies'.[18] Although he was imbued with ideas of democracy and a plural polity, it was not clear whether he would be different when in power. While Bashar's priorities on assumption of power were the economy and Lebanon and talks with Israel, a distant third, recovering the Golan Heights remained a top priority repeating his father's formulaic language that Syria would not make peace unless all the Golan Heights was returned.

Upon his coming to power, three competing perceptions of Bashar persisted—as a closet reformer, as a son loyal to his father's system, and third, as someone who had no idea of what the responsibility entailed.

[16] Ibid. Harvey Sicherman.

[17] Ibid. Harvey Sicherman.

[18] Charles Foster, 'Assad is Dead: Will Assad Live Long?', *Contemporary Review*, October 2000, Vol. 277, No. 1617, pp. 221–222, http://proxyiub.uits.iu.edu/login?url=//search.ebscohost.com/login.aspx?direct=true&db=aph&AN=3,728,560&site=eds-live&scope=site.

It did not take long to understand that he would not change the system left behind by his father except minor tinkering to strengthen its control element and make it even more accountable to the family and its coterie.[19] There would be no attempt to ease the political system by grafting a Western concept of democracy.[20] That soon became evident with the Baath Party increasingly becoming 'a far-reaching instrument of state control of the economy, politics and society rather than a vehicle for political participation'.[21]

'Syria's strategic environment had begun to shift in important ways even before Bashar succeeded his father. In March 2000, two months before Hafiz al-Assad's death, the Syrian track of the peace process effectively collapsed at the Clinton-Assad summit in Geneva, removing the principal framework for structuring Syria's relations with Israel and the United States. Hafez al-Assad had left his son a well-defined set of parameters for an acceptable peace treaty (full Israeli withdrawal from the Golan Heights, comprehensiveness, and a relatively short period for implementation), with a clearly enunciated set of conditions for proceeding with negotiations (most important being, a reaffirmation of Rabin's contingent commitment to full withdrawal—the so-called deposit)'.[22] Yet with Prime Minister Barak's reluctance to take up negotiations, and his succession by Ariel Sharon, the issue never went forward.

In May 2000, weeks before Hafez Assad died, Israel withdrew its military forces from southern Lebanon. In June 2000, the UN Security Council certified that Israel had complied with Security Council Resolution 425 by withdrawing completely from Lebanon, undercutting a critical element of traditional Syrian strategy. This was against the Syrian and Lebanese position that the Sheba'a Farms area was Syrian according to the June 4, 1967 line, that is, back up to the eastern shore of the

[19] Flynt Lawrence Leverett, 'Inheriting Syria: Bashar Assad's Trial by Fire', Brookings Institution Press, Washington 2005, https://kg6ek7cq2b.search.serialssolutions.com/ejp/?libHash=KG6EK7CQ2B#/search/?searchControl=title&searchType=title_code&criteria=TC0000179337.

[20] Susan Sachs, 'Assad Looks at Syria's Economy in Inaugural Talk', *The New York Times*, July 18, 2000, https://www.nytimes.com/2000/07/18/world/assad-looks-at-syria-s-economy-in-inaugural-talk.html.

[21] James Bennet, 'The Enigma of Damascus', *The New York Times Magazine*, July 10, 2005, https://www.nytimes.com/2005/07/10/magazine/the-enigma-of-damascus.html.

[22] Ibid. Leverett.

Sea of Galilee. The Security Council had however maintained that Israeli withdrawal was in accordance with UNSC resolution 425.

In September 2000, just three months after Hafiz al-Assad's death and two months after Bashar's inauguration, the Intifada al-Aqsa erupted, further complicating his task. Syria's strategic environment was also affected by political changes in the United States with President George W. Bush taking office on January 2001. With significantly diminished diplomatic assets Bashar was unable to prevent a decline in US–Syria bilateral relations. This deterioration was the most significant failure of Bashar's diplomacy and remained his most important foreign policy challenge. Thus, even though Bashar veered towards continuity in Syria's foreign policy, events forced him to adapt Syria's policy to the new circumstances. Bashar's efforts to improve Syria's standing, regionally and internationally did not succeed, increasing the isolation of the country.

Bashar al-Assad was unable to go through with genuine reform of the government because of a series of factors. The collapse of the Soviet Union, Syria's close ally and patron, and ascendance of the United States as the world's sole superpower was a major change. The spread of globalization during the 1990s, and a spiralling domestic birth rate coupled with a stagnant economy, made introduction of economic and political reforms a challenge. Bashar was also aware of the need to bridge the deep gulf between Syrian and Western society in areas of technological and scientific progress as well as in the political and the economic sphere to enable its integration with the world economy. 'Yet Bashar al-Assad remained committed to a 'Syrian pace', sufficiently slow and gradual to guarantee political stability'.[23]

Despite a Kurdish uprising in 2004 in Qamishli and Damascus and a terrorist attack by Islamic radicals on the UN office in Damascus, the government still appeared to enjoy the support of most pillars of Syrian society: army officers, economic elites, and the small middle class. In September 2014, the U.N. Security Council passed a humiliating resolution calling for Syria to withdraw its 20,000 troops from Lebanon, which it had occupied since the civil war there in the 1970s. The move co-sponsored by France, Syria's key western backer, took Syria by surprise. It challenged Syria's presence in Lebanon long tolerated by the international community. Hafez al-Assad's shrewd manoeuvring that gave Syria

[23] Eyal Zisser, 'Bashar Al-Assad: In or Out of the New World Order?', *The Washington Quarterly*, Vol. 28, No. 3, pp. 115–131, https://muse.jhu.edu/article/183620/pdf.

an outsize influence in the region had already started to ebb. Bashar's only choice was to become malleable in any peace talks with Israel or in cooperating with the US-installed government in Iraq. 'Syria's half-hearted attempts to secure its borders with Iraq, after Saddam Hussein's fall, left it open to the charge that it backed insurgents fighting the United States. The contrast with the Hafez Assad's decision to join the coalition that defeated Saddam in 1991 was stark'.[24]

Whereas on the domestic front Bashar initially cultivated an image of someone interested in change and reform, in foreign policy he projected an image of maintaining his father's course on major issues. When he assumed the presidency, Bashar stressed publicly the importance of continuity in Syrian foreign policy. Initially, responding to rapidly changing circumstances, he adopted his father's national security script maintaining the same broad strategic and foreign policy objectives. It was the killing in 2005 of Lebanese Prime Minister Rafiq al-Hariri and in March 2011 as regime assertion followed in the wake of the 'Arab Spring' in Syria…that he was forced to take hard decisions much as his father had during the Muslim Brotherhood insurrection at Hama in 1982.[25]

Following the eruption of countrywide opposition flowing from the government's high-handed action in Dara'a, the United States and other Western powers asked Bashar al-Assad to quit like Mubarak in Egypt and Ben Ali in Tunisia had done. They had not considered the different situation in Syria. The upsurge for democracy in Syria essentially was in opposition to the high-handed response of the government. It was a demand to introduce democratic change in decision-making and stop brutal and violent responses. Yet Bashar's constitutional changes in November 2011 and again in early 2012 were too little too late.

The protest against the incarceration of students for displaying anti-Assad graffiti, 'hardly resembled a unified movement for democratic

[24] Stanley Reed & Rose Brady, 'Can Assad Halt Syria's Diplomatic Slide?', *Business Week*, August 11, 2014, No. 3907, p. 68, https://eds.b.ebscohost.com/eds/detail/detail?vid = 0&sid = 95b874d9-7e82-48a5-b316-3b85d486b960%40pdc-vsessmgr05&bdata = JnNpdGU9ZWRzLWxpdmUmc2NvcGU9c2l0ZQ%3d%3d#AN = 14880712&db = mth.

[25] Yasmina Allouche, 'The 1982 Hama Massacre', Middle East Monitor (MEMO), February 12, 2018, https://www.middleeastmonitor.com/20180212-the-1982-hama-massacre/.

principles'.[26] All the opposing groups, nearly 1000 at the height of the civil war, were Sunni, radical, funded by different regional and global powers, particularly Saudi Arabia, Qatar, Kuwait, UAE, UK, France and the United States. 'Throughout the Syrian conflict, [more so after 2015 *added*] the regime of Bashar al-Assad has maintained military superiority over opposition forces'.[27] The discrepancy between the individuals fighting on the ground and the disputes between competing donors created 'a confusing environment that splinters, rather than unifies, the opposition forces against Bashar al-Assad'.[28]

In retaining power, the long-standing loyalty of the Alawi community, built-up since French colonial times, was an asset to the Assad family—both father and son. This went beyond their disagreement with Assad's actions. His continuation in power was due to the fact that once the 'international community' had decided on elimination of Assad's chemical weapons, removing him took lower priority. The conversation had shifted to the elimination of weapons of mass destruction. In so doing, the international community gave the Syrian government a platform to defend their version of events. This was helped by the government's near total control of the distribution of international humanitarian assistance.

To garner support, Assad made many concessions to local interests around the country, allowing allegiances of sect, neighbourhood and region to grow while the civil war dissipated the sense of Syrian nationalism. Yet in encouraging pro-regime local strongmen to operate checkpoints and keep order, he had created parallel local power centres diluting his own authority. Furthermore, with the continued foreign involvement of Hezbollah, Russia and Iran these powers had created assets on the ground introducing uncertainty regarding their departure after the conflict ends. That Assad maintains strong forces throughout the country guarantees that he would be able to reassert the ceded power over local authorities.

In its ninth year, the civil war appears to be waning, leaving many questions open including the uncharted future direction of the war. With Turkey's aggressive action in Afrin and Idlib there does not appear to

[26] Taylor Clausen, 'Why Bashar Assad Remains in Power', *Global Tides*, March 26, 2015, Vol. 9, No. 8, https://digitalcommons.pepperdine.edu/cgi/viewcontent.cgi?article=1182&context=globaltides.

[27] Ibid.

[28] Ibid.

be an early end to the long-running conflict. Starting as a brutal crackdown in Da'raa on peaceful protesters, and then mutating into a raging civil war, the conflict has now morphed into an international scramble for influence over parts of the country not fully under the government. Bashar al-Assad's eventual victory was evident since at least 2015, when Iran and Russia intervened to prop up his flagging army. The absence of an international resolve to prevent an Assad victory was also a factor especially after the collapse of the Obama administration's diplomacy.[29] Under the emerging scenario, Assad remains in power indefinitely, there is no meaningful political settlement to remove or redeem him, as the war grinds on. "For the regime, this has always been about survival, and it's done everything it had to do to ensure its survival," said Yezid Sayigh of the Carnegie Middle East Center. 'We're left with a few bits of tidying up, in Idlib and in the east, and these are still unknowns, but I don't believe they will change the overall trend'.[30]

Russia remains keen to see a political settlement that would win broad consensus, open up access to international funding for reconstruction and legitimize Assad's status and Russia's role in Syria. Under the Russian plan, Assad would run for a third term seven-year term in 2021. Yet Assad has continued to maintain that he expects to rely for reconstruction funding on his friends rather than looking for aid from countries that supported the opposition. Already Russia, Iran and China are lining up for these projects.

In Syria, unlike other countries in the throes popular uprisings, Assad and his inner circle have kept their lock on power and managed to survive nine bloody years of chaos. His resilience could keep him in power for years even with a multitude of challenges, including a rapidly degenerating economy and a persisting insurgency in the northwest.[31] With 'Arab Spring *bis* underway, Bashar al-Assad is the last man standing among the Arab autocrats removed in Algeria and Sudan from long-held power.

[29] Liz Sly, 'The Syrian War is far From Over. But the Endgame is Already Playing Out', *The Washington Post*, September 25, 2017, https://www.washingtonpost.com/world/middle_east/the-syrian-war-is-far-from-over-but-the-endgame-is-already-playing-out/2017/09/24/4361a55e-9d67-11e7-b2a7-bc70b6f98089_story.html.

[30] Yezid Sayegh, personal interview, Carnegie Middle East Center, Beirut, May 2019.

[31] Zenia Karam & Sarah El Dib, 'Syria's Assad: Last Man Standing Amid New Arab uprisings', The Associated Press, April 12, 2019, https://apnews.com/2628467151d94ebd8b92e20fbb67498c.

'With the Syrian conflict in its ninth year, the 53-year-old leader appears more secure and confident than at any time since the revolt against his rule began in 2011'.[32] Perhaps Assad's best asset is Syria's position as a geographic linchpin—a pivotal state—on the Mediterranean and in the heart of the Arab world that attracted crucial political and military assistance from Russia and Iran to move the conflict in his favour.

To avert popular demonstrations, as in the early years, Assad needs to keep rising discontent in check. According to the United Nations, 11.7 million Syrians, nearly 65%, of the present population of 18 million, require humanitarian assistance being displaced from their homes. More than 5 million refugees wait to return.

'After years of war and ever-tightening U.S. sanctions the government's coffers are reeling from lack of resources, and the U.N. estimates that eight out 10 people live below poverty line. Demonstrations reminiscent of the early years of the conflict have resurfaced'.[33]

'In Daraa, where the revolt started in 2011, once again hundreds took to the streets, offended by the government's plan to erect a statue of the president's father, the late Hafez Assad. Other protests took place in some former opposition areas recaptured by the government after authorities moved to enforce military conscription despite promises to hold off. The focus also pivots to Idlib, the last remaining rebel bastion in Syria, where an estimated 3 million people live under control of al-Qaida-linked militants'.[34]

Damascus benefitted from the chaos in Libya, Egypt and Iraq as multiple terrorist groups waged a war not just against Assad and other strong men like Abdel Fatah el-Sisi of Egypt, but also in creating terrorist acts in major European cities. However, Bashar al-Assad reaped the greatest benefit from the character of the state that his father bequeathed to him. Hafez al-Assad's Syria had defied the West and American presidents for three decades becoming the uncompromising Arab leader who would equally support non-state groups that targeted American troops

[32] Ibid.

[33] Ibid.

[34] Ibid.

in Lebanon, yet was an ally needed to ensure the overall stability in the Middle East.[35]

One of the key reasons that Assad, *pere et fils*, has been able to withstand international pressure over their actions is the grudging support they have enjoyed across the region. America's influential policy-makers and diplomats held that an Assad-led strong Syria might be a reliable yet useful nuisance, holding as it did many keys to the Middle East that could risk a regional war. Even Israeli Prime Minister, Ariel Sharon, always warned against the removal of Assad even after the assassination of former Lebanese Prime Minister Rafiq Hariri. 'Henry Kissinger in two key op-eds pieces called for a proper understanding of how the Assads' function, and the need to mitigate the desire to bring democracy to Syria through a military intervention or the forced overthrow of Bashar al Assad'.[36]

Bashar al-Assad survived the fall-out of the assassination of the Lebanese leader, the fall of Saddam Hussein and the early losses of the civil war. He is poised to return into the Arab fraternity, as the major Arab countries reach out to him to curry favour again. Bashar still has wide-ranging support from key elements of Syrian society and his state, in particular, his army and intelligence services. In its make-up, it is one of the most diverse in the Arab world: Christians, Druze, Sunnis are all at key decision-making positions, a legacy he inherited from his father. Syria under Bashar has enjoyed support from the two largest Arab Sunni armies, Egypt and Algeria. The pluralistic state remains the defining factor in his staying power.

The character of the Syrian Army has been crucial to Bashar Assad being able to retain his power throughout the civil war. On assuming power, Hafez al-Assad and Mustafa Tlass, the Army commander, decided that given the external threats, the army… must have a nationalist agenda and be an institution devoid of politics. This ideological agreement between Tlass and Assad led to the complete purging of politics from the military and a separation of powers not seen before in Syria. The army

[35] Kamal Alam,'Pax Syriana: The staying power of Bashar al Assad', *Asian Affairs*, Vol. 50, No. 1, pp. 1–17, https://www.tandfonline.com/doi/pdf/10.1080/03068374.2019.1567099?needAccess=true.

[36] Charles Glass, 'Syrian Archives Add New Details to Henry Kissinger's Disastrous Middle East Record,' The Intercept, June 18, 2017, https://theintercept.com/2017/06/18/syrian-archives-add-new-details-to-henry-kissingers-disastrous-record-in-the-middle-east/.

Bashar inherited 'had firmly erased its sectarian beginnings, which were very much a legacy of French colonial rule. The deft play between rural and urban, tribal and religious sects was evened out through an education system played on party lines rather than those of religion'. The last forty years have shown that the Syrian Army is not a sectarian army. Most of the internal politics within the army has been rooted in power, promotion and performance in the field. As such, the Army saw no major defections of soldiers to the opposing insurgent groups.

Assad has survived through a mix of factors unique to him apart from the loyalty of the Alawite sect. Like them, other minorities in the country and some middle- and upper-class Sunnis have continued to regard his family's rule as a bulwark of stability in the face of Islamic radicalism in the region. 'For now, Assad appears to be secure. With the help of Russia and Iran, he has restored control over key parts of the country, and the world appears to have accepted his continued rule, at least until presidential elections scheduled for 2021. Gulf countries reopened embassies after years of boycott. Delegations from Iraq, Lebanon and Jordan have visited in recent months, discussing restarting trade, resuming commercial agreements and releasing prisoners. Although the Arab League said it was not yet time to restore Syria's membership to the 22-member organization, the issue was discussed at their annual summit for the first time since the country was deprived of its seat eight years ago'.[37] While there was no consensus at the Arab League summit in Tunisia on March 31, 2019, Damascus is more than likely to be re-admitted in 2020.

Assad's main foreign patrons will continue to deepen their military, political and economic ties, while countries that opposed him during the civil war have the most difficult decision. If recent trends are any indication, it seems many of them….are increasingly inclined towards some sort of engagement.[38] Turkey has gone ahead and deployed its Army in Afrin and Idlib even though its motivated performance in the Idlib exclusion zone has revealed its intention. As 2019 ended, an Idlib province, and some far away pockets in Eastern and Southern Syria, remained out of government's control. The Syrian Kurds, without continued support of US arms, appear to be looking at an alliance with the government.

[37] Ibid. Zenia Karam & Sarah El Dib.

[38] Iyad Dakka, 'Syria's Assad is Coming IN From the Cold', World Politics Review, February 15, 2019, https://www.worldpoliticsreview.com/articles/27457/syria-s-assad-is-coming-in-from-the-cold.

For Assad's former Arab foes, there is a counterintuitive geopolitical logic at play here: Having failed to sever Damascus's link to Tehran through military pressure by arming Syrian rebels, they are building economic linkages of their own to prevent Assad from being completely dependent on Iran. Their goal is to prevent Syria from becoming a full-fledged Iranian proxy state.[39] Furthermore, after nine years of conflict, Arab states want to reopen trade and cash in on civil, mechanical and electrical reconstruction projects in the devastated country. Gulf investors and companies are equally eager to get a slice of the rebuilding pie. Direct commercial flights have resumed between Syria, Iraq, UAE, Bahrain and Oman.

What is more, while Washington wants to impose a political process before it agrees to provide funds for reconstruction, the European Union is more flexible due to both its proximity to Syria and the large number of Syrian refugees waiting at its borders. Contrary to its long-held position, UK Foreign Secretary Hunt said that, '…the British longstanding position is that we won't have lasting peace in Syria with that regime. But regretfully we do think he's going to be around for a while and that is because of the support that he's had from Russia'. He further stated that since Syria was now under Russian influence, it was up to them to ensure that there really is peace in Syria.[40]

Russia's crucial role in Assad's regaining his country has been equally important for Israel's view regarding Assad. Israel is likely to be at ease with Assad remaining in power, despite repeated calls by Israeli politicians for the president's overthrow. 'With the growing realisation that the Assad regime will remain in power, there is a tendency in Israel - probably the result of …Israeli-US-Russian consultation - to ensure Israel's acceptance of the Assad regime', said Elie Podeh, professor of the Middle East at the Hebrew University, Jerusalem. 'The bottom line is that Israel wants to ensure the stability and quietness of the Israeli-Syrian border, and if the Assad regime will do its share - as in the past - then Israel will

[39] Ibid. Iyad Dakka.

[40] Larisa Brown, 'Assad is Here For A While Hunt Admits', *Daily Mail*, January 4, 2019, https://eds.b.ebscohost.com/eds/detail/detail?vid=0&sid=afc96eba-130a-4782-8b0b-2c3f855d109c%40pdc-v-sessmgr02&bdata=JnNpdGU9ZWRzLWxpdmUmc2NvcGU9c2l0ZQ%3d%3d#AN=133858680&db=bwh.

be satisfied', added Podeh.[41] Since Russia's intervention in 2015, Israel, with Moscow's acquiescence, has been able to carry out air raids deep inside Syria against Iranian, Syrian and Hezbollah positions. Pointing to Moscow's role as a mediator between the many parties involved in the war, and its control of Syrian airspace, political commentators say Russia's intervention changed Israel's position on Assad, albeit implicitly.[42]

Interestingly, while Western countries and regional powers, such as Turkey and Saudi Arabia, have been vocal in their opposition to Assad, none has taken decisive action to remove the Syrian leader. Similarly, despite rebel appeals, the United States has avoided the kind of military intervention it launched in Libya that helped rebels there bring down Muammar Gaddafi. While arms have come through to rebel groups, opposition leaders said they were insufficient to counter the threat of the Syrian government's air power. The US decision not to supply such weapons was the fear they could fall into the hands of groups like ISIL, and later, used against Western interests.[43] As the war has dragged on both the West and United States appear to have reprioritized Assad's removal.

Syria has always punched above its weight by being maintaining an influential position among its neighbours, Lebanon, Iraq, Turkey and the Palestinian territories. Bashar al-Assad, despite a dire situation, was able to stave off removal from office, or worse, because of a fortuitous constellation of circumstances. First, was the Syrian political and military system honed by Hafez al-Assad that could effectively cope with the splintering of the country. Bashar's assertion of his authority at every turn, particularly vis-à-vis the UN, established the reality of the presence of a sovereign power.

Second, throughout the nine years of internecine civil war, and multiplying foreign participation, majority of the Syrian people, particularly the minorities, reposed confidence that he was the better alternative when compared with the numerous groups professing radical Islamic ideology. Third, the support Bashar al-Assad received from Russia, and

[41] ZenaTahhan, 'Does Israel want Syria's Bashar al-Assad in power?', Al Jazeera, July 5, 2018, https://www.aljazeera.com/news/2018/07/israel-syria-bashar-al-assad-power-180705153500325.html.

[42] Ibid. Zena Taha.

[43] Editors, 'Why is Bashar al-Assad Still in power?', Al Jazeera, April 14, 2018, https://www.aljazeera.com/news/2018/04/bashar-al-assad-power-180414061304833.html.

Iran together with the Hezbollah, in combating his adversaries. Russia's role both in the United Nations, and on the ground, positioned a major power on his side and helped to keep the Israel factor out of the equation. For the Hezbollah and Iran, it was not only a 'pay-back' for long years of support but also a guarantee for the future.

Majority of the 5 million refugees in camps in Turkey, Lebanon and Jordan want to return to a Syria that will be free of foreign interference. For most Syrians, the widespread pluralistic nature of governance, albeit a one-party system, had kept stability in a difficult part of West Asia.

CHAPTER 5

Role of Regional and International Powers

ISIS's collapse and the considerable territorial gains made by Bashar al-Assad's regime have still not ended the civil war. Syria continues to exercise a pull on the region as a whole. Like the international order, itself, the regional order in the Middle East, is in chaos. Any vision of the region finding a workable balance of power is a mirage: the new order is fundamentally one of disorder. 'Although Syria is the most cataclysmic case, the regional powers have created enormous human and political damage elsewhere, too, in their quest for influence and prestige. Their efforts have even destabilized countries that were not embroiled in civil war'.[1]

The active assistance of major global powers through provision of finance, arms and ammunition, and personnel has introduced complexity into the task of bringing in a regional order that will bring peace and meet the aspirations of the people. Rather than the Arab uprisings creating new democracies, there is resurgence of authoritative rule that has consolidated the sectarian divide as the fulcrum of a nascent order based on societal divisions like rural–urban, government-business and army and the rest. In this churning, the Gulf countries endowed with oil and unlimited financial resources could gain an influential profile.

[1] Marc Lynch, 'The New Arab Order: Power and Violence in Today's Middle East', *Foreign Affairs*, September-October 2018, issue, https://www.foreignaffairs.com/articles/middle-east/2018-08-13/new-arab-order.

R. M. Abhyankar, *Syria*,
https://doi.org/10.1007/978-981-15-4562-7_5

The regional agenda will largely hinge on success of the effort to end the Syrian civil war; secondly, the continuation of the Saudi-Iran proxy war; thirdly, the way the Israel–Iran–US triangle plays out, and finally, the positioning and policies of Russia and the United States.[2] Despite their continuing tragedy, in different ways and intensity, the war in Yemen and the Israeli—Palestinian conflict in particular, will have a lesser impact on the overall political developments in the region.

The region appears poised on the brink of a conflagration at multiple points. Since the US withdrawal from the Iran nuclear agreement the situation has become even more fraught with the Iranian drone or cruise missile strike on September 14, 2019 on the Saudi Aramco's Abqaiq facility, causing massive damage and crippling the nation's oil production. The Houthi claim for the attack has been discounted given their capability and the area of attack. Oil production of 5.7 mb per day had to be suspended, according to the company.[3] President Trump promised US action against Iran if proven. Meanwhile, the stalemated war led by Saudi Arabia against the Houthis in Yemen has led to widespread deaths and destruction creating another massive humanitarian tragedy. The UAE has taken the opportunity to establish, for the first time, naval bases across the Horn of Africa to enforce the blockade on Qatar and protect its presence in the south of the country. President Trump has enthusiastically aligned the United States with these like-minded (*read* mainly Sunni) states, Egypt, Saudi Arabia, UAE and Israel.

The diplomatic, trade and travel boycott on Qatar since June 2017 led by Saudi Arabia, UAE, Bahrain and Egypt[4] has virtually destroyed the Gulf Cooperation Council, the only functioning Arab organisation. Qatar has not felt the pinch because of support from Iran and Turkey and an unending store of natural gas for export. Ostensibly imposed on

[2] Volker Perthes, 'Conflict and Realignment in the Middle East', *Survival: Global Politics and Strategy*, Vol. 60, No. 3, pp. 95–104, https://www.tandfonline.com/doi/full/10.1080/00396338.2018.1470760.

[3] Geoff Brumfiel, 'Outside Experts See Iran's Hand In Attack on Saudi Oil Facility', NPR, September 16, 2019, https://www.npr.org/2019/09/16/761378683/outside-experts-see-irans-hand-in-attack-on-saudi-oil-facility.

[4] News Report, 'Riyadh: Qatar Boycott Result of 20 years of Plots', *Gulf News*, September 7, 2019, https://gulfnews.com/world/gulf/qatar/riyadh-qatar-boycott-result-of-20-years-of-plots-1.66278440.

grounds of Qatar supporting 'terrorism' it seemed more like an exercise in domination since Saudi Arabia itself is susceptible to the same charge.

In Syria, Israel's increasingly frequent air strikes on Iranian assets, Turkey's cross-border operations in Afrin and its suspect cooperation on the exclusion zone in Idlib, and the entrenched presence of Russia and Iran is pushing the civil war in new and unexpected directions. In this context, it would be opportune to examine the current goals of the international and regional powers in Syria.

Regional Powers

Saudi Arabia

Saudi Arabia's reaction to the Arab uprisings was fear for their own regime given the fall of Tunisian President Bin Ali and protests in Egypt's Tahrir Square that led to the departure of President Mubarak. The fear resulted from the fragility of the Saudi monarchy described as 'an unstable country in unstable region'.[5] Until the Obama administration was in support of the Mubarak regime, Saudi Arabia pursued its traditional policy of supporting President Hosni Mubarak politically, diplomatically and financially until his resignation on February 1, 2011. US abandonment of Mubarak introduced an element of uncertainty in US policy towards Arab countries in the throes of the Arab Spring. In what was a defensive step, Saudi Arabia adopted an activist policy towards Syria aimed at supporting groups against Bashar al-Assad. They were also concerned that Mubarak's fall created a risk to the balance of power in the region. In particular, loss of the Saudi-Egyptian axis resulted in giving a fillip to Tehran and its regional influence.

At the best of times, Saudi-Syria relations have always fluctuated since they have often found themselves on opposing sides. In the 1950s and 1960s, increased pan-Arabism under Gamal Abdul-Nasser, and the divisive effects of the Cold War, placed Syria and Saudi Arabia in rival camps. The alliance between Syria and Iran, especially during the Iran–Iraq War, caused a deepening of the divide between Damascus and Riyadh. Their

[5] Nazife Selcen Pinar Akgul, 'From Stillness to Aggression: The policy of Saudi Arabia towards Syria after the Arab Spring', *International Journal of Humanities and Social Science*, Vol. 6, No. 9, September 2016, http://www.ijhssnet.com/journals/Vol_6_No_9_September_2016/5.pdf.

bilateral relations became increasingly conflictual after Saudi Arabia held Syria responsible for the 2005 assassination of Lebanese prime minister and Saudi protégé Rafik Hariri. In 2011, after the Syrian government's strong-arm tactics against the protesters in Dara'a, King Abdullah criticizing the violence asking to 'stop the killing machine' and calling for reforms.

Thereafter bilateral relations progressively deteriorated. Although regime opposition to the popular forces of democracy and pluralism were at play 'an ostensibly secular and Alawi Shiite- dominated regime was seen brutally suppressing its Sunni Muslim majority, that became prominent in the view of the overwhelmingly Sunni Saudi population and its leadership'.[6] Saudi Arabia became instrumental in Syria's suspension from the League of Arab States. They were equally cognisant that Iran's growing role in Syria made the country a theatre of the proxy war between the two countries.

This battle is seen both as domestic between Syrian Sunnis and Shias and regional with the Gulf States getting involved because of their fear of Iran extending its regional influence and reach. The sectarianization of the conflict in Syria was due to their realization that only a divisive strategy enabling the political elites to seize control of the emerging political discourse and redrawing the boundaries of political activism would safeguard their power.[7]

'The Syrian crisis opened the door to a more tangible Iranian presence not just in Syria, Lebanon and Iraq, but also throughout the region. It allowed military intervention of a number of Iranian actors on Syrian territory: the Revolutionary Guard Corps (IRGC) and the Quds Force (the external operations branch of the IRGC), the Iranian 65th Airborne Special Forces Brigade (Nohed) and the Iranian Basij forces. Iran is also increasingly active throughout the Levant and Gulf region through a number of connections with Arab proxy forces and a number of Islamist individuals. These forces include both Sunni and Shi'a sub-state actors such as the Hezbollah, the Palestinian Liberation Army (effectively under Syrian control), the Iraqi Badr Organization, the Dawa Party and

[6] Ibid.

[7] Line Khatib, 'Syria, Saudi Arabia, the UAE and Qatar: The 'Sectarianization' of the Syrian Conflict and Undermining of Democratization in the Region', *British Journal of Middle Eastern Studies*, 2019, Vol. 46, No. 3, pp. 385–403, https://www.tandfonline.com/doi/pdf/10.1080/13530194.2017.1408456?needAccess=true.

al-Qaeda senior officials and military chiefs who have taken refuge in Iran'.

For the first two years of the conflict, Saudi Arabia and U.A.E. opted to support the most secular segments of the opposition. Logistical and military support was mainly sent to armed groups viewed as nationalist and secular to bypass the jihadist groups whose roles in the war had alarmed Western and regional powers. It was only in September 2013 that Saudi Arabia started funding Islamist groups such as Liwa' al-Islam (which became part of a coalition known as Jaish al-Islam, the Army of Islam, or Islam Army) in Damascus and the Army of the Sunnis in Deir ez-Zor. This support was to counter the power of the ultra-radical groups such as Nusra Front (now Fatah al-Islam) and ISIS and possibly to create and effectively sponsor Islamist groups that are loyal to and dependent upon the Saudi regime.[8]

The Gulf States intervened in Syria because of their perception that the Syrian government was manipulating the conflict, as were the outside forces, to threaten the Gulf kingdoms, particularly Saudi Arabia and UAE. It fostered a myriad of armed groups, both Shi'a and Sunni, whose politico-religious message and agenda served to portray the Gulf sheikhdoms as corrupt and un-Islamic. Saudi and Emirati leaderships perceived the Syrian uprising and ensuing conflict as a microcosm of the wider threat to their regimes.[9] GCC leaders felt compelled by both domestic imperatives and the fear that their autocratic regimes would be challenged by the multiplicity of Shi'a and Sunni actors in Syria strengthening existing domestic opposition.

The Saudi-engineered Islamic Military Counter Terrorism Coalition (IMCTC)[10] presently active in Yemen had an additional objective in its formation in 2016. Its ultimate objective in Syria, apart from the ISIS, was to take on Syrian President Bashar al-Assad and the Iran-created Shi'a militias. Were the Islamic coalition to move into Syria, it would become the nucleus of a regionally coordinated military approach towards

[8] Ibid.

[9] Ibid. Line Khatib.

[10] Arab News, 'Islamic Military Counter Terrorism Coalition (IMCTC),' *Arab News*, November 30, 2019, https://www.arabnews.com/tags/islamic-military-counter-terrorism-coalition-imctc.

ISIS, Assad and the Shia militias.[11] This thinking was the result of the Obama administration policy to lead from behind in the Syrian situation. The bogging down in Yemen of the IMCTC ensured that these plans remained on paper.

Saudi Arabia has accepted that the Iranian-backed Assad government has triumphed even though the state will remain conflict-ridden for years to come. It has given up on both the military fight as well as political attempts to engineer a near-term transition. Riyadh is expecting Moscow to limit Iranian influence in Syria even hinting at the possibility of strengthening Assad at Iran's expense. Iran, on its part, is more focused on the Israeli threat, rather than Saudi Arabia, that could shape the next phase of the Syrian war.[12]

Turkey

Turkey's continued intervention in Syria should be seen in the backdrop of a revival of a neo-Ottoman sentiment towards the region. It has three distinct threads. First, 'Foreign Minister Davutoglu argued that Turkey sits at the main power corridors and energy routes in the Black Sea and Mediterranean. Therefore, Turkey must assume its pivotal status by resurrecting its Ottoman legacy. Its long-term strategy seeks to transform Turkey from a regional into a global power. Turkey's expansion was to start from the closest basin, especially the Middle East.' Not surprisingly, Davutoglu attributed a strategic importance to Syria given Turkey longest common border with Syria enabling it to dominate the wider Mediterranean geopolitics.[13]

Second, pipeline politics dictates Turkey's energy-related geoeconomic involvement in Syria. Turkey aspires to diversify its energy

[11] Nawaf Obaid, 'Saudi Arabia's Master Plan Against ISIS, Assad and Iran in Syria', *The National Interest*, February 16, 2016, https://nationalinterest.org/feature/saudi-arabias-master-plan-against-isis-assad-iran-syria-15221.

[12] Julien Barnes-Darcy, 'Saudi-Iranian Rivalry and the Impact of the Syrian Conflict', Middle East Centre Blog, London School of Economics and Political Science, May 7, 2018, https://blogs.lse.ac.uk/mec/2018/06/22/saudi-iranian-rivalry-and-the-impact-on-the-syrian-conflict/.

[13] 245Efe Can Gurcan, 'Political Geography of Turkey's Intervention in Syria: Underlying Causes and Consequences', *Journal of Aggression, Conflict and Peace Research*, December 2017, https://www.emerald.com/insight/content/doi/10.1108/JACPR-10-2017-0329/full/html.

sources, revisit its excessive dependence on Russian and Iranian energy, and eventually become an energy hub that connects eastern energy to Europe. To this end, its two projects, the Trans-Anatolian Natural Gas Pipeline from Azerbaijan and the Qatar-Saudi Arabia-Jordan-Syria-Turkey pipeline, both compete with the Iran–Iraq–Syria pipeline project. Turkey sees Syria as a rival sharing the same regional aspiration. Thirdly, the ruling AKP has relied on a pragmatic use of Sunni sectarianism and Kurdish ethno-politics to politicize religion and ethnicity characterized by inconsistent appropriation of the Sunni tradition and of enmity with the Kurds.[14]

Syria and Turkey bilateral relations in the past two decades have been subject to extraordinary turnarounds. With very brief interludes, the relationship between them from Syria's independence in 1946 upto 1998 varied from outright enmity to very strained, exacerbated further by the Cold War dynamics. After Turkish interventions in the long conflict in Syria, President Erdogan maintains that it has a long-term role in that country. According to him, it will include an 'intensive vetting process to reunite child soldiers with their families, oversight of the creation of local governing councils, serving as an intermediary between the United States and Russia in ending the eight-year-old Syrian civil war and to ensure that Islamic State doesn't resurrect itself'.[15]

Addressing the future of Kurds in Syria, Erdogan stated that Turkey would help create a stabilization force with fighters from diverse Syrian milieu since it would best serve all Syrian citizens and bring law and order.[16] From summer 2016, Ankara settled on specific interrelated goals in Syria: 'blocking westward expansion of the American-backed Syrian Democratic Forces (SDF); frustrating American military operations east of the Euphrates River; working through Russia to ensure that Syria remains a unitary state after the conflict ends; resettling displaced people in Turkish-controlled territory in northern Syria'.[17]

[14] Ibid.

[15] Bill Faries, 'Erdogan signals Lasting Turkey Role in Syria Amid US Confusion', Bloomberg, January 7, 2019, https://www.bloomberg.com/news/articles/2019-01-07/erdogan-signals-lasting-turkey-role-in-syria-amid-u-s-confusion.

[16] Ibid.

[17] Aaron Stein, 'Turkish Policy in Syria: Divining Intent and Options for the United States', Atlantic Council, November 16, 2018, https://www.atlanticcouncil.org/blogs/menasource/turkish-policy-in-syria-divining-intent-and-options-for-the-united-states/.

In July 1998 with 10,000 Turkish troops massed at the Syrian border the tenuous situation forced Assad to expel the Turkish Kurdish leader Abdullah Ocalan and terminate support for PKK (Kurdistan Workers' Party). In 2002 Erdogan's foreign policy of 'zero problems with neighbors' saw a dramatic improvement in bilateral relations from familial cordiality between the leaders to joint military exercises in 2009 and a visa abolition agreement. Along with an earlier agreement to allow free trade, it ensured that people and goods could pass freely over the same borders that had barbed wire and landmines less than a year earlier. On December 3, 2010 Turkey, Syria, Lebanon and Jordan signed an agreement to form the 'Levant Quartet', which was hailed as the prospective 'EU of the Middle East'.

When the Syrian conflict started Erdogan continued to publicly support Assad calling him 'a good friend who was loved by his people'. Yet he started surreptitiously sending arms and Arab Islamist fighters into Syria, and providing a haven for defecting Syrian Army officers and soldiers. Erdogan, the pre-eminent patron of the Muslim Brotherhood in West Asia, perceived the unrest as an excellent opportunity for them to take power in Syria. Until November 2011, Turkey canvassed Assad for the return to Syria of the Muslim Brotherhood's leaders, release of its cadres and a power-sharing agreement with them. In response, Assad released many Muslim Brotherhood and other political prisoners. When these suggestions turned into demands and threats, Assad rejected them and the relationship soured rapidly.[18]

Turkish 'denunciations of Assad started getting stronger with Assad being termed a "butcher" and a "brutal dictator"; sanctions were put in place. Turkey became the foremost supporter of a variety of Islamist groups fighting in Syria, and its conscious purchase of smuggled oil from the ISIS-controlled areas helped the Islamic State enormously. Taking advantage of the unsettled conditions in Syria, Turkey started proactively pursuing "Turkiization" of northwestern Syria by infiltrating Turkic-speaking Islamist fighters and Chechens'.[19]

[18] Ranjit Gupta, 'Understanding the War in Syria and the Roles of External Players: Way Out of the Quagmire?', *The Commonwealth Journal of International Affairs*, January 25, 2016, Vol. 105, No. 1, pp. 29–41, https://www.tandfonline.com/doi/full/10.1080/00358533.2016.1128630.

[19] Ibid.

In the context of its growing involvement in northern Syria, Turkey's relations with both Russia and Iran have remained fraught. The downing of a Russian fighter aircraft by Turkey on November 24, 2016 became the cause for a downswing in their bilateral relations. Erdogan's priorities have made him launch open war against the PKK. At the same time, Turkey also fears that Syria's Kurds, backed by the United States in their fight against Daesh, will attempt to carve out their own autonomous enclave in the future, thus reviving Kurdish calls for independence from Turkey.[20]

As the Syrian civil war progressed, Turkey has become a key supporter of the Syrian revolution and a major critic of President Bashar Assad. It has also received the largest number of Syrian refugees during the last nine years. Turkey hosts the Syrian National Coalition (SNC) and most of the anti-Damascus opposition groups. Its influence over the Syrian opposition is considerable. It was in recognition of this fact that Russia and Iran, at Sochi, agreed to set up an exclusion zone in Idlib and give Turkey time to persuade the Islamic groups to enter the 'cordon sanitaire' around the province. Yet nearly eighteen months after the exclusion zone was set up Turkey's action has not inspired confidence that the job will be completed soon.

Turkey's intervention into Afrin adds another messy dimension to the Syrian conflict, not least for Turkey itself. Turkey's military push opens up another front and further consolidates foreign occupation of the country. Yet it has deepened the cleavages among the opposing groups, relieving pressure on Assad including halting the regime's ongoing military campaign in Idlib. It reflects a deepening conflict between Turkey and the United States, both NATO members. 'Ankara remains focused on preventing the consolidation of an autonomous Kurdish zone in Syria, whereas Washington has been working to a Syrian strategy that positions (non-Afrin-based) Kurds as the spearhead of a combined anti-ISIS, anti-Assad and anti-Iran approach'.[21]

Afrin was Ankara's second major incursion in Syria but the Turkish army's first showdown with Syrian Kurds. 'Afrin is at the western tip

[20] Osama Al Sharif, 'Turkey's Role in Syria Essential', *Arab News*, January 1, 2016, https://www.arabnews.com/columns/news/858336.

[21] Julien Barnes-Dacey, 'What it means for the Syrian War' in 'Three Views on Turkey's Syrian intervention', *European Council on Foreign Affairs*, January 25, 2018, https://www.ecfr.eu/article/commentary_three_views_on_turkeys_syria_intervention#.

of the Kurdish region in Syria isolated from the rest of the Kurdish-controlled zone liberated from the Islamic State. Ankara intends to create a 30 km-deep safe zone there and eventually link that with the Jarablus-Azez pocket already controlled by the Turkish military since the end of 2016. The Turkish government says the target of its 'Olive Branch' operation is the YPG that it regards as 'terrorists' linked to the Kurdistan Workers Party (PKK). The YPG attaches huge importance to Afrin and believes that if the Turkish army manages to defeat them in Afrin, they will try to do the same in other regions across Northern Syria.[22]

Nevertheless, the YPG is also a key US ally and the backbone of the US-backed anti-ISIS ground force.[23] Afrin has become a political hot potato with the intersection of Turkish, Russian, and American interests, all with competing designs for the future of Syria. 'It hosted Russian troops and was seen as a Russian 'protectorate' since the early days of the Syrian war. Ankara had to secure Moscow's blessing to start the incursion. Russia agreed to it as a *quid pro quo* for gaining concessions on the Astana process—Ankara's acquiescence on the Syrian regime's advances on Idlib—than any real sense of a Kurdish threat'.[24] Furthermore, Russia also expects that a prolonged Turkish-Kurdish confrontation would force the Syrian Kurds to arrive at a political agreement with the Assad regime. Nevertheless, the Turkish onslaught on the Kurds has the danger of causing difficulties with the United States. The continuing uncertainty of President Trump's focus on reducing Iran's influence in the region makes for unpredictable US support of the Kurdish groups.

With the Turkish ambition to advance on the Kurdish-held town of Manbij,[25] on the westernmost outskirts of SDF controlled territory in Aleppo province, there was fear of direct conflict with the US forces. US troops have a military base in Manbij, currently held by a local militia

[22] GunayYildiz, 'What it Means for the Kurds'in 'Three Views on Turkey's Syrian Intervention', European Council on Foreign Affairs, January 25, 2018, https://www.ecfr.eu/article/commentary_three_views_on_turkeys_syria_intervention#.

[23] 253AsliAydintasbas, ' What it means for Turkey' in 'Three Views on Turkey's Syrian intervention', European Council on Foreign Affairs, January 25, 2018, https://www.ecfr.eu/article/commentary_three_views_on_Turkeys_syria_intervention#.

[24] Ibid. Asli Aydintasbas.

[25] Farrah Najjar, 'New Front in Syria's War: Why Manbij Matters, Al Jazeera', October 10, 2019, https://www.aljazeera.com/news/2019/10/front-syria-war-manbij-matters-191015143157365.html.

allied to the YPG, that Turkey deems a security threat. The centrepiece of this impossible balancing act is that United States and Turkey had agreed to the so-called Manbij Roadmap, conditions-based document that calls for coordinated, independent patrols; joint patrols; and then the vetting of men and women for leadership positions.

A spokesperson for the US-led coalition fighting the IS group confirmed that government forces were not inside Manbij but rather on the outskirts of the city. Syria's army is outside Manbij responding to calls by the Kurdish YPG (Peoples Protection Units), part of the US-backed SDF, against possible attack by Turkey.

US cooperation with the PKK and their affiliates dates back to the beginning of Washington's involvement in the anti-ISIL campaign. Despite the PKK's terrorist designation, the organization has played an instrumental role in both the Syrian Civil War and the fight against ISIL. Its longstanding transnational presence in both Iraq and Syria has ensured their deep involvement in both conflicts. Multiple credible sources indicate that the PKK is the driving force behind the Syrian Kurdish People's Protection Units (YPG) and the YPG-led SDF. Their partnership successfully repulsed the ISIL offensive from Iraqi Kurdistan and helped retake much of northern Syria from ISIL control. Despite vehement Turkish objections, the US government has only continued to ramp up support for the YPG and SDF.[26]

To pursue its goal to keep a hand in Syrian affairs Turkey made a strategic u-turn in its policy vis-à-vis Syria moving from antagonism towards Russia and Iran to collaborating with these countries to secure a role in determining Syria's future. It begs many questions, above all, of the sanctity of Syrian sovereignty. Erdogan's primary goal is also to deny the Kurdish YPG groups, seen as part of the PKK, from securing autonomy from the Syrian state. Erdogan threatened to order the Turkish military into northeastern Syria eight times since January 2018, the last three warnings coming between late July and early August 2019.

'Erdogan's threat to invade northeastern Syria was a bluff designed to coerce concessions from Washington. In August 2019 he secured a three-point agreement that calls on the United States "to address Turkey's

[26] John Holland-McCowan, 'War of Shadows: How Turkey's Conflict with PKK Shapes the Syrian Civil War and Iraq Kurdistan', ICSR, King's College, London, 2017, https://icsr.info/wp-content/uploads/2017/08/ICSR-Report-War-of-Shadows-How-Turkey%E2%80%99s-Conflict-with-the-PKK-Shapes-the-Syrian-Civil-War-and-Iraqi-Kurdistan.pdf.

security concerns," set up a joint operations center in Turkey's southeast, and establish a safe zone in northern Syria'.[27] Erdogan has not only managed to get a US commitment to remain engaged in the situation but also secured a no-cost option to berate his NATO partner.

The problem arises because of a difference in understanding between the United States and Turkey. United States sees the Sunni-majority transnational terrorist groups as requiring a military response to deny safe haven that has driven the rationale and legal justification for the Syrian military campaign. For Turkey, the Sunni-majority terrorist groups are a law-enforcement problem, whereas the PKK (and its affiliates) are a military threat requiring the elimination of their and expansion and safe-haven.[28]

In this situation, the role of Russian President Vladimir Putin becomes crucial. 'He is now the undisputed broker of the future of Syria, but Moscow will have to handle the competing interests of Syria and Turkey. In this context, Turkey's feint to invade northwestern Syria was intended to ensure that the United States would commit to defending Turkey. If Putin can manage this complicated situation without a major confrontation between the Turks and Kurds, and between the Turks and Syrians, he will solidify his role as a regional leader'.[29]

Qatar

Qatar's involvement in the Syrian civil war is attributed to desire of the Emir of Qatar, Sheikh Hamad bin Khalifa Al Thani,[30] 'to secure a legacy for himself as the man who took the Arab world into a more

[27] Steven E. Cook, 'Erdogan Plays Washington Like a Fiddle', Council on Foreign Relations, September 3, 2019, https://www.cfr.org/article/erdogan-plays-washington-fiddle.

[28] Ibid. Aaron Stein.

[29] Steven A. Cook, 'Syria's Changing Power Grid: What Turkey Wants', Council on Foreign Relations, December 21, 2018, https://www.cfr.org/in-brief/syrias-changing-power-grid-what-turkey-wants.

[30] John Hall, 'Emir of Qatar profile: Who is Sheikh Hamad bin Khalifa Al Thani, how did he turn Qatar the world's richest nation and why has he decided to abdicate?', *The Independent*, June 25, 2013, https://www.independent.co.uk/news/world/middle-east/emir-of-qatar-profile-who-is-sheikh-hamad-bin-khalifa-al-thani-how-did-he-turn-qatar-into-the-world-8672997.html.

activist phase of multilateral action…to stand up and solve Arab problems with Arab action, backed by the use of force'.[31] In Qatar's view, its national interest and raison d'état dictated support for the myriad regional Islamist groups against the Assad regime and in other countries beset by the 'Arab Spring', Tunisia, Egypt, Libya or Yemen. These groups were positioned to play leading roles in the upheavals in their countries. In contrast with Saudi Arabia, Qatar was more in control of its domestic setting without the same concern regarding both foreign and home grown political dissidence and growing Islamist militancy.

Their largesse covered Sunni political Islamists, mainly the Muslim Brotherhood, that were 'better organized, more vocal and better at galvanizing the public masses than the region's secular and pro-democracy dissidents'.[32] 'Qatar secured two forms of leverage in the states in transition, individual connections through Doha-based exiles who returned to their countries of origin and institutional influence through the Muslim Brotherhood.'[33] Qatar has supported the Muslim Brotherhood in Egypt and Tunisia's Islamist al-Nahda party, which won the first elections after the popular revolts.

Interestingly, the Qatar Emir was once a close friend of the Assad family. 'Qatari institutions were big investors in Syria, with a $5bn joint holding company set up in 2008 to develop everything from power stations to hotels. The emir also championed the international rehabilitation of Assad during his ostracisation by the United States, Europe and his Arab peers; Sheikh Hamad was instrumental in restoring Syrian relations with France in the years before the uprising, when he counted the former president Nicolas Sarkozy as a friend. Back then, Syria was part of an alliance—with Iran and Lebanon's Hezbollah—that seemed on the ascendant, and Qatar, with typical pragmatism and opportunism, saw a chance to ride the wave as well as to moderate Assad's policies'.[34]

Qatar created formidable advantages for itself even before the Arab Spring. It maintains cordial relations with Iran and is seen as a mediator

[31] Michael Stephens, 'What is Qatar Doing in Syria?', *The Guardian*, August 8, 2012, https://www.theguardian.com/commentisfree/2012/aug/08/qatar-syria-opposition.

[32] Ibid. Line Khatib.

[33] Ibid.

[34] Roula Khalaf & Abigail Fielding-Smith, 'How Qatar Seized Control of the Syrian Revolution', *Financial Times*, May 17, 2013, https://www.ft.com/content/f2d9bbc8-bdbc-11e2-890a-00144feab7de.

in the region. It has contacts with Israel while simultaneously backing the Palestinian group Hamas and Lebanon's Hezbollah.[35] In the Afghanistan quagmire, it has provided the venue for talks between the Taliban and the US Administration. It hosts the US military base at al-Udeid Air Base, with 10,000 American troops, the overseas headquarters for US Central Command in the region.

Following the Arab Spring, however, Qatar dynamically responded to the political opportunity the region presented. The increasing militarization of the Syrian uprising made Qatar a major external source of funds for the radical militant groups. It attempted to influence the course of events through its local proxies. It soon became the main supplier of arms to the rebels in northern Syria, which became the principal axis of Qatari influence to develop networks of loyalty among rebel groups and set the stage for influence in a post-Assad era. Despite Qatari efforts to maintain exclusivity regarding the funding of specific Syrian opposition groups, more often, the latter have kept re-branding themselves to secure funds from Saudi Arabia also. This has been the cause of long-standing suspicion between the two countries. With the multiplicity of outside sources of sponsorship and no stable organisational structures, rebel groups have lurched from sponsor to sponsor.

Qatar lobbied the 22-member Arab League to hand over Syria's seat to representatives of the Syrian opposition, and in March 2013, it inaugurated a new Syrian embassy representing the Syrian opposition, the only country to have taken this step. Overall, Qatar has provided very significant amounts of financial support, diplomatic leverage and armaments to Syria's opposition, including sending up to US $1 billion in aid to the rebels.

Qatar's Syria policy was primarily pragmatic neither ideological nor religious. Its networks with Islamists evolved from the emirate's tradition of maintaining a place of refuge for the politically persecuted and the belief that political Islam provided the only functional opposition to authoritarianism. It also believed that the charitable work of the Islamist groups was more effective, reliable and inclusive than that of secular charities. With the disintegration of the political order in the Middle East,

[35] Ibid. Khalaf and Fielding-Smith.

Qatar saw the Islamist groups as the only available force able to fill the socio-political void left by the failing regimes.[36]

Nevertheless, Qatar could not retain operational and tactical control over its Syrian protégées, while Obama administration's hesitant policy prevented Qatar's support to the moderate rebels. With the geopolitical environment becoming difficult, Qatar withdrew its military liaison officers from Syria in 2014. Qatar's charities continued providing aid to local councils. 'Qatar had tried to help the Syrians build a post-authoritarian future. It did so relying on Syria's moderate opposition groups promising to embrace pluralism, civil liberties and socio-political inclusion. With the proliferation of salafi-jihadists in Syria, it was no longer feasible for Qatar to provide military support to these groups on the ground'.[37]

Qatar's unilateral action in funding and supporting the Sunni Islamist groups in Syria were viewed by UAE and Saudi Arabia as undermining their domestic stability and regional position. Qatar was accused by them of supporting Sunni Islamist militias, opposed to the Saudi and Emirati dispensations that challenged their current territorial borders, and like Iran, had a revisionist plan for the entire region.

The competition between Qatar and Saudi Arabia in Syria is historical. Both have had longstanding ties to the Syrian regime. The Saudi regime was a benefactor of Hafez al-Assad for close to three decades, and the two regimes' interests in the region often converged. The Saudi-Syrian convergence during these years was also important to US's role in the region. The divergence between Qatar and Saudi Arabia arose from the late 1990s when the new Qatari emir, Hamad bin Khalifa, overthrew his pro-Saudi father. When Bashar al-Assad began consolidating his power in Syria, he shifted his foreign policy in Lebanon against the interests of Saudi Arabia and Lebanese Prime Minister Rafic Hariri. As a result, Qatar became Assad's natural ally, while Saudi Arabia pulled away from the Syrian regime. This divergence and competition between Saudi Arabia and Qatar has exacerbated throughout the Syrian civil war.[38]

[36] Andreas Krieg & Andrew J. Bowen, 'Qatar's Pragmatic Syria Gamble', *The National Interest*, October 4, 2017, https://nationalinterest.org/feature/qatars-pragmatic-syria-gamble-22602.

[37] Ibid.

[38] As'ad Abu Khalil, 'How the Saudi-Qatari Rivalry has Fueled the War in Syria', The Intercept, June 29, 2018, https://theintercept.com/2018/06/29/syria-war-saudi-arabia-qatar/.

The resulting diplomatic tension between these countries has eventually led since June 2017 to a continuing four-nation—Bahrain, Egypt, UAE and Saudi Arabia—embargo of Qatar led by Saudi Arabia and UAE. Riyadh and Abu Dhabi have accused Doha of financing terrorism, cosying up to Iran and harbouring fugitives. The embargo forced changes to airplane routes and severed Qatar's only land border. Qatar has repeatedly denied allegation of sponsoring 'terrorism', a euphemism for supporting radical Islamic groups equally opposed to Saudi Arabia. 'It has also troubled American forces and strategy in the region, which envisions a united Arab effort to combat terrorism and contain Iran'.[39]

Qatar emerged a clear winner with the Quartet having failed to force Qatar to accept its demands (including shutting down of Al Jazeera and stopping support for Islamic groups), and failed in its intention to interfere in Qatar's foreign policy. Qatar's public relations campaign, particularly in the United States, was able to lobby in its favour and against the Quartet regimes. Furthermore, as Qatar became less involved with extremist groups in Syria and Mohammed bin Salman became the Saudi Crown Prince, Qatar was better able to position itself as a supporter of grassroots Arab causes.[40]

During his visit in early April 2018 the Qatari Emir was able to convince President Trump that the holdout against settling the embargo is not Qatar but the United Arab Emirates and its crown prince, Mohammed bin Zayed. The US President has pushed for a settlement so that it does not become an unwanted distraction in a region roiled by conflict. The blockade boosted Qatar's impressive diplomatic capabilities and helped to deepen its ties with Iran, Russia, the United States and Turkey. The blockade also assisted the Emirate in speeding its economic reforms and diversification of its economy and in extending ties with other countries, that will, be beneficial in the end.[41] Qatar's sovereign wealth fund valued at $335 billion could secure a favourable standing in Syria's

[39] Gardiner Harris and Mark Landler, 'Qatar Charm Offensive Appears to Have Paid Off, US Officials Say', *The New York Times*, https://www.nytimes.com/2018/04/09/us/politics/qatar-trump-embargo-charm-offensive.html.

[40] Hassan Hassan, 'Qatar Won the Saudi Blockade', Foreign Policy, June 4, 2018, https://foreignpolicy.com/2018/06/04/qatar-won-the-saudi-blockade/.

[41] Joze M. Pelayo, 'Doha's Diplomatic Potential in Syria', International Policy Digest, April 19, 2019, https://intpolicydigest.org/2018/04/19/doha-s-diplomatic-potential-in-syria/.

reconstruction while its close relations with both Russia and the United States could bring its influence to bear on the final resolution to Syrian conflict.

As Qatar's cooperation with Russia grows, it will be in the interest of the United States to keep Doha a close ally and further its relationship if it continues to be interested in exercising leverage and diplomatic efforts on Moscow and Tehran.[42] In a fanciful opinion, it has been suggested that 'if Qatar was to rescue Syria when the war there is over—if it's vast wealth could rebuild that ancient land—then Qatar would have an empire for its emperors. Not that Qatar would ever own Syria—far from it, Syrians would fight to stop that—but it would have, as we say in the Middle East, "considerable influence". It would have power. And a power—with a Mediterranean coastline—that even Saudi Arabia doesn't have'.[43]

After eight years following Iraqi mediation, Syria and Qatar are taking steps towards normalization to break their respective regional isolation. In 2014, the two countries had worked together, via Lebanese mediation, on the release of 13 nuns kidnapped by the Islamist Jabhat Al-Nusra group. Their rapprochement began in March 2018, with their sports federations signing a low-profile cooperation agreement in the training and exchange of athletes. A state-imposed Syrian ban over Al Jazeera channel's website was lifted, for both the Arabic and English versions. There are other Arab countries equally interested in restoring bilateral relations with Syria reasoning that Bashar al-Assad is there to stay.[44]

Turkey, Qatar and Saudi Arabia have been the leading Middle Eastern states seeking the overthrow of Syrian President Bashar al-Assad. All three saw the Syrian civil war as a key arena for their regional ambitions. While they sought to expand their own influence they lacked the capacity to achieve their goals without high US involvement. Since 2011, having set

[42] Ibid. Joze M. Pelayo.

[43] Robert Fisk, 'Once the Syrian War is Over, Qatar Could Become an Empire Once More', *The Independent*, May 3, 2018, https://www.independent.co.uk/voices/syria-war-assad-qatar-saudi-arabia-israel-golan-occupation-a8334056.html.

[44] Sami Moubayed, 'Syria and Qatar Silently Mend Broken Fences', *Gulf News*, April 25, 2019, https://gulfnews.com/world/gulf/qatar/syria-and-qatar-silently-mend-broken-fences-1.63545446.

regime change as the goal, they found themselves in a contradictory position with US policy in retreat damaging their ties to Washington and worsening their situation in Syria.[45]

Iran

Syria is the geopolitical lynchpin for Iranian influence in the Levant and the wider Arab world. If the Syrian regime fell, it would affect the flow of arms and aid to Iran's most important Arab ally, the Lebanese militia and political party Hezbollah that has thousands of rockets aimed at Israel and the main Iranian deterrence against Israel.[46]

Iran and Syria have been close allies since the 1979 Iranian revolution and have provided the other with critical assistance at critical times. Syria was one of only two Arab nations (Libya was the other) to support Iran during the eight-year war with Saddam Hussein in the 1980s. It was an important conduit for weapons to an isolated Iran. Tehran's privileged relationship with Damascus has facilitated its support for the Shiite Hezbollah group in Lebanon, and for Hamas and other Palestinian factions. The constellation of allies, which Tehran calls the 'axis of resistance', or the 'front of refusal', has given Iran strategic depth in the heart of the Arab World, spread its influence across the eastern Mediterranean, and widened its room for maneuver and dissuasion in Iran's confrontation with the Israel and the United States.[47]

Since 2013 along with its military interventions in crucial battles, Iran has steadily grown its military, economic, political, and ideological influence within Syria. Its support was Bashar al-Assad's mainstay to survive until the launching in September 2015 of Russia's air operations against al-Assad's opponents. 'While Russia's political cover in the international arena and its vital air support have been no less essential to Assad's survival, Iran has invested far more than Russia, when measured in blood

[45] Christopher Phillips, 'Eyes Bigger Than Stomachs: Turkey, Saudi Arabia and Qatar in Syria', *Middle East Policy*, March 19, 2017, https://onlinelibrary.wiley.com/doi/full/10.1111/mepo.12250.

[46] Alireza Nader, 'Iran's Goals in Syria', The RAND Blog, January 1, 2015, https://www.rand.org/blog/2015/01/irans-goals-in-syria.html.

[47] Mohammad-Reza Djalili & Thierry Kellner, 'Scramble for Syria', *The Cairo Review of Global Affairs*, The American University in Cairo, Summer 2017, https://www.thecairoreview.com/essays/scramble-for-syria/.

and treasure'.[48] Over the last decade, Iran's Revolutionary Guards have trained, equipped, and aided Syria's security and military forces. More than five hundred Iranians have died in Syria since 2012 including Iranian Revolutionary Guard General Mohammed Allahdadi in January 2015, as well as more than 1200 Lebanese Hezbollah fighters and more than 800 Afghan fighters.

Major General Qassem Soleimani,[49] chief of the Quds Force—foreign branch of the IRGC—was the architect of Tehran's strategic efforts from Lebanon through Syria and Iraq to Yemen. A significant influence in shaping the Syrian government's military campaign he was seen on major battlefields in Syria with pro-regime fighters and Shiite militias. Iran's Shia'a foreign legions have filled the gaps for the Syrian Arab Army when it began struggling to fill its ranks in 2015. Iran not only trains and equips these fighters, but it also pays their salaries. Iran's economic support kept the Assad regime afloat in 2012 and 2013 with $14 to $15 billion, and since then, Iran's provides between $15 and $20 billion annually. Iran's unwavering commitment to Syria makes it certain that will spare no effort to preserve its hard-fought strategic gains.[50]

With Iranian guidance, the National Defence Forces were set up in 2012 to organize Syria's informal paramilitary arm *(shabiha)* as a partial response to the Syrian Army's manpower shortage. The so-called 'Hezbollah in Syria' was created by Iran in 2014, with the help of Lebanese Hezbollah and Iraq's Badr Organization and Kata'ib Hezbollah. This diverse group of Shi'i militias subscribing to Iran's revolutionary ideology, has played an important role in advancing Iran's interests and fighting on behalf of the regime in the Aleppo and Homs areas, along the Lebanon–Syria border, on the Jordanian-Syria border, and on the Golan Heights.[51]

In Syria, as well as in Iraq, Iran has used the war against the Islamic State's Caliphate to further legitimise its presence and expand the scope

[48] Brandon Friedman, 'Iran's Hezbollah model in Iraq and Syria: Fait Accompli?', Orbis, 2018, Vol. 62, No. 3, pp. 438–453, https://www.sciencedirect.com/science/article/pii/S0030438718300413.

[49] Peter Beaumant, 'Making of a Martyr: How Qassem Suleimani Was Hunted Down', *The Observer*, January, 5, 2020, https://www.theguardian.com/world/2020/jan/05/making-of-a-martyr-how-qassem-suleimani-was-hunted-down.

[50] Ibid.

[51] Ibid.

of its influence. Echoing Bashar al-Assad, it has also projected the war as a fight against terrorism. Yet, despite the destruction of the Caliphate, the war continues. Since 2015, Iran has expanded its militias in Syria, introducing units that are comprised of Iranian-trained Afghan and Pakistani Shi'is. Tehran was fully cognisant of the need to maintain one of its most important alliances in the region.

In southern Syria, Iran is attempting to establish a permanent military presence close to Israel's border on the Golan Heights, where a number of jihadi opposition groups have already established themselves. Holding this territory appears to be part of Iran's broader plan to link the territory that its clients control in Lebanon and Iraq through what some have referred to as a land bridge, extending from Tehran across western Iraq and eastern Syria to the Mediterranean coast. However, a major obstacle to Iranian expansion into the eastern Syrian territories of the former IS Caliphate are the US-backed SDF, which control the resource-rich territories that lie east of the Euphrates River.[52]

In eastern Syria, the US-supported Kurdish SDF are coming into conflict with Assad's ground forces, supported by Iran militias, that could end up challenging the Kurdish bid for autonomy that the United States supports. Conversely, U.S. military presence in southern and eastern Syria thwarts Assad's bid to consolidate territorial sovereignty and Iran's ambition to control the Syrian-Iraqi frontier and border crossings. Iran has focused on controlling three main transit points between Syria and Iraq: the southernmost al-Waleed border crossing (where the Syrian, Jordanian and Iraqi borders converge); al-BuKamal/al-Qaim border crossing; and, the northern al-Yarubiya/Rabia border crossing. Iran's forces are active on both sides of the Syrian-Iraqi border. It views its interests in Syria and Iraq as inextricably linked. Therefore, Turkey's expansion into both northwest Syria and northeast Iraq will force Iran to recalibrate its own plans along the Syrian-Iraq border.

Russia has attempted to manage competing Iranian and Turkish interests in Syria by dividing its sphere of influence in western Syria into four de-escalation zones that delineate the areas that fall under its partners' control. While Iran is looking to establish a permanent military presence in southwestern Syria, Turkey has occupied a wide swathe of territory in

[52] Ibid. Brandon Friedman.

northwest Syria and declared that it will create a security belt to prevent Kurdish autonomy in northeast Syria.

At the same time, the Iranian-directed militias are trying to establish a permanent presence along Israel's border with Syria, replicating Hezbollah's presence in southern Lebanon. Israel, for its part, has drawn a red line on any Iranian attempt to change the status quo along its border with Syria and has responded with air strikes destroying Iranian military assets in Syria.[53] Iran continues to work towards establishing permanent influence and protecting its long-term interests, whatever the outcome of the civil war, as part of its strategy to reinforce its 'axis of resistance'.

Cultural diplomacy through religious tourism is among the activities encouraged and supported by Iranian authorities to deepen the links between Syria and Iran. Annually, thousands of Iranian pilgrims come to Syria, like before the civil war, to visit the shrines of Shi'a saints—e.g the tomb of Sayyida Zeinab[54] near Damascus, the daughter of Ali, the first Shi'a Imam, considered the holiest site in Syria. Iran has also sought to protect the dozens of Shi'a holy sites in Syria even encouraging Shi'a from other parts of Syria to settle there.

Interestingly, armed opposition groups fighting the Assad regime have opined that Iran has been able to strike bargains with some of the anti-Assad forces on the ground. Iran has even been able to make a number of deals with hard-line rebel groups to undertake population exchanges or ceasefires. Iran would appear to be a useful and direct interlocutor on the ground. While it may be unable or unwilling to compel the Syrian government to change its behaviour, it is able to change realities on the battlefield.[55]

Both Iran and Saudi Arabia have exploited the increasingly sectarian tone of conflicts across the Arab World to their advantage. Tehran has found a foothold in Arab countries with significant Shi'a populations, like Lebanon, Iraq, and Syria, while Riyadh has consistently claimed the

[53] Ibid.

[54] Editor, 'Zainab bint Ali(as): The Woman who saved Islam', Khamenei.IR, March 23, 2020, http://english.khamenei.ir/news/4376/Zainab-bint-Ali-as-The-woman-who-saved-Islam.

[55] Aniseh Bassiri Tabrizi & Rafaello Pantucci, 'Understanding Iran's Role in the Syrian Conflict', Royal United Services Institute for Defence and Security Studies (RUSI), August 2016, https://rusi.org/sites/default/files/201608_op_understanding_irans_role_in_the_syrian_conflict_0.pdf.

mantle of leading the orthodox Sunni world. Their regional cold war includes proxy campaigns in Iraq and Yemen. Yet 'Syria remains the critical battlefield given its strategic position in the heart of a Sunni-majority region that includes not only Syria itself but Turkey, Jordan, Lebanon, Palestine, and Israel'.[56]

Diplomatically, Tehran, in collaboration with Moscow and Ankara, has marginalized not only Riyadh and the other Gulf monarchies, but also Washington and the Western bloc in negotiating a settlement in Syria. At the same time, Iran's entrenched position in Syria has also caused negative friction among the other Gulf powers. It is one of the reasons for UAE, Qatar, Egypt and others to rebuild bridges to Bashar Assad and propose his re-entry into the Arab League.

The Iran–Syria alliance has been one of the most enduring in the region. Both countries projected themselves as the vanguard of resistance against the interests of United States and Israel in the Middle East. They have a shared interest in Iraq and Lebanon, with the Hezbollah as a front to oppose Israel. Thus, the relation between Syria and Iran has a historical basis as well as a pragmatic intent at its heart: the survival of both the Assad dynasty and Islamic Republic. The Islamic Republic can pitch its assistance to Syria in terms of core revolutionary values, namely maintaining independence and keeping foreign influence in the region in check. Tehran will remain a significant factor in any resolution of the Syrian conflict and will significantly influence the extent to which Damascus can deliver any political deal.

It remains axiomatic that without Moscow's support, and an emboldened Russia, it is unlikely that Assad would have survived. With Russia seeking to project its regional role at the expense of a vacillating United States, it has enabled this alliance to persist at the expense of Western aims in the Middle East.[57] Despite high cost, Iran will continue spending billions supporting President Bashar al-Assad in an open-ended commitment lest it undermine Iran's credibility as a revolutionary and regional power. Geopolitically, loss of the decades-old Syrian alliance would be a

[56] Ibid. Djalili & Kellener.

[57] Edward Wastnidge, 'Iran and Syria: An Enduring Axis', *Middle East Policy*, 2017, Vol. 24, No. 2, pp. 148–159, https://eds.b.ebscohost.com/eds/pdfviewer/pdfviewer?vid=1&sid=9ac35453-4be3-442f-ad2d-c81df0a43dc3%40pdc-v-sessmgr06.

major foreign policy setback partially closing Tehran's access to Lebanon, depriving Iran of a frontline ally against Israel and isolating the Islamic Republic.

International Powers

Russia

Russia justified its foray into Syria as part of an effort to reduce terrorism by shoring up the Assad government, which by the summer of 2015 was facing military setbacks. As Putin said in October, 'The collapse of Syria's official authorities will only mobilize terrorists. Right now, instead of undermining them, we must revive them, strengthening state institutions in the conflict zone'. Moscow was adamantly opposed to anything that would weaken the rule of secular strongmen in the Middle East—hence Putin's repeated denunciations of U.S. support for opposition forces during the Arab revolts of 2011 and his anger over the NATO military action against Libya that year, which led to the ouster of Libyan dictator Muammar al-Qaddafi.

Putin also equated the issue of Chechnya with the civil war in Syria. He was comfortable with calling it terrorism in Chechnya without making any distinction based on cause, religion or motivation. In Syria also, like Bashar Assad, he accepted the characterization of the opposing groups as terrorists. Yet the fundamental difference in the situations in Chechnya and Syria is that the effects of the former could not spread to Russia as whole whereas in the latter case the span of effects is wide both ideologically and geographically.

Moscow was also convinced that humanitarian intervention under the banner of R2P in Libya—in spite of the procedural legitimacy conferred by UNSC Resolution 1973, and Moscow's own acceptance that Gaddafi had lost legitimacy and that the Libyan National Transitional Council could take over—was ultimately an elaborate cover for regime change, perceived by Moscow as illegitimate.[58]

[58] Derek Averre & Lance Davies, 'Russia, humanitarian intervention and Responsibility to Protect: The Case of Syria', *International Affairs*, July 2015, Vol. 91, No. 4, pp. 813–834, https://search-ebscohost-com.proxyiub.uits.iu.edu/login.aspx?direct=true&db=24h&AN=108358727&site=eds-live&scope=site.

In Putin's eyes, the disorder in Iraq, Syria, and North Africa, combined with the rise of the self-proclaimed Islamic State (ISIS), demonstrates the West's failure to think through the consequences of undermining the authoritarian states in the region. Putin fears that chaos in the Middle East will strengthen Islamic extremism on Russia's borders, in the neighbouring states of the former Soviet Union, and potentially in Russia itself.[59]

Russia took strategic advantage of an international policy vacuum when it decided to intervene militarily in Syria. In doing so, it was building on a long-standing relationship, primarily based on supply of arms and military material that the former USSR had with Syria. Like the Soviet Union in Afghanistan, the United States and its allies were bruised from interventions in Afghanistan and Iraq. There was little public stomach for more military involvement in the Middle East. Russia saw an opportunity to act decisively, both in the UN Security Council and on the ground in Syria. Putin was equally conscious that in March 2011 Russia was played by the Western powers, when it abstained in the UNSC in pushing a unanimous decision for intervention in Libya.[60]

'Russia's intervention in Syria altered the course of the war ensuring the survival of Bashar al-Assad's presidency. All those countries that share borders with Syria or have also become involved there have had to recognize Russian power. It has regained a leading role on the international stage of the kind that Moscow has not enjoyed since the time of the Soviet Union…Russia's return to a powerful global role has gone some way to reverse its sense of trauma. The challenge now is to consolidate those gains'.[61]

[59] Angela Stent, 'Putin's Power Play in Syria: How to Respond to Russia's intervention', *Foreign Affairs*, 2016, Vol. 95, No. 1, pp. 106–113, https://eds.b.ebscohost.com/eds/detail/detail?vid=0&sid=905b4591-43cd-4571-b3a7-ff82a6fbdb1c%40pdc-v-sessmgr01&bdata=JnNpdGU9ZWRzLWxpdmUmc2NvcGU9c2l0ZQ%3d%3d#AN=ICHA975725&db=ich.

[60] Hannah Van Hoose, 'Understanding Russian Response to Intervention in Libya', Center for American Progress, April 12, 2011, https://www.americanprogress.org/issues/security/news/2011/04/12/9529/understanding-the-russian-response-to-the-intervention-in-libya/.

[61] James Rodgers, 'Russia and Syria: Policies, Problems, Perspectives', *Forbes*, January 11, 2019, https://www.forbes.com/sites/jamesrodgerseurope/2019/01/11/russia-and-syria-prospects-and-prizes/#2397dfc36852.

Putin took the decision to deploy Russian forces to Syria in September 2015. Syria had, for many decades, been an ally first of the Soviet Union and then of the new Russia. They were being sent, it was stated, in order to fight 'international terrorism' and thus to help ensure that such terrorists were less likely to visit their atrocities on the Russian homeland. A Russian military presence in Syria (with forces-based largely at Hmeimim airbase near Lakatia and at the port of Tartus) was also required to help prop up the regime of President Bashar al-Assad.

As a great power, Russia also wanted a presence in Syria to give Moscow leverage in the Middle East, a vitally important area of the world. Here was a region whose oil wealth and underlying instability virtually demanded interference from a large number of great-power actors. Russia had to be one of them. It was a region, moreover, that had come to draw added attention post-2011 due to the Arab Spring, including the destabilizing of Syria.

Once Russia demonstrated its degree of commitment, the leaders of all these regional states and groupings, along with the representatives of the other great powers, had to make calls on Kremlin luminaries. The opinion of those luminaries regarding Syria, and of Putin most notably, came to matter. For the Russian media it was a demonstration of Putin's 'personal diplomacy [as] a force multiplier'. A further driver behind the commitment to Syria was the desire to project *derzhavnost or* 'great-powerness'. Successive Tsarist, Soviet and Russian governments had believed that their country should always have a prominent role on the international stage.

From 2010 onwards, with his waning personal popularity among the Russian people Putin began to put considerable stress on the projection of Russia's great-power credentials. The intervention in Syria tapped into this nationalist sentiment. It came to symbolize a return to the supposed imperial glory of the Soviet Union. Having ordered this intervention, Putin would doubtless hope to bask in the reflected glory.

Russia has gained most at the higher strategic level from its regional presence in Syria. The vital combat experience gained by the Russian forces on the ground in Syria coupled with that in Georgia, made for a markedly more powerful and efficient Russian armed forces than just ten years earlier. The Syria operation also provided a significant proving ground for testing new equipment and weapons systems.

'Russia, whether in its Tsarist or Soviet incarnations, has always sought to maintain maritime forward defensive zones just as, on land, it has sought to maintain defensive "buffer states" between its own territory and those of its main adversaries'.[62] The Russian Navy will be operating in the Eastern Mediterranean and out of Tartus port for a long time with Russia extending in 2017 its lease—dating from the Soviet period—by 49 years on its naval facilities. The continuing upgrading, repair and replenishment of the port will allow Russian vessels to remain for longer in the Mediterranean and not have to return often to Black Sea ports.[63] The growth of Russian naval power in the Eastern Mediterranean contrasts with the US Navy's reduced activity since much of its assets were moved to the Asia-Pacific.

Increasingly, the Russian Navy is operating frigates and corvettes from the Caspian Sea Flotilla to launch Kalibr cruise missiles at targets in Syria. They are the latest, most flexible and most potent cruise missiles in the Russian naval arsenal. The use of these missiles was both a technology demonstrator and a warning to NATO in the context of US's Prompt Global Strike (PGS) capability. PGS capability provides United States with the capacity to launch within Russia 6000 non-nuclear cruise missiles, all within one hour, aimed at operational and strategic targets (including nuclear weapons silos).[64]

The Russian air base at Hmeimim is equipped with 'A2/D2 bubble' for air defence and to combat hostile NATO activity from the British air base at Akrotiri in Cyprus and United States bases in Turkey at Incirlik and the Kurecik ballistic-missile defence radar station (part of the European Phased Adaptive Approach system). Russian air defence assets guard the airspace above Syria to allow the unfettered in-theatre movement of Russian military assets/troops and other friendly forces. Its weapons systems include, for instance, the Kalibrs and Iskander-M neither of which have NATO equivalents. This bubble also makes significant use of ground-based missile air defence using the highly sophisticated S-300 (range 150 km) and the S-400 (range 400 km).[65] Russia explains that its presence at Hmeimim will be 'permanent' in the context of its counter-PGS role in the defence of Russia itself. An irony is the fact that Putin has

[62] Rod Thornton, 'Countering Prompt Global Strike: The Russian Military Presence in Syria and the Eastern Mediterranean and Its Strategic Deterrence Role', *The Journal of Slavic Military Studies*, 2019, Vol. 32, No. 1, pp. 1–24, https://www.tandfonline.com/doi/full/10.1080/13518046.2019.1552655.

[63] Ibid.

[64] Ibid. Rod Thornton.

[65] Ibid. Rod Thornton.

declared a permanent Russian military presence in support of a regime that, at least presently, is 'permanently insecure'!

Moscow has gained substantive advantage since its involvement given it significant ability to leverage events to its own geopolitical advantage in Syria. Yet it has been equally mindful to balance it with its close relationship with Israel. Their growing relationship has led to the setting up of a joint military committee to ensure that Russia's military armament in Syria, and to Hezbollah, does not harm Israeli jets operating in Syrian airspace. At the same time, with Russia controlling Syrian airspace any Israeli air strike in Syria requires Russian clearance.

Economic Reconstruction

With President Assad's political survival seemingly assured, much remains to be done to ensure a stable future for Syria and its people. In this context, Moscow continues to tread an independent course on the Syrian reconstruction process by pushing for funding from the United States and EU who continue to link it to a political process that excludes Assad. Many EU countries, including Germany, appear willing to fund reconstruction in Syria, but only after reaching a political settlement. The Syria Working Group believes that after the Russian-backed military "victory" of the regime, funding for reconstruction is the only tool the international community has to pressure Assad and his allies to accept a political solution to the conflict.[66] Russia, in contrast, wants reconstruction to be detached from any political process.

Under these circumstances, Russia has had to rely on funding coming from China. Russia has positioned itself to reap the largest windfalls from future investment in Syria's war-ravaged economy by snagging a number of reconstruction and rehabilitation contracts in oil and gas and in manufacture. While Russia could emerge as a short-term winner in the reconstruction process, Moscow's limited financial resources and emerging rivalry with China and Iran for contracts, could erode its long-term leverage.

Russia's has strategic objectives in rapidly increasing its interest in the Syrian reconstruction process. First, it wants to reconnect Syria to global

[66] Marwan Kabalan, 'Russia's New Game in Syria', Al Jazeera, October 29, 2018, https://www.aljazeera.com/indepth/opinion/istanbul-summit-failed-181029102112796.html.

financial markets so that Bashar al-Assad can consolidate his hold on power and begin securing the $400 billion necessary for rebuilding the country. Second, Russia wants to benefit from its gradual positioning as the main actor in the Syrian reconstruction process as foreign capital influx into the Syrian economy could provide vital hard currency for Russian businesses.[67]

Russia & Iran

Iran and Russia have a different degree of influence over Damascus. While Iran and Russia coordinate closely on the ground to advance the war, there is little trust between them over their respective long-term aims in Syria. Tehran views Russian policy in Syria as a way of controlling Iran's links to Europe and helping the Russian state-owned energy company Gazprom to continue its dominance of European energy supplies. Regardless of the reality of these perceptions, they reflect a high level of mistrust between the two countries. Putin understands that while Iran, and Hezbollah, may also be supporting Assad, their vision of Syria is quite different from his own.

Damascus, on its part, is more comfortable dealing with Russia than the seemingly sectarian agenda of Iran. While the Syrian regime recognizes Iran's pivotal role in preventing its collapse, both militarily and economically, it much prefers Russian support, which is devoid religious zeal, has less focus on the role of militias, and in many respects demands less politically intrusive control over the regime's security apparatus. Neither does the Syrian regime want to end up as a pawn fought over and used by Saudi Arabia and Iran. It remains concerned about Hezbollah fighters mobilized—and in some cases directed—by Iran. They are also apprehensive about Iranian militias trying to convert secular Syrian forces with ensuing tensions between the two sides. While aware of these tensions, Damascus and Tehran have prioritized regime stability as the basis of their cooperation and coordination.[68]

Given their strategic role, neither Russia nor Iran can be excluded from talks over Syria's future. Iran is likely to have greater influence on local

[67] Samuel Ramani, 'Russia's Eye on Syrian Reconstruction', Carnegie Endowment for International Peace, January 31, 2019, https://carnegieendowment.org/sada/78261.

[68] 297 Ibid. Aniseh Bassiri Tabrizi & Rafaello Pantucci.

issues, such as ceasefires and humanitarian access in specific areas while Russia's greater interest will factor in its own security. Russia would also see its status as guarantor in any final Syrian political settlement. Moscow's ultimate goal remains a change the global geopolitical balance that would increase its influence on the international stage. At the same time, Putin cannot withdraw from Syria yet as it will essentially hand the country to Iran.

Russia & Turkey

Russian–Turkish relations have witnessed major vicissitudes during the Syrian conflict. Their interests have clashed in Syria even though they are energy and economic partners. While Ankara funded and hosted Syrian opposition members, Moscow has been Assad's most prominent backer. Turkey's shooting down in November 2015 in Syria of a Russian jet was a major crisis. It was only when Turkish president Erdogan apologized in June 2016 that the Russia's retaliatory sanctions were lifted. Since then, they have been involved with Iran in a multilateral strategic partnership in the Astana peace process.

Nevertheless, fundamental differences in their views on Syria have coloured a continuous clash of interests. Moscow may have played a role in softening Ankara's approach towards Assad's regime, yet it could not limit Turkey's military intervention in Afrin or secure that Ankara observes the Idlib understanding.

Turkey has conducted five separate military operations on Syrian soil since 2015 from fighting ISIS, and in Rojava (Autonomous Administration of North and East Syria),[69] to the relocation of a tomb. Rojava consists of self-governing sub-regions of Afrin, Jazira, Euphrates, Raqqa, Tabqa, Manbij and Deir Ez-Zor. The region gained its de facto autonomy in 2012 as part of the ongoing Rojava conflict and the wider Syrian civil war. Its official military force, the SDF, composed primarily of Kurdish, Arab and Assyrian/Syriac militias as well as some smaller Armenian, Turkmen and Chechen forces, has maintained its autonomy.

The People's Protection Units (YPG), a mostly Kurdish militia, militarily leads the SDF. YPG are the ideological partners of the Turkish Kurds from PKK (Kurdistan Workers' Party) that Ankara is determined to

[69] Mireille Court & Chris Den Hond, 'Is this the end of Rojava?', The Nation, February 18, 2020, https://www.thenation.com/article/world/rojava-kurds-syria/.

annihilate. Turkey's most recent military operation thus was its invasion of Syria's Afrin in January 2018, where it has aimed to drive out the Kurdish YPG fighters. Bashar al-Assad publicly criticized it recognizing it as a violation of Syria's sovereignty. Moscow's recent alignment with Syria's Kurds, by recognizing their autonomous rule in a draft constitution could exacerbate Turkish military action in Afrin.[70]

'Ensuring the survival of Assad's authoritarian regime in Damascus was never the sole goal of Russia's intervention. Instead, its purpose was, at least as much, to inject itself into a crucial geopolitical battleground and force Washington to realize that Russia cannot be overlooked. It was also to keep Syria from becoming an Iranian vassal'.[71] Moscow and Tehran while happy to try to marginalize the United States in Syria are also fierce competitors seeking influence in the Middle East and South Caucasus.

The Assad government now has momentum and is far from collapse. Moscow has been able to demonstrate that it is 'a power broker in the Middle East, a spoiler in North Africa, and a partner (of sorts) in Asia, making it at least a global player if not a superpower'.[72] It also remains true that in 2015–2016 Russia's military involvement in Syria 'distracted Western and Russian attention from Putin's Ukrainian operations and the buildup of his forces in Syria'.[73] Russia equally feared regional spillover from civil war in Syria, especially the infiltration of radical Islamist extremists into Central Asia and Russia proper.[74] Further, by using military force in Syria, Moscow sent a message to other regional players: unlike the United States, Russia will support leaders and governments against popular uprisings and will not desert them as the US abandoned Egyptian President Hosni Mubarak in 2011.

[70] Zeidon Alkinani, 'Russia's Cautious Role in Syria', Open Democracy, June 20, 2018, https://www.opendemocracy.net/en/north-africa-west-asia/russia-s-cautious-role-in-syria/.

[71] Mark Galeotti, 'Putin is Playing a Dangerous Game in Syria', *The Atlantic*, February 15, 2018, https://www.theatlantic.com/international/archive/2018/02/the-costs-of-russian-intervention-in-syria-are-rising/553367/.

[72] Ibid.

[73] Maksymilian Czuperski et al., 'Distract, Deceive, Destroy: Putin at War in Syria', The Atlantic Council, April 2016, https://publications.atlanticcouncil.org/distract-deceive-destroy/assets/download/ddd-report.pdf.

[74] Hanna Notte, 'Russia in Chechnya and Syria: Pursuit of Strategic Goals', *Middle East Policy*, 2016, Vol. 23, No. 1, pp. 59–74, https://onlinelibrary-wiley-com.proxyiub.uits.iu.edu/doi/pdf/10.1111/mepo.12174.

Nevertheless, Russia's Syrian involvement continues to have political costs to Putin. For the Russian people, it is not a popular war especially after the combat deaths of his regular soldiers and mercenaries' belonging to Wagner, a Russian-funded and led outfit for frontline duty. Russian nationalists are also demanding some kind of response to the U.S. airstrikes that killed Russian fighters. The odds of a Russian-US confrontation escalating into an outright confrontation remain low, yet the risk that Moscow, as in the past, might be forced to back down to avoid one is much greater. 'For now, Putin has won his desired role as a geopolitical player. So far, he probably feels he is winning in Syria. But the game is not over, and the costs are rising'.[75]

Neither the scale of the humanitarian tragedy nor other issues, have led the Russian president to abandon Syria. His best option, with Bashar al-Assad having regained most of his country, is to promote, within the UN Security Council, the need to pool and jointly provide funding for restoring a country destroyed by the P-5 themselves. He will also continue to insist that in negotiations for a political settlement inclusion of Bashar al-Assad is the only way forward.

United States

During the eight years of the Syrian civil war US's strategy and military presence in the country has been changing under presidents Obama and Trump.[76] Under neither president has the United States taken a leading role given the public fatigue after two long wars in Iraq and Afghanistan. Nevertheless, United States' policy still broadly followed three strands: defeating ISIS, deterring the use of chemical weapons and countering Iran's influence. 'The United States also seeks a peaceful resolution to the multifaceted Syrian conflict in a manner that protects U.S. interests, preserves a favorable regional balance of power, protects our allies and partners and alleviates suffering'.[77]

[75] Ibid. Galeotti.

[76] Peter Juul, 'The United States Still Needs a Syria Strategy', FP, October 15, 2019, https://foreignpolicy.com/2019/10/15/the-united-states-still-needs-a-syria-strategy/.

[77] Jim Garamone, 'DOD Official Explains US Strategy in Syria to House Panel', U.S. Department of Defense, September 26, 2018, https://dod.defense.gov/News/Article/Article/1646188/dod-official-explains-us-strategy-in-syria-to-house-panel/.

In the final months of the Obama administration, the foreign policy elite sought to correct the perceived mistakes of the president and influence his successor's choices. The bipartisan nature of the recommendations reflected a remarkable consensus when the country was polarized on the best option. While not recommending going back to the costly wars in Iraq and Afghanistan, 'they were advocating something of a middle ground between Bush's interventionism and Obama's retrenchment in the Middle East'.[78] Yet the advisory studies and reports towards the end of Obama's term called for more aggressive action (including US airstrikes against Assad's use of chemical weapons and barrel bombs) to counter Iran in the Middle East and Russia in Europe. Their focus was on building a 'centrist internationalism' that would not reach the level of involvement under Bush. It remained unclear whether such a policy had any support among an American public weary of war in the Middle East and largely opposed to foreign intervention.

President Obama was elected on a mission to end America's wars in Iraq and Afghanistan by a people tired of paying the cost in blood and treasure. He was also extremely reluctant to be sucked into another messy Middle East conflict. Despite the pressing moral imperative of the human suffering in the civil war, Obama remained convinced a military intervention would be a costly failure. It would be difficult for the United States to keep the peace without the commitment of a huge number of troops. The battlefield was too complex: fragmented into dozens of armed groups and supported by competing regional and international powers. The lack of support for military intervention from key allies such as the UK and Germany also influenced his decision to back away from his famous 'red line' threat in response to Assad's use of chemical weapons. NATO intervention in Libya while carefully planned had yet left the country in a mess. 'It was also part of a larger pessimism about what the United States could achieve in the Middle East'.[79]

[78] Greg Jaffe, 'Washington's Policy Elite Breaks With Obama Over Syrian Bloodshed', *The Washington Post*, October 20, 2016, https://www.washingtonpost.com/politics/washington-foreign-policy-elites-not-sorry-to-see-obama-go/2016/10/20/bd2334a2-9228-11e6-9c52-0b10449e33c4_story.html?utm_term=.01cfdeaf34cf.

[79] Barbara Plett Usher,'Obama's Syria Legacy: Measured Diplomacy, Strategic Explosion', BBC News, January 13, 2017, https://www.bbc.com/news/world-us-canada-38297343.

Obama was a foreign policy realist with a keen sense of the limits to American power and 'rejected what he saw as the moralizing interventionism of the president he replaced, George W. Bush'.[80] His successful policies on Iran's nuclearization and the opening to Cuba and Myanmar illustrate his emphasis on measured diplomacy and progressive multilateralism. Syria did not respond and Obama decided against trying to push it through. Obama had calculated early on that the Syrian civil war did not directly endanger America's national security. Obama also took the lead on combating what he saw as one of the biggest threats, climate change. Neither did he hesitate to use drones against terrorist suspects when he felt America's security was at stake.

He was convinced that both Iran and Russia would put far more into Syria than the United States should. He focused on using US military might against the Islamic State (IS), as a threat to the homeland, organizing an international coalition that had considerable success in achieving that limited goal. Obama unsuccessfully sought to diffuse the power of Islamist fighters by covert military aid to moderate Syrian rebel groups to shape them into a force that could defeat Assad.[81] Yet the presence of radical Islamist groups turned the administration's view against an early removal of Bashar al-Assad.

Entering the war in 2015 Russia reversed rebel gains and turned it in Assad's favour. Its anti-aircraft weapons closed the door on even the remote chance of a US intervention. Russian air force solidified Assad's grip on Syria's cities, culminating in the military victory over Aleppo and giving Moscow new lever in the Middle East. Many in the US foreign policy establishment believed that Obama's narrow definition of US interests in Syria ended up sidelining it. Nevertheless, the US administration did focus on providing humanitarian aid, and on promoting a ceasefire and political negotiations aimed at Assad's departure. Some argued that stepping back from his red line on chemical weapons damaged US credibility, shook the confidence of allies, and emboldened its adversaries. In Syria, they believe, his administration left a perception of American weakness. This consensus was the result of a broad-based backlash against a president who had repeatedly stressed the dangers of overreach and the need for restraint, especially in the Middle East. It accorded with Obama's

[80] Ibid.

[81] Ibid. Barbara Plett Usher.

belief that while US leadership was essential in international affairs, it should selectively lead only where it has clear definable interests. In this respect, 'Barack Obama and Donald Trump are on the same page when it comes to non-interventionism'.[82]

Both Obama and Trump had a remarkably common position on the war in Syria. Neither president considered Syria involving any US geostrategic interest. They both held the view that Syria was not America's fight. Trump is clear that in Syria, the United States seeks to protect the American people, and that means liberating territory once controlled by the Islamic State, not liberating territory controlled by Assad or removing the Syrian leader.[83] In elaborating his approach to Syria, Trump also indicated something more fundamental about his outlook: the Middle East's problems, including Syria, are not for America to fix. 'The United States will be a partner and a friend', Trump said, 'but the fate of the region lies in the hands of its own people'.[84]

Thus, the evolution of Trump's Syrian policy was first, to deter the Assad regime from using chemical weapons. The only difference between the two presidents is that Obama backed down after nearly striking Syria for chemical weapons usage, whereas Trump executed such strikes twice. Second, defeating the Islamic State's as a vital U.S. interest that **included preventing a terrorist resurgence**, targeting Salafi-jihadist groups like al-Qaeda that threaten the United States and its allies. It also could include persuading the Gulf countries to stop funding of the radical Islamic groups still holding out in Syria. The third, added later, was to put pressure on Iran in Syria. This could include deterring Iranian forces and militias from pushing close to the Israeli border, disrupting Iranian lines of communication through Syria, preventing substantial military escalation between Israel and Iran, and weakening Shia proxy forces.

President Trump has stated his preference to extricate America from the Syrian quagmire. Only images of Syrians killed by chemical weapons seem to arouse Trump's willingness to put Americans in harm's way in Syria. Although 'Assad may now think twice before using chemical weapons again, at a decisive moment in a future battle, he may again

[82] Ibid. Barbara Plett Usher.

[83] Robert M. Danin, 'President's Syria Strikes Are Not About Syria', Middle East Matters, Council on Foreign Relations, April 16, 2018, https://www.cfr.org/blog/president-trumps-syria-strikes-are-not-about-syria.

[84] Ibid. Robert M. Danin.

calculate that an American reprisal is a price worth paying if chemical weapons allow him to gain further control over vital Syrian territory'.[85] While Trump, commenting on US strikes, has cited both Russia and Iran for supporting Assad to shame them 'for associating their countries with mass murder', he has continued to keep the diplomatic channel open with both countries.

The United States is working to a strategy in Syria that keeps several hundred military and intelligence personnel in the country and in neighbouring countries like Iraq and positioning supporting air and naval assets in the region. In Syria, the United States has kept a small force to safeguard the Al-Tanf base and to buttress the Kurdish SDF. US forces are equally present in Manbij, in eastern Syria.[86] Yet, the prospect of an imminent U.S. military withdrawal could be used to increase pressure on Syrian Kurdish elements to come to a workable compromise with both Damascus and Ankara and thus, bolster prospects for an eventual political resolution in Syria. In Iraq, the US forces provide limited funding, training, and assistance to the Iraqi Army with an additional remit to watch Iranian moves in Syria, although its relations with the Iraqi government are on a downward path.

As Bashar Assad has won back all but one province, his country has transitioned from an active conflict zone to a 'grey zone', an area of ambiguity that sits uncomfortably between peace and war. In areas in Syria where the Islamic State has withdrawn or been defeated, the United States has been competing with Iran to secure these newly liberated territories. Given their more active involvement, it seems inevitable that forces linked to, or supported by, Iran will come into direct contact with the U.S. military, as they did in southeast Syria in early June 2017 when U.S. forces struck Iranian-backed militias on multiple occasions near the al-Tanf border post. Part of Iran's gray zone strategy is to minimize direct conflagration with the US forces to concentrate on completing a permanent military base approximately eight miles south of Damascus.[87]

[85] Ibid. Robert M. Danin.

[86] Seth G. Jones, 'Developing a Containment Strategy in Syria', Center for Strategic and International Studies, May 17, 2018, https://www.csis.org/analysis/developing-containment-strategy-syria.

[87] Colin P. Clarke, 'Countering Iran's Grey Zone Strategy in Syria', Lawfare, January 24, 2018, https://www.lawfareblog.com/counteracting-irans-gray-zone-strategy-syria.

The concept of gray zone warfare is not new, but the United States still lacks a clear and coherent strategy to respond to actions undertaken by nation-states and their proxy forces that fall short of conflict. As such, Russia, China, and Iran will operate around the edges attempting to stop just short of provoking the United States. United States needs to devote significant resources to design its own gray zone strategy to prevent Tehran from taking advantage of the current conflict and humanitarian crisis. It could also be used to restrict Iranian efforts to cement its influence in Syria and throughout the region.[88]

It is undeniable that since 2014 there has been progress in defeating ISIS in Syria after it had swept across much of Syria and into Iraq declaring a caliphate covering the captured provinces in both countries. While Coalition efforts have contributed to the liberation of more than ninety-nine percent of the territory captured by the ISIS it is not fully eliminated. It has been estimated that nearly 3000 ISIS members in the Syrian desert. Tough fighting remains in the middle Euphrates River valley and while the hard-won gains in Iraq and Syria remain vulnerable. Using military force is never easy, but it can only be effective if it is part of a coherent and realistic political strategy.

At the same time, US military strategy in Syria has to be part of a political strategy about bigger issues than Syria itself. The first objective is to push back against the increasing "normalisation" of chemical weapons use in wars of any kind despite the strong taboo since the end of World War I. The Chemical Weapons Convention of 1993 has been one of the most effective disarmament measures in modern history. Syria is a signatory to it. 'Despite firm denials from the Assad government, there is an abundance of evidence that Syrian forces, with Russian connivance, have been using chemical weapons against their own people on a regular basis. Many Western politicians feel that—with all the moral grey areas of this situation—they cannot sell the pass on this issue yet again. It has become a test case for international rule of law already under severe pressure on many fronts'.

Some argue that effective military action would represent an acceptance that Western powers continue their interest in the Middle East at a time when Western influence on events from Lebanon to the Yemen is in steep decline. The calculation is whether long-term Western interests are

[88] Ibid.

served better by involvement rather than indifference to a region sliding out of control. The hope for the Syrian population is that an effective military campaign could possibly push President Assad back into negotiations so that the war might end with something more humane than a vicious victory.[89]

In conclusion, US's main interests have largely advanced in Syria—the weakening of ISIS and the reduction of chemical weapons use by Bashar Assad. ISIS has been degraded via aggressive campaigning and, for the present, does not present a major risk. President Trump's basic instinct in Syria remains to declare victory over ISIS and withdraw U.S. forces as soon as practical. Second, actors with major interests in Syria—Russia, Iran and Turkey—will continue to push their own agendas, regardless of US actions, so that the United States will be unlikely to make any moves that violate their interests. Growing tensions with Russia, especially regarding the greater potential for military confrontation, will continue to constrain US action. At the same time, 'the Syrian crisis will need to be managed within the broader context of many other global security challenges that are of greater consequence to the United States. These include addressing the nuclear threat posed by North Korea, managing the longer-term competition with an increasingly assertive China in Asia, confronting a resurgent Russia in Eastern Europe, and preventing Iran from developing a nuclear weapons capability'.[90]

Third, Bashar al-Assad is likely to remain in power after the civil war ends following a lasting ceasefire. The long civil war has left the country destitute requiring hundreds of billions of dollars in reconstruction costs that few, if any, seem willing or capable of bearing. Syria will remain a broken, devastated, poor and weak country for the near future. The United States has a major role in providing this assistance while working with Russia and other UNSC P-5 members to promote and guarantee, in accordance with UNSCR 2254(2015) of December 18, 2015, an

[89] Michael Clarke, 'Syria: What Can Western Intervention Achieve?', BBC News, April 12, 2018, https://www.bbc.com/news/world-middle-east-43738713.

[90] Christopher J. Bolan, 'Strategic Insight: After the Smoke Clears in Syria: Dilemmas for US Strategy Remain', Strategic Studies Institute, US Army War College, May 18, 2018, https://ssi.armywarcollege.edu/index.cfm/articles/After-The-Smoke-Clears-in-Syria/2018/05/18.

acceptable political settlement in Syria.[91] 'The potential of U.S. financial assistance to the massive international reconstruction effort, required in post-civil war Syria, should be leveraged to ensure aid is delivered through a multinational group of competent nongovernmental organizations directly to the Syrian people, and aimed at strengthening effective and representative....governance'.[92]

'The U.S. and Russia may be at odds from Ukraine to North Korea, but they appear to be much more aligned in Syria, where neither wants to see Iran gain a substantial foothold. As the Syrian civil war winds down, Moscow wants to make sure that it—not Tehran—remains the primary benefactor of President Bashar al-Assad; that it retains its bases at Tartus and Hmeimim; and that Iran's presence in the Middle East is curbed'.[93] U.S's aim of trying to halt Iran's progress in the Middle East creates convergence with Russia, with the former's goal to reduce Iranian ground forces in Syria to prevent Tehran from having a contiguous overland route to the Mediterranean Sea and threaten the Syria-Israel border. This possibility for cooperation between Russia and United States is opportune with the civil war winding down. It is the thin end of the wedge by which Russia and United States, together, with the remaining UN P-5, can work to guarantee a new acceptable political structure in Syria and provide funding for humanitarian relief to rebuild a devastated country.[94]

Despite its unhappiness with continued US presence in Syria, it serves Russia's interest by preventing Iran from seizing territory in northern and northeastern Syria and keeping the Islamic State contained to a limited insurgency with no real ability left to threaten Bashar al-Assad. For its part, the U.S. may be willing to exchange cooperation against Iran in Syria for sanctions relief for Russia. In its view, U.S. presence in northern Syria also mitigates the threat of a Turkish invasion from the north. 'A complete U.S. withdrawal—the kind that U.S. President Donald Trump threatened in December 2018 but subsequently backtracked from—would open the path for Turkey to push further into northern Syria, and possibly gain

[91] An analysis of UNSCR 2254 (2015) can be seen at Chapters 6 and 7.

[92] Op. cit. Bolan.

[93] Xander Snyder, 'In Syria, An Opportunity for US-Russian Cooperation, Geopolitical Futures (GPF),' June 20, 2019, https://geopoliticalfutures.com/in-syria-an-opportunity-for-us-russian-cooperation/.

[94] Ibid.

more ground, hence, more leverage in negotiations with SDF'.[95] Russia would rather see an early settlement reached between Damascus and the SDF.

A three-way agreement between Russia, Israel and the U.S. to counter Iran would neither end the Syrian civil war nor guarantee Iran's complete expulsion from Syria, but it could conceivably represent a step towards establishing a shared cause to find a meaningful political resolution to problems that have mired Syria in an all-consuming war for nearly a decade.[96]

United Kingdom

Britain has always considered the Middle East as a region of vital interest that has dictated a long historical relationship. British foreign policy in the Middle East has sought to preserve stability to ensure Britain's access to its resources and to the East. Although the UK has had little direct interests in Syria, its wider involvement in regional issues has 'often set the interests of the two states in conflict with each other'.[97] UK's involvement in Syria is a legacy of earlier UNSC interventions in Iraq and Libya

The incremental nature of Britain's role in Syria from 2013 to 2015 was in the background three factors: the major refugee crisis building up with the European Union, Russia's growing support to the Syrian government and Australia and France extending their Iraqi air operations to Syria. Prime Minister David Cameron appeared confident that he would get a majority in the Commons in favour of extending UK air and drone strikes against IS from Iraq to Syria.[98] In this context, Labour Party leadership passing to Jeremy Corbyn, was also important.

As early as 2013, the British parliament had turned down military action against the Syrian government. It continued to remain divided

[95] Ibid. Xander Snyder.

[96] Op. cit. Xander Snyder.

[97] Sarah Scott, 'British Foreign Policy Towards Syria: Its Importance, Its Distinctiveness and Its Relation to the Policy of Other Actors in the Region' Ph.D Thesis, University of St. Andrews, 2016, https://research-repository.st-andrews.ac.uk/bitstream/handle/10023/9903/SarahScottPhDThesis.pdf?sequence=2&isAllowed=y.

[98] Paul Rogers, 'The UK's Creeping Intervention in Syria', Oxford Research Group, September 16, 2015, https://www.oxfordresearchgroup.org.uk/the-uks-creeping-intervention-in-syria.

on launching an offensive against Bashar Assad or supporting regime change. Many believed that an escalation in conflict could lead the UK into a proxy war with Vladimir Putin's forces supporting Assad against the radical Islamic groups. The Government repeatedly insisted it had no plans for military action and instead was working with the international community to end the civil war. It was felt that if the UK prime minister wished to become further involved military against the Assad government she would have to seek a mandate in the Commons with no guarantee of success.

UK government was, nevertheless, able to increase its involvement in Syria in three ways while skirting the need for parliamentary approval. First, embedding RAF pilots with the Royal Canadian Air Force engaged in airstrikes in Syria, most likely flying CF-18 strike aircraft. Second, British Special Forces, probably members of the Special Reconnaissance Regiment, were involved with US Special Forces in a raid, earlier in 2014, on a compound near Deir ez-Zor, to capture Abu Sayyaf, a senior Islamic State logistics organizer. Although Pentagon represented the raid as a success, it failed in its main task when Abu Sayyaf was killed during the raid. Third, in August 2015, to kill two British IS paramilitaries, Reyaad Khan and Ruhul Amin, on grounds they were was orchestrating major attacks in the UK, a British MQ-9 Reaper drone attack with Hellfire missiles was used.

The prospect of a more prominent UK role increased as the attempt to bring the parties to the table receded while ISIS became resurgent. It was feared that it could increase the internally displaced and refugees while stepping up ISIS recruitment in Britain. At the same time, Britain came out clearly for attacks on Syria's chemical weapons capability on grounds that it threatened a humanitarian disaster. British Prime Minister Theresa May in 2018 stated that 'the UK is permitted under international law, on an exceptional basis, to take measures in order to alleviate overwhelming humanitarian suffering. The legal basis for the use of force is humanitarian intervention, which requires three conditions to be met: (1) convincing evidence, (2) no alternative and(3) necessary and proportionate use of force.[99]

The British government further stated that 'the chemical weapons attack on Khan Sheikhoun in April 4, 2017 killed approximately 80

[99] BBC, 'Syria Air Strikes: The UK Government's Legal Position in Full', April 18, 2018, https://www.bbc.com/news/uk-43768145.

people and left hundreds more injured. The attack on April 7, 2018 in Douma killed up to 75 people, and injured over 500 people. Since 2013, neither diplomatic action, tough sanctions, nor the US strikes against the Shayrat airbase in April 2017 have sufficiently degraded Syrian chemical weapons capability or deterred the Syrian regime from causing extreme humanitarian distress on a large scale through its persistent use of chemical weapons. There was no practicable alternative to the truly exceptional use of force to degrade the Syrian regime's chemical weapons capability and deter their further use by the Syrian regime in order to alleviate humanitarian suffering'.[100]

Thus, given parliamentary scrutiny, the British government had to justify its joining in the air attacks on Syria's remaining chemical facilities. Nevertheless, it did not prevent UK from getting involved in covert operations from 2012 to overthrow Bashar Assad. By July 2015, Britain was training Syrians in Saudi Arabia, Turkey, Jordan and Qatar to fight IS, but the war against Assad also continued. British operations in Syria with its allies have for years involved working alongside extremist and jihadist groups, in effect supporting and empowering them. The UK-supported rebels had an even closer relationship with Nusra, a close ally of the Free Syrian Army. Britain is unlikely to have directly armed or trained jihadist groups in Syria, but its covert war has continued in the certainty that these groups benefited from its policies. In 2017, the British government revealed that since 2015 it spent £199 m ($277 m) supporting the 'moderate opposition' opposed to Assad and IS. This support included 'communications, medical and logistic equipment' and training journalists to develop 'an independent Syrian media'. 'But details of more recent UK covert operations remain murky, and few recent media reports have uncovered the UK role'.[101] Peter Ford, the former British ambassador to Syria, told a parliamentary enquiry in 2016 that the existence of "moderate" groups among the armed opposition was "largely a figment of the imagination".[102]

At the same time, Britain has equally given aid to Syria reflecting its open policy whose obverse face was its operation in the shadows. 'At an

[100] Op. cit. BBC.

[101] Ibid. Mark Curtis.

[102] Mark Curtis, 'How Britain Engaged in a Covert Operation to Overthrow Assad', Middle East Eye, April 25, 2018, https://www.middleeasteye.net/opinion/how-britain-engaged-covert-operation-overthrow-assad.

EU-UN Summit in Brussels April 2018 Britain pledged that will commit to providing £450 million for Syria and the region in 2018, with £300 earmarked for 2019, bringing the total UK aid to the region to £2.71 billion. The announcement consists of £250 million of new money spread across the two years'.[103] The aid was earmarked for medical facilities and health workers.

Boris Johnson, as Foreign Minister in 2017, had reversed UK policy on Syria stating that 'UK accepts that Bashar al-Assad should be allowed to run for re-election in the event of a peace settlement in Syria.'

With an often contradictory Syria policy, 'the Global Network for Syria, which includes peers from the Conservatives, Labour, Liberal Democrats and also independents, [wrote] to [prime minister] May demanding a change in the government's policy. The group has accused the government of funding "so-called moderate armed opposition forces" the "vast majority" of whom they claim are "dominated by Jihadist militants"'.[104]

They opined that the continuation of these policies would instead of stabilizing Syria, ensure that stabilization and reunification under a unitary authority will remain a distant possibility, prolonging the suffering of the Syrian people and weakening the stability of the Middle East as a whole. 'They called on government to lift sanctions, work for diplomatic solutions and allow the Syrian people to determine their own future …including allowing President Bashar al-Assad to remain in power'.[105]

France

France's policy towards Syria had three components to the scale of its intervention. First, France was using its interventionist foreign policy in Syria, and more broadly the Middle East, to reinforce its self-perception as a great power. Second, in fulfilment of its historic role France was

[103] Jon Stone, 'Britain to Ramp up Aid to Syria Over the Next Two Years', *The Independent*, April 25, 2018, https://www.independent.co.uk/news/uk/politics/syria-brussels-summit-uk-aid-penny-mordaunt-a8320436.html.

[104] Shehab Khan, 'Theresa May's Policy on Syria is 'Prolonging Suffering, Cross-Party Group Including Ambassadors Says', *The Independent*, July 19, 2018, https://www.independent.co.uk/news/uk/politics/theresa-may-syria-foreign-policy-suffering-cross-party-group-a8455126.html.

[105] Ibid. Shehab Khan.

presenting an alternative foreign policy to that of the United States. Third, France considered its steadfast opposition to Assad an opportunity to enhance security cooperation with anti-Assad Sunni countries that also shared France's deep distrust of Iran.[106]

France's interventionism in the Middle East is a new development. President Jacques Chirac, much to the chagrin of U.S. policymakers, opposed the 2003 Iraq war and continued France's trade relations with Iraq. France's relations with Baathist Syria, a former French colony, were similarly cordial. In France's penchant for exploiting the economic dimension of a relationship, it encouraged deeper security cooperation with Sunni Arab states, particularly Saudi Arabia and Egypt. 'Nevertheless, the continued sponsorship of the Islamic State by Saudi private donors remained a point of tension'.[107]

French political elite considered Bashar al-Assad's succession in 2000 heralding a new era in Syrian politics. President Nicolas Sarkozy openly praised Assad for defending the rights of Syrian Christians. French fashion magazine Elle voted Asma al-Assad the most stylish woman in world politics. 'The major shift came with Sarkozy's August 2011 statement that Assad's actions caused "irreparable damage" to his legitimacy.' In January 2012, Sarkozy demanded that Assad should resign after massacres that caused 'disgust and revulsion around the world'.[108] French support for regime change in Syria evolved from its actions in Libya and aimed to build a perception of France as a humanitarian leader. With its escalation in Syria, France aimed to mobilizing the Arab League to follow its lead, thus, strengthening its partnerships in the region.

In the aftermath of 2015, Paris terror attacks the fruits of its alliance-building secured France a display of solidarity by the Sunni-majority Muslim countries. France stepped up airstrikes in conjunction with Russia. The distinction between the radical and moderate groups came to the fore when Russia, echoing the French, expressed readiness to back the latter against the Islamic State. Yet eventually Russia found it opportune to classify all opposing groups as terrorists and whole-heartedly back Assad.

[106] Samuel Ramani, 'Why France is So Deeply Entangled in Syria', *The Washington Post*, November 11, 2015, https://www.washingtonpost.com/news/monkey-cage/wp/2015/11/19/why-france-is-so-deeply-entangled-in-syria/?noredirect=on&utm_term=.673d50a87498.

[107] Ibid.

[108] Ibid. Samuel Ramani.

Russia stepped up its attacks on the ISIS after intelligence confirmed its hand in the crash on October 31, 2015 of a Russian aircraft in the Sinai killing 224. The multiple coordinated attacks that struck Paris on Friday November 13, 2015 marked a new operational phase of France's war against the self-declared Islamic State. French President François Hollande launched an unsuccessful diplomatic offensive to unite the two international coalitions in the war against Islamic State (IS). Yet it was clear that domestic popular support for troops on the ground was theoretical making it clear that France would not overtly send troops on the ground.[109]

The Moscow-Tehran-Damascus axis sought to keep Syrian President Bashar al-Assad in power while the other, led by the United States and including France, laid down Assad's departure as a precondition for military cooperation. The glaring fissures in the latter coalition made Turkey prioritize preventing a Kurdish state, while Saudi Arabia and other Gulf Arabs—the main financiers of the rebellion—rabidly opposed Assad and were ambiguous on IS.[110] The same local and geopolitical obstacles to a broader consensus on the conflict in Syria continued to hamper efforts to design a new strategic approach for eradicating ISIS. However, the attacks lent France more leverage in diplomatic talks during the Vienna process.[111]

France's military operations in Syria grew out of its involvement in Iraq when, in response to an Iraqi government request, in September 2014 it joined in the fight against the Islamic State, or ISIS. At the time, its aims were clear. It sought to demonstrate solidarity with its American ally by joining the US-led coalition fighting the Islamic State's self-proclaimed caliphate in Iraq. In targeting ISIS in Iraq, France was responding to national security concerns relating to the risk to numerous young French people seduced by jihadism.

[109] Karina Piser, 'Despite Falls, France Ramps Up Its Role in Syria', WPR Trend Lines, October 1, 2015, https://www.worldpoliticsreview.com/trend-lines/16840/despite-pitfalls-france-ramps-up-its-role-in-syria.

[110] Lara Marlowe, 'François Holland in bid to Form 'Grand Coalition' Against IS', *The Irish Times*, November 18, 2015, https://www.irishtimes.com/news/world/europe/fran%C3%A7ois-hollande-in-bid-to-form-grand-coalition-against-is-1.2433869.

[111] Judah Grunstein, 'Paris Attacks Signal New Phase in France's War Against Islamic State', WPR Trend Lines, November 16, 2015, https://search-ebscohost-com.proxyiub.uits.iu.edu/login.aspx?direct=true&db=wpr&AN=111233254&site=eds-live&scope=site.

'France's military campaign in Iraq, known as "Operation Chammal," consisted of three types of operations: air support, advice and training. In September 2015 the concentration of Islamic State foreign fighters near Raqqa and Deir ez-Zor led France to expand its operations with reconnaissance flights to be followed by airstrikes against foreign jihadist training camps in Syria'.[112] The shock of the November 2015 Paris terrorist attacks by the ISIS, based in Raqqa, that killed 137 people had validated the decision to expand the campaign into Syria.

France had deployed detachments of Special Forces since 2015 to fight alongside Kurdish militias in northern Syria and in April 2018 increased their number. These units also provided targeting information to guide French airstrikes against French jihadists in Raqqa and Deir ez-Zor. With the territory under the Islamic State's shrinking, French soldiers began to move closer to the front and at times engaged directly with Islamic State forces. The deployment of French military assets had the advantage of demonstrate their weapons systems, especially the Rafale multirole aircraft and the Caesar heavy artillery cannon. India has already contracted for the former.

President Emmanuel Macron election in May 2017 continued France's Syria policy except stating that France no longer sought regime change in Damascus for itself. This tacit policy shift had started under his predecessor, Francois Hollande. Still, France continued to insist on the need to deter and counter the Syrian government's use of chemical weapons and to preserve Syrians' access to humanitarian aid.

President Trump's abrupt announcement—since partially restructured—on US withdrawal from Syria left France in a quandary on its future role. It threatened to tie the hands of Washington's allies in the Middle East, particularly the Israelis and Kurds, and America's European allies who sought to continue the war against the Islamic State. The French Army minister qualified the defeat Daesh stating that it was not yet an enduring defeat. Opinion veered between government, and outside, between votaries of following the U.S. lead relying on Special Forces and airstrikes, and those advocating a greater commitment of troops on the ground to increase the chances of a lasting victory. France's historical ties

[112] Mas Cedric, 'After US Withdrawal, What's Next for France's Military Operations in Syria', World Politics Review, February 22, 2019, https://search-ebscohost-com.proxyiub.uits.iu.edu/login.aspx?direct=true&db=wpr&AN=134908914&site=eds-live&scope=site.

and geographical proximity made, for the French, the complete defeat of ISIS a more pressing matter.

Further, US withdrawal would also raise France's ongoing commitment to the SDF and YPG in the Kurdish areas especially as Turkey may be encouraged to move into Kurdish territory. In the medium to long-term, France also raised the question of a European army to balance against both Russia and the United States. Other Europeans, however, feared that a European army would be little more than a platform for French strategic goals.[113]

The fate of French nationals captured in Syria during the fighting raised a major controversy. France had targeted Islamic State training camps for foreign fighters aware they could be potentially killing French citizens, who could launch terrorist attacks on French territory. In the context of an abrupt U.S. withdrawal from Syria, French authorities had to decide the future of French ISIS fighters captured by Iraqi or Kurdish forces. Paris had initially insisted that they be tried there and not return to France. 'Washington has now asked France, as well as other European countries, to repatriate their ISIS foreign fighters—about 150 French citizens amongst the 800 ISIS detainees in northern Syria—or risk having them released'.[114]

Despite some calls from the French political right to refuse them entry back into the country, the French government had to bring them back for trial in France. This decision underscores an aspect of the challenge—radicalization in jail—of achieving lasting victory over the Islamic State. 'Ultimately, whether in French prisons or in Syria and Iraq, the long-term success of France's intervention hinges on finding a solution to the problem of disillusioned youth being attracted to violent jihadism'.[115]

France has always considered the use of chemical weapons a serious violation of international law, particularly the Chemical Weapons Convention (CWC) of 1993 of which Syria since 2013 was a signatory. In its national assessment on April 13, 2018, France stated that it was highly probable that the Syrian armed and security forces were responsible for this attack. On April 14, 2018, France, with its British and American

[113] Robert Zaretsky, 'France's Existential Loneliness in Syria', December 21, 2018, https://foreignpolicy.com/2018/12/21/frances-existential-loneliness-in-syria/.

[114] Ibid. Mas Cedric.

[115] Ibid.

partners, carried out targeted attacks on the Syrian government's illegal chemical weapons arsenal. France has held that it was crucial to dismantle the entire Syrian chemical weapons programme. The Organisation for the Prohibition of Chemical Weapons (OPCW) must have complete, immediate and unhindered access to all the information required for independently verifying this fact.[116]

On January 23, 2018, France launched the International Partnership against Impunity for the Use of Chemical Weapons. Its current membership has 34 States and aims to bolster the regime for the non-proliferation of chemical weapons, support international organizations and international enquiry mechanisms and underline the worldwide ban on using such weapons.

France is also working to ensure that long-term stability can be built in the zones freed from Daesh in order to avoid any resurgence from terrorist groups. It has supported several NGOs and multilateral bodies that are active on the ground. France announced, during the Brussels II conference on April 25, 2018, on the future of Syria and the region that its contribution for 2018–2020 would total over €1 billion for the Syrian people and host communities in countries receiving refugees: over €250 million in grants and €850 million in loans.[117] This allocation would include the emergency response programme for Syria, announced by the French President, on April 16, 2018, of €50 million.

France supported the establishment of an agreed on a political framework to end the Syrian crisis through United Nations Security Council resolution 2254 of December 2015 and supports early resumption inter-Syrian negotiations in Geneva. In pursuit of its goal to create the conditions for a credible political transition 'France has encouraged negotiations to resume with all partners present in Syria to facilitate an end to the crisis and build together the convergences which will help provide a political solution to the conflict'.[118]

[116] France Diplomatie, 'War in Syria: Understanding France's Position', June 2018, https://www.diplomatie.gouv.fr/en/country-files/syria/war-in-syria-understanding-france-s-position/.

[117] Ibid.

[118] Ibid.

Conclusion

This chapter has traced the involvement of four major powers and four regional powers who have been involved ever since the civil war in Syria erupted in March 2011. The spark lit in Dera'a became a fire as it spread across the country in the process destroyed it. The humanitarian tragedy that the Syrian situation represents is unparalleled since the Second World War. The civil war is far from over although waning. At the same time, it could renew it in unexpected directions. It points to the imperative need for a durable ceasefire that would enable discussions to commence on the elements of UNSCR 2254 (2015).

Over the last nine years we have seen history repeat itself with Syria becoming a battleground for different outside forces to settle their disagreements. We have traced the history and the justification of each of the eight powers enmeshed in this country. Each power has pursued its own agenda regardless of the effects on Syria or its people. With four of the five permanent members of the UN Security Council on the ground, there has been no incentive to use that failing mechanism to work towards peace rather than continue the war.

The only exception was the unanimous UNSC agreement that enforced on Bashar Assad the elimination of his chemical weapons facilities and stocks. The UNSC has nevertheless worked on creating forums to discuss the process of building the peace through the Geneva forum (2012), the Vienna forum and the limited Astana Forum (2015) and instituting an acceptable political structure. UNSC Resolution 2254 (2015) is the only agreed document that provides a blueprint for the basis of a settlement.

The reasons are not far to seek for the absence over nine long years of a lasting ceasefire. The analysis above shows that each power—whether regional or global—has only pursued its own interest and those of its proxies unmindful of the UN's cardinal principles. Yet the future of Syria and the well-being of its people depend on the same powers even more than it does on Bashar Assad. The last nine years have completed one cycle of violence and counter-violence with Bashar al-Assad retrieving most of his country. It is again up to the UNSC members how the situation will evolve. Will they start the carnage once again or work jointly to alleviate the suffering of the Syrian people and help in rebuilding a country their bombs have destroyed?

CHAPTER 6

International Efforts Towards Peace Agency and Results

The international community, represented by the United Nations, has been regularly engaged since the beginning of the civil war in Syria. Between April 2012 and February 2018, the UN Security Council and the UN General Assembly unanimously approved fourteen resolutions while the Russian Federation and China vetoed twelve. The UN General Assembly also considered the matter twice during 2017–2018. It was thus not the absence of energy, of political will, that was responsible for their inability to bring about a lasting ceasefire leading to peace. This is equally true of negotiations under the multiple peace processes—Vienna, Geneva, Astana and other major power consultations—through which the United Nations has been striving to move forward. Their difficulty was compounded by the presence, on the ground, of all great powers, except China, and important regional powers with their defence material in support of their own troops, irregulars and the chosen militant opposition group.

Nevertheless, on Syria-related issues whenever interests of the P-5 aligned it did reflect that the Syrian government was in accord with the decisions taken. The tabular presentations in Appendices 2 and 3 explain in detail the decisions taken at Geneva and the Geneva-related peace processes bringing out the complexity of the issues. A detailed analysis of the steps taken between 2011 and 2019 will demonstrate that agreement on particular issues was difficult at the best of times, yet it was productive when it did transpire.

R. M. Abhyankar, *Syria*,
https://doi.org/10.1007/978-981-15-4562-7_6

UNSC Resolution 2254 (2015) of 18 December 2015 became the guiding text for ushering a lasting ceasefire, and eventually, a peaceful and democratic evolution out of the long civil war. The text of the resolution is at Appendix 4. Its all-encompassing mandate cites, importantly, the following:

1. Close linkage between a ceasefire and a parallel political process;
2. A Syrian-led and Syrian-owned political transition in order to end the conflict and for the Syrian people to decide the future of Syria;
3. United Nations facilitating the Syrian-led peace process leading to the establishment of a credible, inclusive and non-sectarian governance;
4. It gives the process of drafting a new constitution an important place with elections, administered by the United Nations, in keeping with the highest standards of transparency and accountability;
5. It suggests the establishment of mechanisms for regular ceasefire monitoring, verification and reporting; and the need for confidence-building measures by all parties;
6. Prevention and suppression of terrorist acts by the ISIL (Da'esh), An-Nusra Front, ANF and other Al-Qaeda associated groups on the UN list;
7. To allow humanitarian agencies immediate, rapid, safe and unhindered access throughout Syria so that such assistance reaches widely;
8. That all parties cease attacks against civilians including on medical facilities and comply with 'their obligations under international humanitarian and human rights laws';
9. Underscores the critical need to create conditions for safe return of refugees and internally displaced to their home areas and urges members to provide assistance.

The UN and its Special Representative, and other parties and groups, have accepted the resolution as the blueprint for the negotiating process. Yet, it is remarkable that nowhere is there an injunction in any UNSC resolution for *all* foreign forces to withdraw from the country. No doubt, that would have proved divisive and defeated an agreement on other goals cited above.

A detailed study of the meandering nature of the negotiations illustrates the tortuous nature of the multiple forums engaged in Syria's peace process between parties with multiple interests, stakes and backers. Furthermore, the resultant progress still leaves it uncertain whether it is ephemeral or lasting. An important factor remains President Bashar al-Assad's policy after the fall of the final rebel-held redoubt of Idlib. The continuing stalemate at Idlib threatens to tip the balance in favour of continuing the conflict. The following paragraphs analyse the multiple peace processes following the major themes contained in UNSC Resolution 2254 (2015).

Syrian Political Process: Moving Towards a New Constitution

Anticipating the failure of Kofi Annan's mission, the 'Group of Friends of the Syrian People' held four conferences in 2012, reiterating UNGA resolution 66/253 of 2012, that the political process will have to be Syrian-led and inclusive to form a democratic, pluralistic political system. While they stated that, the Syrian people must determine the future of Syria, each of the parties streamlined their actions around political transition away from Assad. At their conference on December 12, 2012, they recognized the Syrian National Council (SNC) as the legitimate representative of all Syrian people forcing its merger with the Syrian National Coalition.

UNSC Resolutions 2042 (2012) of March 2012 essentially supported the Annan Plan emphasizing an inclusive and Syrian-led process.

The Vienna Process, guaranteed by Russia, Saudi Arabia, Turkey and the United States, met October 23 and 30, 2015 and November 14, 2015 to take the issue further after the successive failures of UN Envoys Kofi Annan[1] and Lakhdar Brahimi.[2] The purpose of the meetings was to discuss the situation and the potential for peace including the future of Assad. The meetings asserted 'the importance of Syria's unity, independence, territorial integrity and secular character'. They further stated

[1] Reuters, 'Text of Annan's Six-point Peace Plan for Syria', April 4, 2012, https://www.reuters.com/article/us-syria-ceasefire-idUSBRE8330HJ20120404. Envoy Kofi Annan's six-point peace plan included an inclusive, Syrian-led political process, ensuring humanitarian assistance and release arbitrarily detained persons.

[2] Raymond Hinnebusch and I. William Zartman, 'UN Mediation in the Syrian Crisis: From Kofi Annan to Lakhdar Brahimi', International Peace Institute, March 2016, https://www.ipinst.org/wp-content/uploads/2016/03/IPI-Rpt-Syrian-Crisis2.pdf.

that state institutions would remain intact [unlike in the Iraq case[3]] and reconfirmed that the political process will be Syrian-led and Syrian-owned. However, there was no agreement on the future of Bashar al-Assad. At their last meeting on November 14, 2015, the sponsors produced a road map and timetable for a political solution on two tracks, political and military. To this end, they supported the establishment of a UN Monitoring mission. Importantly, for the first time, they asserted the need to convene a conference, under UN auspices, of the government and the opposition groups.

The unanimous passage of UN Security Council 2254 (2015) spurred parallel efforts by interested countries and the opposition to converge around its operative provisions.

Moscow Principles[4]

The four-day peace talks in Moscow from January 26 to 29, 2015 between about 40 representatives of the Syrian opposition and the Syrian government signed the 'Moscow Principles' including a guarantee of Syrian sovereignty and territorial integrity, the need for a political settlement, non-interference by outside powers and 'the end of Israeli occupation of the Golan'. In parentheses, this issue became alive in March 2019 after President Trump formally declared the area part of Israel. The format of the meeting suggested that Moscow and Damascus were trying to establish a new political coalition to buttress the Syrian government. During their meetings from April 6 to 9, 2015, they called for boosting humanitarian aid and easing of sanctions. There was no major outcome on the former. The Moscow meeting saw signs of change as to how the opposition views the basics of the Syrian peace process, namely the 2012 Geneva I Communiqué that establishes a road map for ending violence in Syria. Reports on January 28 suggested that the opposition had withdrawn the demand for immediate establishment of a transitional government, as outlined in the Geneva Communiqué, and Assad's departure from power.

[3] Miranda Sissons and Abdul Razzaq Al-Saidi, 'Iraq's de-Baathification Still Haunts the Country', aljazeera.com, March 12, 2013, https://www.aljazeera.com/indepth/opinion/2013/03/201331055338463426.html

[4] Yuri Barmin, 'Moscow's 11 Principles for Peace in Syria', Russia Direct, January 29, 2015, https://Russia-Direct.Org/Analysis/Moscows-11-Principles-Peace-Syria

Geneva Process

Much priming to move the peace and constitution process led to consultations on May 4, 2015, without much success, to gauge the prospects for negotiations. Taking from the initiatives under the Vienna process meetings on October 23 and 30, 2015 and November 15, 2015 and a meeting under the Geneva process from February 1 to 3, 2016 decided to convene a conference to negotiate a plan for the political process.

At **Geneva III** from **March14–24 and April 13 to 27, 2016**, the aim was to bring the parties together to form a transitional body with elections in eighteen months. It agreed on a new constitution and the setting up of a transitional government including representatives from the government, the opposition and independents. Yet Riad Hijab, chair of the Saudi-backed Syrian High Negotiating Committee[5] stopped the negotiations citing the escalation of violence and the inability to deliver humanitarian relief. The ceasefire equally ended with the aerial bombardment of Aleppo. Eventually, Mohammad Alloush, the HNC negotiator, a member of Jaish al-Islam, resigned from the HNC in May 2016 because of the lack of progress in the Syrian peace process.

The Syrian High Negotiations Committee (HNC) consists of several opposition platforms backed by Cairo, Moscow and Riyadh that reflect the view of its backers. It also includes members of the National Coordination Committee for Democratic Change, independent oppositional figures and representatives of other opposition factions. It has seen divisions arise among its members on their positions towards Turkey's continuing military operation against the Kurdish People's Protection Units (YPG) in al-Jazira.[6]

Following Russian military intervention and Syrian Army's gains President Bashar al-Assad held parliamentary elections after nearly five years of the civil war and ensuing negotiations for a ceasefire. The Ba'ath Party-led National Progressive Front claimed it won 200 of the 250 seats, while the opposition inside and outside the country boycotted the elections;

[5] Editors, 'Head of Syrian Opposition's HNC Resigns', Reuters, November 20, 2017, https://www.reuters.com/article/us-mideast-crisis-syria-hnc/head-of-syrian-oppositions-hnc-resigns-statement-idUSKBN1DK26N.

[6] Editor, 'Divisions Within the High Negotiations Committee on the Turkish Offensive', Enab Baladi, October 21, 2019, https://english.enabbaladi.net/archives/2019/10/divisions-within-the-high-negotiations-committee-on-the-turkish-offensive/.

voter turnout was 57.56%.[7] Furthermore, the Idlib Governorate was already in rebel hands and almost entirely outside government control while the ISIL occupied Raqqa and Deir ez-Zor Governorates. Elections did not take place in these provinces. Anti-government forces also held parts of Aleppo, Homs, and Da'raa governorates. Rojava, the Kurdish area, had been semi-autonomous since the civil war began.

After **Geneva III** from **February 23 to March 3, 2017**, the scene shifted to negotiations under the **Vienna process** on **May 17, 2016**, the September 20, 2016 meeting in New York of the International Syria Support Group (ISSG) and the Astana process sponsored by Russia, Iran and Turkey.

At the Vienna meeting, the participants urged full compliance of the ceasefire and hoped it would become comprehensive and nation-wide. An emergency meeting on September 25, 2016 of the UN Security Council discussed attacks in the context of the September 9, 2016 ceasefire. It targeted August 1, 2017 to develop the framework for a Syrian-owned and Syrian-led political process yet failed to agree on a commencement date for it. It also urged concrete steps for reaching humanitarian aid. At the ISSG meeting, the United States called for cease flights over aid routes while Russia called for a three-day ceasefire with no results. UN Security Council Resolution 2268 (2016) endorsed the cessation of hostilities from February 27, 2016 as a first step for a lasting ceasefire and called for immediate implementation of UNSCR 2254 (2015).

The three sponsors of the Astana process met on December 20, 2016 in Moscow and agreed that their aim would be to realize UNSCR 2254 (2015). They called for a countrywide ceasefire from December 29, 2016 brokered by Russia and Turkey. They also established a 'No Fly Zone' over the Euphrates Shield allowing Turkish troops to supervise military operations and governance in the area. On December 13, 2016, Russia and Turkey also agreed to a ceasefire and evacuation of civilians and opposition fighters from Aleppo to Idlib.

Meeting in **Astana**, the capital of Kazakhstan, in **Round I** on **January 23 and 24, 2017,** the three co-sponsors, Iran, Russia and Turkey, agreed to set up a trilateral mechanism for ceasefire monitoring and agreed to further implementation of UNSCR 2254 (2015). The meeting rejected

[7] News Wires, 'Assad's Party Wins Majority in Syrian Election', France 24, April 17, 2016, https://www.france24.com/en/20160417-syria-bashar-assad-baath-party-wins-majority-parliamentary-vote.

a Russian proposal for a draft constitution. While the coalesced opposition group, Ahrar al-Sham, attended the meeting, the Tahrir al-Sham was opposed to the Astana meetings. Despite no result at their technical meeting on **February 6, 2017**, Astana II convened on **February 15–16, 2017** establishing a Joint Monitoring Group to report to the UN to formalize the ceasefire of December 16, 2016. They prepared draft provisions on 'reconciled areas' though no joint statement was released.

Nevertheless, at the Geneva conference convened from February 2 to March 3, 2017 UN Envoy Staffan de Mistura[8] divided the discussion on the proposed political process in four baskets: first, Governance, second, Constitution, third Elections and four Security and Confidence-building proposed by the Syrian government. It was also agreed that 2254 (2015) will be the point of negotiation and that talks under the Astana process were complementary. It thus brought about a degree of concordance between the multiple forums in which talks were proceeding simultaneously.

During **Astana Round III** on **March 14 and 15, 2017** Russia accused the United States of not upholding the ceasefire. Nevertheless, the discussions went forward under the next round of the Geneva conference. Meanwhile, UN Envoy Mistura continued discussions in **Geneva V from March 23 to 30, 2017** on the four baskets. It was heartening during this time that donors at the Brussels conference raised US $6 billion in addition to $10 billion for humanitarian relief in Syria. Meanwhile, **Astana IV** on **May 3 and 4, 2017** reiterated in a Joint Statement that the goal remained a Syria-owned, independent political process that safeguarded the unity and territorial integrity of Syria.

While discussions under the Geneva forum continued to concentrate on the four baskets, talks ended without a breakthrough during **Geneva VI** from **May 15 to 19, 2017**. US airstrikes on the Hezbollah at al-Tanf vitiated the atmosphere. Yet, a ceasefire agreement by the **Astana Heads of Government** at Hamburg on July 7, 2017 provided a shot-in-the-arm to the political process with the agreement on setting up the first 'De-escalation Zone' (DEZ) covering Dara'a, al-Quneitra and Suweida. Its borders were defined and it was agreed that the perimeter would be policed by Russia. **Geneva VII** from **July 10 to 14, 2017** and **VIII** from

[8] Wireservice Reports, 'Syria War: UN Envoy Staffan de Mistura to Step Down', BBC News, October 17, 2018, https://www.bbc.com/news/world-middle-east-45893986.

November 29 to December 15, 2017 equally ended without a breakthrough, primarily because the Syrian government restricted the talks only to the basket on terrorism—by which they meant all the diverse radical Islamic groups opposing them.

Nevertheless, at **Astana VII** on **October 30 and 31, 2017** the sponsors agreed to convene a congress of National Dialogue. At the Astana guarantors' meeting on November 19, 2017 at Antalya, they discussed plans for the proposed National Dialogue. The **leaders' Summit** on November 22, 2017 at Sochi reviewed developments in Afrin and Idlib and noting the breakthrough in the battle against terrorism agreed to push Da'esh out of its last major stronghold. They also noted the success of DEZs' and agreed to coordinate efforts to achieve a political solution. Under **Astana VIII** on December 21 and 22, 2017 they agreed that the National Dialogue would be scheduled in January 2018 in Sochi. At their **Astana IX meeting** on January 19 and 20, 2018 the guarantors agreed on a list of participants for the Sochi congress.

Nevertheless, **Geneva IX** on January 25 and 26, 2018 noted the need for political will on the part of all sides for the talks to succeed. Meanwhile, **Astana X** at Sochi on July 30 and 31, 2018 continued to review their trilateral cooperation. A high-level meeting at Geneva on September 10 and 11, 2018 also discussed the formation of a new constitutional committee while another meeting in Geneva on December 18, 2018 emphasized its determination to facilitate the setting up of a constitutional committee. It eventually met in Geneva for the first time in October 2019[9]—comprising opposition, civil society, and regime members—beginning its work with UN facilitation on November 20, 2019. The committee is mandated within the context of a UN-facilitated Geneva process, to prepare and draft for popular approval of constitutional reforms paving the way for a political settlement in Syria. The Syrian delegation left the meeting on November 24, 2019, due to non-acceptance of their proposals on fighting terrorism, lifting of sanctions and condemnation of Turkey's operation in northern Syria.

Meanwhile, earlier at a four-way **Summit on Syria on October 27, 2018**, France, Germany, Russia, Turkey and UN Envoy Mistura reaffirmed Syrian sovereignty, welcoming the agreement on Idlib of

[9] Barbara Bibbo, 'Long-awaited Syrian Constitutional Committee Meets for the First Time', Al. Jazeera J Impact, October 30, 2019, https://www.aljazeera.com/news/2019/10/long-awaited-syrian-constitutional-committee-meets-time-191030151424363.html.

September 17, 2018, stressed the importance of a lasting ceasefire and urged the convening of the constitutional committee. However, **Astana XI** on November 28 and 29, 2018 did not come to an agreement on forming a constitutional committee. Syria said that all illegitimate (read except Russia, Iran and the Hezbollah) must leave the country. **Astana XII** guarantors Summit on February 14, 2019 at Sochi recognized US troop withdrawal as positive and reiterated the need to facilitate a constitutional committee. However, given other opinions in the US Administration a delay of the withdrawal was possible.[10]

Separately, Russia raised tensions when President Putin told President Erdogan that without consent of President Assad they had no right to create a safe zone inside Syria. He also advised the Turkish president to follow the Adana Agreement of 1998 between the two countries. In that agreement the Syrian government had declared its readiness to cooperate with Turkey that would require Damascus to crack down on the presence of the Kurdistan Workers' Party (PKK) and 'affiliated organizations' in its territory on the condition that Turkey first removed its proxies and troops from the country. Russia came out directly stating that any action by Turkey should not lead to the emergence of any quasi-autonomous territorial entities and threaten Syria's territorial integrity. The Turkish government has continued to violate the agreement since 2011 through its support, financing, training and facilitating the transit of terrorism into Syria as well as its occupation of Syrian lands in Afrin and Idlib. Russia also nudged the Turkish government to engage with the Syrian government.[11]

Humanitarian Assistance

The Kofi Annan Plan[12] contained in UNSC resolution of March 2012 was the first mention of ensuring humanitarian assistance to the internally displaced as well as the refugees. This was taken further by UNSC Resolution 2139 (2014) of February 22, 2014 emphasizing the need to urgently respond to the growing humanitarian crisis. It exhorted the need

[10] Anthony H. Cordesman, 'Taking All the Wrong Steps in Syria, Iraq and the Fight Against Terrorism', CSIS, April 4, 2018, https://www.csis.org/analysis/taking-all-wrong-steps-syria-iraq-and-fight-against-terrorism.

[11] Sinem Cingiz, 'Why Is the 1998 Adana Pact Between Turkey and Syria Back in the News', Arab News, January 25, 2019, http://www.arabnews.com/node/1441931.

[12] Reuters, ibid.

to facilitate the expansion of humanitarian relief and to allow safety and free passage of medical and humanitarian aid workers. In the same year, UNSCR 2165 (2014) dealt with the issue of aid access giving authority for aid convoys to use routes across conflict lines and border crossings. It also set up a monitoring mechanism for humanitarian relief. This mandate regularly extended and holds until January 2020. UNSC resolution 2254 (2015), as stated above, comprehensively dealt with the issue. The Astana leaders' Summit in Sochi underscored the need for humanitarian aid and confidence building. **Astana IX** on **May 14–15** reiterated these issues while **Astana X** on **July 30 and 31, 2018** emphasized on the UN and international community the need to step up humanitarian assistance.

The provision of humanitarian relief, and improving access to it, has never been far from the minds of the various forums deliberating on the Syrian situation. By UNSCR (2018) of December 13, 2018, UNSC members concentrated on the issue of delivery and decreed a thirty-day pause to facilitate it. In this context, it called for respecting this cease-fire and providing safe and unimpeded access to UN and UN-partnered humanitarian convoys. Their fear was the continued partisan use of relief by the Syrian government in order to capture areas held by the insurgent groups.[13] UNSCR 2449 (2018), in the same year, renewed paras 2 and 3 of UNSCR 2165 (2014 for twelve months).

A major concern has been the inadequate humanitarian assistance reaching the affected populations and returning refugees.[14] At its meeting 8471, 1st Meeting (UNSC/3 13718) the United Nations Emergency Relief Coordinator expressed grave concern at the serious suffering among civilians exacerbated by severe weather, flooding and a spike in fighting. He underlined the urgency to facilitate aid deliveries and prevent a humanitarian catastrophe calling the situation dire, with more than 11.7 million Syrians requiring aid in 2019 and thousands continuing to be displaced by violence. At the same time, serious concerns also persisted on the protection of civilians in areas held by Islamic State in Iraq and the

[13] Robert Ford and Mark Ward, 'Assad's Syria Plays Dirty with US Humanitarian Aid', *The Hill*, December 2, 2018, https://thehill.com/opinion/national-security/373449-assads-syria-plays-dirty-with-us-humanitarian-aid.

[14] UN Security Council, 'Amid Staggering Levels of Need, Aid Delivery in Syria Crucial to Prevent Humanitarian Catastrophe, Relief Coordinator Warns Security Council', Reliefweb, February 26, 2019, https://reliefweb.int/report/syrian-arab-republic/amid-staggering-levels-need-aid-delivery-syria-crucial-prevent.

Levant (ISIL) and elsewhere where increased military operations remain a risk.

Release of Detainees and Missing

UNSC resolution of March 2012 raised the issue of the release of arbitrarily detained persons as part of the discussions relating to the Annan Plan. The issue was subsequently discussed at the various forums.

The Opposition meeting in Cairo from January 22 to 24, 2015 exhorted the release of detained, imprisoned and kidnapped persons. Eventually, in **Astana VIII** on December 21 and 22, 2017 decided to set up a Working Group on the release of detainees. The first meeting of the Working Group was held in parallel with Astana guarantors meeting on March 14 and 15, 2018. Further discussions of the Working Group, with the participation of the UN and the International Committee of Red Cross (ICRC) facilitated a prisoner swap on November 24, 2018 between the government and the opposition.

According to the UN, reports suggest that more than 100,000 people in Syria have been detained, abducted or gone missing during the eight-year conflict, with the government mainly responsible.[15] UN Security Council based its figures on accounts corroborated by the Commission of Inquiry on Syria authorized by the U.N. Human Rights Council and other human rights organizations since the conflict started. UNSG Antonio Guterres' 'also called for the Syria conflict to be referred to the International Criminal Court, saying accountability for serious violations of international human rights and humanitarian law' 'is central to achieving and maintaining durable peace in Syria'.[16]

Supervision Force (SF) and Related Issues

As provided in the Annan Plan, by UNSCR 2043 (2012) of April 21, 2012 the supervision force (SF) established to monitor the ceasefire, UN Supervision Mission in Syria (UNSMIS), lasted only until July 2012. UNSCR 2139 (2014) of February 22, 2014 exhorted the lifting of the

[15] Edith M. Lederer, 'More Than 100,000 People Detained, Missing in Syria', Global News, August 7, 2019, https://globalnews.ca/news/5737295/syria-conflict-detained-missing/.

[16] Ibid.

siege of populated areas: Homs city, Muble Zahra (Aleppo), Madaniyat al-Sham, eastern Ghouta and Darayya (Damascus rural) and Yarmouk (Damascus). It was only on December 18, 2015 by resolution UNSCR 2254 (2015) that ceasefire monitoring was emphasized and the ending of attacks on civilians.

De-Escalation Zones (DEZ)

The Astana Three—Russia, Turkey and Iran—took the responsibility to move forward the issue of designating, demarking and policing the most vulnerable areas in Syria. In the process, the three powers decided to protect the most sensitive and vulnerable areas in Syria knowing that they would determine the course of the war. Each country ended up consolidating its assistance to the Assad government but equally made their presence indispensable to the government. They made it increasingly difficult to visualize their departure from Syria.

Astana IV on May 3 and 4, 2017, agreed on the creation of De-escalation Zones (DEZ) at Idlib, Homs, eastern Ghouta and southern Syria, including Quneitra and Dara'a. It also agreed on a ceasefire in the DEZ's. **Astana V** on July 4 and 5, 2017 finalized details of the DEZ's and agreed to manage each DEZ under separate policies but failed to agree on its boundaries. A Ceasefire Agreement in Hamburg on July 7, 2007 in the presence of President Putin, Foreign Minister Lavrov, President Trump and Secretary of State Tillerson decided to implement the first ceasefire in the **DEZ covering Da'raa, Quneitra and Suweida**.

They agreed to define the borders of the zone and to deploy Russian forces on the DEZ perimeters. With the De-escalation Agreement, they extended the process to demarcate the **eastern Ghouta DEZ** while again agreeing to the deployment of Russian Military Police. Aerial strikes on July 23, 2017 by the Syrian air force in the Ghouta disrupted the situation. Astana sponsors' meeting in Cairo from July 31 to August 3, 2017 established the **third DEZ in Homs city** mandating a ceasefire in the area. Two Russian checkpoints and three observation posts were established on the perimeter. It resulted in the unblocking of the Homs-Hama section of the highway in the DEZ.

Astana VI on September 14 and 15, 2017 established the **fourth DEZ in Idlib governorate** with automatic extension until March 2019. The deployment of forces in the DEZ was on the basis of the agreed map of September 8, 2017. They also agreed to set up a Joint Iran-Russia

DEZ Coordination Center. They agreed that Russia, Iran and Turkey would post Observers on the periphery of the Idlib DEZ. **Astana VII** on October 30 and 31, 2017 set up twelve Observation posts along the Idlib DEZ.

UNSCR 2401 (2012) of February 24, 2018 once again asked for lifting of the siege of eastern Ghouta, Yarmouk, Fuaa and Kefraya. Following this on February 27, 2018, President Putin ordered daily five-hour pauses in eastern Ghouta that were ignored. On May 8, 2018, the last opposition-held area near Homs surrendered and insurgents were transported to Idlib. The Astana Guarantors meeting on March 14 and 15, 2018 decided to focus on the DEZ's in eastern Ghouta and Idlib. While the rebels were allowed to keep their weapons, following the cease-fire, a prisoner exchange was arranged between the Hezbollah and the al-Nusra Front. As earlier, the al-Nusra rebels were sent to the Idlib governorate.

Astana IX on May 14 and 15, 2018 reviewed the DEZ's one year after their initial decision. The Astana Guarantors summit in Tehran on September 7, 2018, considered the imminent offensive by the Syrian forces on Idlib with Russia and Iran rejecting the Turkish call to back ceasefire in the DEZ. While President Putin did not include the ceasefire, President Rouhani insisted that there should be no compromise on Idlib. Eventually, at Sochi on September 17, 2018, the Guarantors reached an agreement to create a 'buffer zone' around the Idlib DEZ and a cease-fire in Idlib by October 15, 2018. The buffer zone which is between 15–25 kilometres throughout the entire length of the Idlib province and the ceasefire continues to hold. **Astana XI** on November 28 and 29, 2018 reaffirmed the determination of the Guarantors to implement the Idlib agreement. The Astana Guarantors Summit at Sochi on February 14, 2019 expressed concerns that in Idlib the Hayat Tahrir al-Sham is increasing control over the province, while Turkey continues to seek more time to segregate the radicals from the civilian population. Turkey has called for international military support to halt the Syrian Army's offensive started in May 2019 on Idlib supported by Russian aircraft. It has decided to flood the EU with Syrian refugees in its camps. Although the EU has proposed a no-fly zone over Idlib, United States, that controls airspace over Syria's northeast, has not yet considered the suggestion. A no-fly zone over Idlib would require the capability and political will to shoot down Russian and Syrian aircraft.[17]

Syria and Chemical Weapons

The vexed issue of use of chemical weapons has been a running thread during the nine years of the Syrian conflict. Russia in 2013 persuaded Syria to disarm its chemical weapons capacity including production facilities and stockpiles of chemical weapons. Essentially, Bashar Assad was convinced to trade his longevity in power against his chemical weapons capacity.[18] Given that the civil war was already raging, Bashar Assad's continued presence at the helm would alone would ensure Syria's commitment under the CWC.

Israel having destroyed all Bashar Assad's attempts to develop nuclear weapons, in his own estimation, Assad gave up his foil to Israel's nuclear weapons capability. The Assads', both Hafiz and Bashar, have used Israel's possession of nuclear weapons to justify Syria's development of its own weapons of mass destruction (WMDs) while asserting that a host of factors prevented Israel or even the United States from using their own nuclear capability in any realistic way. They surmised that 'in this intemperate middle ground of strategic escalation, Syria could pursue its own WMD programs with impunity, secure in the knowledge that it is unlikely to face anything other than conventional weapons on the battlefield'.[19]

UNSCR 2118 (2013) required Syria to sign the Chemical Weapons Convention (CWC) that covers the 'Prohibition of the Development, Production, Stockpiling and Use of Chemical Weapons and on their Destruction'. U.S and Russia made a joint announcement on July 14, 2013 that Syria had acceded to the CWC. The OPCW approved the procedure and became responsible for verification. On October 31, 2013,

[17] Staff Writer, 'Syria: Russia and Turkey Agree to Ceasefire in Battered Idlib', The Defence Post, March 5, 2020, https://thedefensepost.com/2020/03/05/syria-idlib-ceasefire-putin-erdogan/.

[18] William Schabs, 'Why Are Chemical Weapons Worse Than Other Weapons of Mass Destruction', *The Guardian*, April 25, 2018, https://www.theguardian.com/commentisfree/2018/apr/25/chemical-weapons-mass-destruction-syria-nuclear.

[19] Brian Benoit, 'Sins of the Father: Syrian President Hafez Assad's Legacy of Chemical Weapons and the Balance of Power in the Middle East', Readex Blog, March 5, 2018, https://www.readex.com/blog/sins-father-syrian-president-hafez-assad%E2%80%99s-legacy-chemical-weapons-and-balance-power-middle.

CWC confirmed the destruction of Syria's chemical weapon stockpiles and equipment. On April 1, 2016, Veolia, CWC's sub-contractor, completed the destruction of the Syrian chemical weapons stockpile. A Joint Investigating Mechanism (JIM) of the UN and OPCW, to identify perpetrators of chemical attacks in Syria, was set up in terms of UNSCR 2235 (2015) of August 7, 2015. The JIM continued to be extended under UNSCR 2314 (2016) and 2319 (2016) until Russia vetoed further extensions.

Yet OPCW's verified destruction of Syria's chemical weapons production facilities and stockpiles did not remove the use of chemical weapons in the long-running civil war. All belligerents, including the Syrian government and the Islamic State, were held culpable for using them.[20] The OPCW Fact-Finding Mission, in its report in July 2018, concluded that a toxic chemical, most likely chlorine, was used frequently, most recently on April 7, 2018 in Douma. Russia contested this view in the UN Security Council that called the attack 'staged' by the rebels in Ghouta for their own ends.[21]

Nevertheless, on April 15, 2018, United States, along with Britain and France, bombed Syria. It is the second time the United States had waded into the country's conflict in response to a chemical weapons attack. The allies hit three targets, including the capital of Damascus and the facilities relating to Syria's chemical weapons programme, an important research centre, a storage facility, and an equipment facility and command post.[22] Neither has Israel stopped itself from aerial attacks on Syria's alleged chemical weapons facilities[23] even though it has a prolific chemical weapons programme itself.[24]

[20] Daryl Kimball, 'Timeline of Syrian Chemical Weapons Activity 2012–2019', Arms Control Association, March 2019, https://www.armscontrol.org/factsheets/Timeline-of-Syrian-Chemical-Weapons-Activity.

[21] BBC News, 'Syria 'Chemical Attack': Russia and US in Fierce Row at UN', April 9, 2018, https://www.bbc.com/news/world-middle-east-43706579.

[22] Alex Ward, 'The US Has Bombed Syria to Punish It for a Chemical Attack', Vox, April 16, 2018, https://www.vox.com/2018/4/13/17221420/trump-syria-attack-strike-assad-russia-response-chemical-weapon.

[23] Stuart Winer, 'Israeli Jets Said to Hit Chemical Weapons, Missile Sites in Syria', Times of Israel, September 7, 2017, https://www.timesofisrael.com/israeli-planed-reportedly-hit-chemical-weapons-site-in-syria/.

[24] Melanie Garson, 'Is It Time for Israel to Reveal the Truth About Its Chemical Weapons', The Conversation, May 21, 2018, https://theconversation.com/is-it-time-for-israel-to-reveal-the-truth-about-its-chemical-weapons-95604.

The use of chemical weapons, alleged or real, will remain a factor so long as the civil war continues. There have been no confirmed reports on their use by the government since the ceasefire in the final DMZ in Idlib. Yet Russia carried out air strikes against Syrian rebels it accuses of launching a chemical attack on the government-held city of Aleppo. Both Syria and its Russian allies say shells carrying toxic gas injured about 100 people. The rebels deny carrying out a chemical strike and say the claims are a pretext for an attack on opposition-held areas.[25]

The repeated strikes by British, French and American governments on Syria's alleged use of chemical weapons have been justified on grounds of ensuring respect for international law. Yet such use of force without UNSC authorization is contrary to the UN charter. There is a contradiction in blithely violating international law to promote the enforcement of international law. 'If there is a taboo on the use of chemical weapons, why is there not also a taboo on the unilateral use of armed force, contrary to international law? Does one taboo trump the other?'[26]

Terrorism

A fall-out of the long-running Syrian conflict is the spawning of multiple meanings of 'terrorism'. Over its course, a diverse range of entities has earned the dubious distinction of being labelled 'terrorist' including the Syrian government itself. Terrorism is a controversial label abused all over the world, not the least in Syria. The Assad government has labelled all the radical Islamic groups opposing it as terrorists while Assad's supporters, Russia and Iran have also adopted that classification.

On the other hand, the Western P-5 members call the government a terrorist and since December 29, 1979 Syria is on US's list of 'States Sponsors of Terrorism'. The label signals to the international community that the state is an 'international pariah'. The label does not have universal validity and many states still maintain diplomatic relations with Syria. Yet, the designation carries a wide range of sanctions, including a ban on arms-related exports and sales, prohibitions on economic assistance, and the imposition of other financial restrictions. In the US view, Bashar Assad's

[25] BBC News, 'Syrian War: Aleppo 'Gas Attack' Sparks Russian Strikes', November 25, 2018, https://www.bbc.com/news/world-middle-east-4633714.

[26] Ibid., William Schabs.

government supports a variety of terrorist groups that have a destabilizing effect well beyond the region. It provides political and weapons' support to the Lebanon-based Hezbollah and makes it possible for Iran to provide war material to the group.

Nevertheless, terrorism in Syria has a long history dating from the Islamist uprising in the early 80s, from the brutal state-sponsored attack on Hama in 1982 to the ongoing Civil War.[27] Since March 2011 peoples' protests against the government and their mutation into radical Islamic groups led the government to label them terrorists. The subsequent rise of radical Islamist groups such as ISIL,[28] al-Nusra Front[29] and other al-Qaeda-affiliated groups[30] has been a phenomenon of the civil war. While ISIL has been defeated, seven per cent of the country remains under control of radical rebel groups.[31] UNSCR 2139 (2014) of February 27, 2014 was an early condemnation of terrorism sponsored by al-Qaeda. Subsequently UNSCR 2254 (2015) of December 18, 2015 exhorted the need to suppress terrorism.

Under the Astana process, at their third meeting on March 14 and 15, 2017 the co-sponsors discussed creating a 'single map' indicating positions of terrorist groups like ISIL, Al-Nusra Front and other armed opposition groups. At both Astana VIII on December 21 and 22, 2017 and Astana X, the co-sponsors affirmed their determination to eliminate terrorism. As President Assad's control over Syria has expanded Idlib is holding out following the ceasefire worked out by Russia, Iran and Turkey since September 2018. However, the situation in the province remains fragile as the Hayat Tahrir al-Sham (HTS)[32] (Organization for

[27] US State Department, 'State Sponsors of Terrorism'.

[28] AJ Impact, 'The Rise and Fall of ISIL Explained', Al Jazeera, June 20, 2017, https://www.aljazeera.com/indepth/features/2017/06/rise-fall-isil-explained-170607085701484.html.

[29] Staff Writer, 'Profile: Syria's Al-Nusra Front', BBC News, April 10, 2013, https://www.bbc.com/news/world-middle-east-18048033.

[30] Bruce Hoffman, 'Al Qaeda's Resurrection', Council on Foreign Relations, March 6, 2016, https://www.cfr.org/expert-brief/al-qaedas-resurrection.

[31] Charles Lister, 'In Syria We Are Getting Counter-Terrorism All Wrong', MEI, February 3, 2020, https://www.mei.edu/publications/syria-were-getting-counter-terrorism-all-wrong.

[32] DPA, 'Blast Rocks Hayat Tahrir al-Sham Headquarters in Syria's Idlib', Daily Sabah, January 18, 2019, https://www.dailysabah.com/syrian-crisis/2019/01/18/blast-rocks-hayat-tahrir-al-sham-headquarters-in-syrias-idlib.

the Liberation of the Levant), another al-Qaeda offshoot, commands the loyalty of as many as 10,000 fighters in Idlib controlling more than half of the territory. It has an estimated 70,000 fighters including Arabs, Turks, Chechens, Uzbeks and Muslims from China's Xinjiang province. Some of their groups, like the Turkistan Islamic Party, are HTS allies.[33] Continuing clashes end-December 2018 between HTS and the Free Syrian Army-backed National Liberation front (NLF) threatened the agreement at Sochi between Russia and Turkey on the DEZ at Idlib.[34] Turkey designated the HTS as a terrorist group in August 2018 while the moderate opposition groups in the province apprehend that HTS would overlook of the deal on Idlib and expanding its territory within Idlib.

Syria has been the focus of the world's counter-terrorism efforts in recent years. Although ISIS remains alive albeit without a territorial entity under its control, there is increasing international disinterest in continuing a campaign against ISIL. The apathy and inaction towards the situation in Idlib has created conditions for extremists like HTS to thrive. The cause for continuing violent extremism is mainly socio-political with young men seeing HTS as the best option to resist the Syrian Army. Given Syria's unstable environment an early end to terrorism in the country is unlikely.

Despite the developments aimed at bringing peace to Syria, nothing has changed to reduce the longer-term pressures on Syria and the region—the problems of governance, economics, and internal unity—that have led to the rise of extremism and terrorism. It introduces a note of caution in the fight against terrorism in Syria.

Refugee Return and Facilities

The Group of Friends of the Syrian People (GOFSP) at their second conference on April 1, 2012 for the first time expressed concern about the refugees and internally displaced persons (IDP) because of the civil war. It

[33] James Phillips and Austin Avery, 'This little-Known Terror Group Poses a Greater Threat Than ISIS in Syria', The Heritage Foundation, December 3, 2018, https://www.heritage.org/middle-east/commentary/little-known-terror-group-poses-greater-threat-isis-syria.

[34] Nur Ozkan Erbay, 'Turkey, Russia Cooperation Over Idlib Continues Amid Worrying Regional Developments', Daily Sabah, January 13, 2019, https://www.dailysabah.com/diplomacy/2019/01/14/turkey-russia-cooperation-over-idlib-continues-amid-worrying-regional-developments.

was only UNSCR 2254 (2015) that emphasized the need to create conditions for return of refugees and IDP's thereby giving the issue sanctity of all UNSC permanent members.

At the same time, despite having collected international funds to succor the IDP's there has been a difference of opinion on the timing of disbursing foreign aid for rebuilding the country and making it possible for refugees and IDP's to return to their home areas.

Syrian Opposition

The international effort, by interested parties, to agree on a common position between the numerous combative opposition groups started soon after the passage of UNSCR 2254 (2015). Meeting in Cairo on January 22–23, 2015 agreed that the goal was to transform Syria into a civilian democracy adding that any realistic solution would require national, regional and international cover in addition to popular support. It significantly stated that all non-Syrian military presence must end. The meeting convened by the Saudi government in Riyadh on December 10, 2015, to prepare for a common opposition position in Geneva process, stated that international guarantees and support must not go against national sovereignty. It supported the transitional period proposed in the Geneva communique and setting up of a UN monitoring mechanism. It also agreed to establish a High Negotiating Committee (HNC) of the opposition groups. It had 133 members from the National Coalition, National Coordination body, independents linked to political groups, armed groups like the Free Syrian Army, Ahrar al-Sham and Jaish al-Islam, while fifteen other opposition groups were represented by Turkey. Yet the conference suffered because, for ideological reasons, other important opposition groups were not invited. As a result, the Kurdish groups held a separate conference in Damascus while the government held another also in Damascus.

Future of Bashar al-Assad

The question of whether Bashar al-Assad should leave or stay has been a moving target ever since the start of the Syrian conflict. Each party to the conflict has had its own view, from the multiple radical Islamic groups and the foreign powers in Syria to the larger population itself. The GOFSP at its first meeting on February 24, 2012 agreed that each country's national policy should cater for political transition away from Assad. Yet as the civil war continued endlessly, opinion has veered dependent on the need to combat the Islamic State (ISIL) and its depredations. With their military and other support to the chosen insurgent group, the foreign powers have adopted the view of their proxies in the expectation of building equities in their favour.

The United States under President Obama exhorted Assad to leave, although his subsequent policy remained confused without following through on his 'red line' on Assad's use of chemical weapons. Under President Trump US policy has been equally confusing with the dual goals to fight ISIL and ensure Assad's departure, the former taking priority. Trump's announcement of withdrawal of US troops from Syria was in 'fulfilment' of the former. Yet in March 2019 Trump called on Assad to leave, paradoxically at a time when he had regained control of most his country. 'There's a reason why two such disparate presidents have suffered this common dilemma: For Washington, the Syrian civil war is a no-win situation. If you want to back the rebels, you end up supporting radical Islamists who could exploit yet another dysfunctional Arab state and harbour anti-American terrorists. If you seek to support the only force capable of defeating the rebels, you end up backing a war criminal and Iran's close friend, President Bashar al-Assad'.[35]

Russia's policy in Syria was never about Syria alone but was seen an instrument to assert Russia's global power. While Russia has rescued Assad, it has also acquired, for the first time, a port on the Mediterranean. 'After three years of nonstop bombing and throughout the previous year's summits in Sochi, Russia, and Astana, Kazakhstan, it became obvious that Russia was championing a political settlement. Its foreign adventures seemed to have paid off. The Kremlin's actions helped it to secure access to all conflicting parties in the region, and its voice is now heard from the corridors of power in Tehran and Cairo to the ritzy palaces of the Gulf monarchies'.[36]

[35] Michael Hirsh, 'The Problem with America's Syria Policy Isn't Trump. Its Syria', Foreign Policy, January 8, 2019, https://foreignpolicy.com/2019/01/08/the-problem-with-americas-syria-policy-isnt-trump-its-syria/.

[36] Dimitriy Frolovskiy, 'What Putin Really Wants in Syria', Foreign Policy, February 1, 2019, https://foreignpolicy.com/2019/02/01/what-putin-really-wants-in-syria-russia-assad-strategy-kremlin/.

Iran's policy is based on the close and supportive relations between the two countries since the Iranian Revolution of 1979. They have a common interest in the future of Palestine and the Arab struggle against Israel. The Iran–Syria alliance is pragmatic at its heart: the survival of both the Assad dynasty and Islamic Republic. However, it has proved to be mutually beneficial during the long-running civil war. Their common interest in Lebanon for expressing their 'resistance', common interest in Iran and apathy to the United States has had an overlay of religious underpinning that has benefitted both countries. 'There is also a strong defensive element in the Islamic Republic's thinking towards Syria, with Iran seeking to maintain its position in the region…The strengthening of Hezbollah's position in Lebanon has also further tied their strategic outlook to one another. Thus, while their views of pan-Arab nationalism and Islamic universalism may be widely divergent, their common desire to promote "resistance" in the Middle East binds them closely together'.[37] Iran also seeks economic benefits in Syria in the process of the country's reconstruction and as succour during heightened US economic sanctions.[38]

The European powers, particularly France and UK, have had a divergent though changing view on Bashar al-Assad's exit. France, Germany and the United Kingdom want to maintain a tough anti-Assad stand, though others with populist governments in southern and eastern European nations, want to moderate it. The latter view his continuation as helping with the return movement of the Syrian refugees. They have been the first within the EU to face the brunt of their numbers. EU's policy is based on U.N. Resolution 2254 (2015) which demands 'political transition' in Syria. The wording is deliberately ambiguous, allowing Western countries opposing Assad to demand that he step down while Russia, China, and others can say it merely means agreed political reforms. With Assad staying on the resolution's ambiguity has led to disagreement

[37] Edward Wastnidge, 'Iran & Syria: An Enduring Axis', Middle East Policy Council, 2017, https://www.mepc.org/journal/iran-and-syria-enduring-axis.

[38] Hamidreza Azizi, 'Iran Seeks Economic Benefits From Syria', Atlantic Council, February 22, 2019, https://www.atlanticcouncil.org/blogs/iransource/iran-seeks-economic-benefits-from-syria.

within the EU'.[39] EU members Italy, Hungary, Austria and Poland are of the opinion that giving Assad the recognition of a winning the war is a better way to do business with him on the return of the refugees. France, Germany and UK opine that with his near control of Syria the only way left to leverage a constitutional change is through their financial assistance.

The Syrian and Opposition forces, reflecting the view of Saudi Arabia, at their Riyadh meeting of December 10, 2015 wanted Assad to leave the scene. They nevertheless accepted the Geneva Communique recommendation to implement a transitional period. Yet UNSCR 2254 (2015) of December 18, 2015 did not address Assad's future and left it vague in the interest of unanimity on its other provisions. Meeting in Riyadh from November 23 to 25, 2017, the Syrian opposition groups reiterated that Assad play no role in the political transition although condemned the presence of foreign military forces in the country.

Conclusion

Bashar al-Assad's control of most of his country has made it possible for him to impose a version of 'victor's justice' on the Syrian people or at least those who opposed his continuance. It has heightened the greatest challenge of moving towards a political process driven by the wishes of the Syrian people.

The complex negotiating process on UNSCR 2254 (2015), albeit slow and arduous, has nevertheless catered for the widest diversity of opinion and interests. It will now be necessarily have to await a cessation of hostilities so that the political process to start. Much will depend the willingness of the involved powers to withdraw militarily from the country while moving to instituting the process and rebuilding the country.

The political process in Syria, anchored in UNSCR 2254 (2015), was pursued on contiguously coterminous multiple tracks with the increasingly complex conflict. It starkly differs from similar processes in Afghanistan and Iraq both marked by the absence of a UNSC resolution and primacy of the United States. In Iraq, the majority Shi'a, while asserting their numerical and political primacy, have in place the

[39] Anchal Vohra, 'Europe Doesn't Even Agree on Assad Anymore', Foreign Policy, March 8, 2019, https://foreignpolicy.com/2019/03/08/europe-doesnt-even-agree-on-assad-anymore/.

accoutrements of democracy while undermining the minority Sunni, in a payback for their dominance for four decades under Saddam Hussein—in their version of 'victor's justice'. In Afghanistan, the evolution of the political process, over the eighteen years of the war, has primarily been in US hands with growing marginalization of the 'elected' government in its final denouement. Another contrast between Syria and the two other situations is that Bashar al-Assad, whose family has ruled over forty years, is still in place whereas in the others multiple leaders have emerged dictated by tribal and religious linkages.

CHAPTER 7

Future Evolution

The fall-out of the Syrian civil war is seen in the military engagement between ISIL and the Iraqi Army in Mosul and continues in the military engagement between the Saudi-sponsored 'multinational' forces fighting the *Houtis* in Sanaa. With the vast refugee outflow stranded at the EU's borders and in Turkey, ISIL-inspired terrorism in France, UK, United States and elsewhere in Europe has further internationalized the Syrian conflict.

With ninety per cent of Syria's territory under Bashar al-Assad's control the endgame in Syria has started. Its outcome will determine whether Syria continues to retain its existing borders. The fate of Idlib province, the last rebel stronghold after nine year of the conflict, had hinged on Russia's agreement with Turkey to withhold military operations until the armed opposition groups led, by the dominant Hayat Tahrir al-Sham (formerly Jabhat al-Nusra), exited the province. With Turkey delaying its commitment, in May 2019 the Syrian army, supported by Russian airpower, launched a military operation that after ten months has yet to achieve its objective. However, after the deaths of at least 30 Turkish troops on February 2020, most likely by a Russian airstrike, both sides are in a standoff from which neither can afford to back down. 'More importantly, the next moves will define the dying stages of the Syrian war and determine the fate of up to 3 million desperate people who have

R. M. Abhyankar, *Syria*,
https://doi.org/10.1007/978-981-15-4562-7_7

been trapped between a Russian-led onslaught and a Turkish pushback'.[1] While Turkey would seek to retaliate against the Syrian army, it is unlikely that its NATO partners would agree to pitch in. The outcome will affect the numerous regional and international state actors, domestic rebels, and foreign fighters each with conflicting interests and concerns on post-war configurations.

The fall of Idlib would not be the end of Syria's nightmare. The long-term political, social, economic and strategic implications for the future of the country will be massive. The stability of Assad regime's hold over much of the country, albeit at a high cost, would crucially depend on continuing Russian and Iranian presence. The tasks of reconstruction and resettlement are huge and costly: problems with which nobody seems ready to engage. Here again much will depend on Russia's willingness and ability to bring about a minimal understanding among the P-5 particularly the four directly involved.

What began as a local uprising against an unpopular regime has mutated into a regional struggle. It has drawn in proxies for organizations like al-Qaeda and the Islamic State group. Syria has become a cockpit for wider international tensions, with Russia, Turkey, Iran, Israel, the Gulf States and the United States all seeking their own advantage. An Assad victory will not reduce these pressures. 'The US, Israel, and Washington's Gulf allies are now all intent on seeing Syria as yet another battlefront in the strategic struggle against Iran'.[2]

Nevertheless, it highlights the need to plan the future political map of the country's governance. It is as important as the parallel need to provide international humanitarian assistance to facilitate the return to their homes of the refugees and internally displaced. This chapter will examine alternative humanitarian and reconstruction scenarios and the social and political options for Syria. It will also elaborate future options for the Bashar al-Assad and the Alawite community as a whole. At the

[1] Martin Chulov, 'Russia and Turkey's Next Moves Will Define the Syrian War's End', *The Observer*, February 28, 2020, https://www.theguardian.com/world/2020/feb/28/russia-and-turkeys-next-moves-will-define-the-syrian-wars-end.

[2] Jonathan Marcus, Diplomatic Correspondent, 'Will Idlib Spell the End of Syria's War?, BBC News, September 5, 2018, https://www.bbc.com/news/world-middle-east-45397704.

minimum, the possibility cannot be excluded of his continuing as a participant in the process of government formation as part of a revived peace process.

It may be best, at the outset, to consider the multiplicity of parameters involved in the situation before attempting a possible post-war political scenario. The steps, nearly simultaneous, towards de-escalation will cover:

1. Ushering an enduring ceasefire,
2. Return of refugees and the internally displaced to their homes,
3. Commencing the rebuilding of hospitals, roads, schools, housing, conservancy services and water supply,
4. Deciding on a political structure for the country,
5. Rejuvenation of agriculture and industry,
6. Internal peacekeeping.

Durable Ceasefire

A lasting ceasefire is only possible once regional and international actors are persuaded that prolonging the conflict will give no further advantage. This can only happen if the UN peace process under Special Envoy Gier Pederson[3] can move the discussion to the post-war scenario. Assad's re-establishment of control over most of his country could persuade the remaining rebel groups and their foreign backers. Russia, one of the four permanent members on the ground, is best placed to provoke such an agreement within the UNSC with China expected to support any Russian initiative in this direction.

Bashar Assad is in a cleft stick despite near-control of the country. The presence of both Russia and Iran[4] militates against a resolution of the civil war given the United States' statement to remain in Syria as long as Russia. Much depends on President Trump following through with this US commitment. Israel has also stated that they would continue their air operations over Syria so long as Iran remains there.

[3] Report, 'United Special Envoy Geir O.Pedersen Briefing to the Security Council', Reliefweb, February 19, 2020, https://reliefweb.int/report/syrian-arab-republic/united-nations-special-envoy-geir-o-pedersen-briefing-security-council-0.

[4] TOI Staff & agencies, 'Kremlin Says Iran's Presence in Syria a Top Issue at Trump-Putin Meeting', Times of Israel, July 14, 2018, https://www.timesofisrael.com/kremlin-says-irans-presence-in-syria-a-top-issue-at-trump-putin-meeting/.

Bashar al-Assad's continuation is another issue that needs resolution given that western opinion has been fluctuating. Even though priority to the elimination of the Islamic State, it is more than likely that the western powers will now seek Assad's ouster unmindful that a similar strategy in 2011 in Libya has not lead to a stable government. A durable peace is possible only when the four permanent members have no further interest in continuing to sponsor the various anti-Assad groups in Syria. It is in this context that Russia can play a major role in culling out a minimum acceptable agreement aimed at promoting a durable ceasefire. It would signal that Russia itself is ready to give up its interest in the country in return for similar understandings by the western powers involved.[5]

Regarding the continued interest of the regional powers, particularly Turkey, Saudi Arabia and UAE, the task is more difficult. Their concern with the sectarian dimension of the ongoing civil war conditions their response to the possibility of a durable ceasefire. With the assertive Shi'a majority in Iraq, supported by Iran, the intention of the regional powers would be to correct the sectarian balance in Syria. With the majority Sunni population ruled by the Alawis, a minority Shia sect, their intentions are clear. In fashioning a new constitution for Syria, the major powers would have to assure the regional powers that the new Syrian constitution would recognize the Sunni majority. It could be an important condition for them to accept a durable ceasefire.

Another contentious issue needing resolution relates to the status of the Syrian Kurds in relation to the Kurds in the contiguous areas of Turkey, Iran and Iraq. Without the acquiescence of the regional powers, particularly Turkey and Iran, maintaining a durable ceasefire will be difficult.[6] For Turkey, the Syrian Kurds have provided sanctuary and armaments to the PKK led by Ahmed Ocalan,[7] currently in a Turkish jail, for militarily asserting the fundamental rights of the Kurds in that country. In the past, the Syrian government has allowed the Turkish army to enter

[5] Report, 'US Rejects Russian Plan for Syrian Ceasefire at UN Security Council', DW, March 7, 2020, https://www.dw.com/en/us-rejects-russian-plan-for-syria-ceasefire-at-un-security-council/a-52673415.

[6] Majority of the Kurds are Sunni yet historically are seen as an ethnic group different from the Arabs.

[7] AJImpact, 'Jailed PKK Leader Abdullah Ocalan 'Ready for a Solution' with Turkey', Al Jazeera, August 9, 2019, https://www.aljazeera.com/news/2019/08/jailed-pkk-leader-ocalan-ready-solution-turkey-190809003125441.html.

its territory in 'hot pursuit' of Ocalan's group. Furthermore, the Kurds have been responsible for the military success of the Iraqi army in Mosul and for the routing of the ISIS from Aleppo. As things stand, they benefit from US support in asserting their importance to the government. Their significant numbers and military prowess makes them an important interlocutor in assuring a durable ceasefire. It provides Turkey with a pretext to maintain its army in Idlib while continuing to seek a longer pause in the combined Russian-Syrian attack on that province.

The maintenance of a durable ceasefire, after the fall of Idlib, will effectively re-establish Syria's sovereignty within its existing borders. Assad's control over more than 90% of the country provides an opportune moment for the UNSC to shift discussion to a ceasefire and its concomitant consequences. It is only then that meaningful steps can be taken to commence the return of refugees back to Syria and for the internally displaced to return to their homes. This will have to be the first step before the process of rebuilding the country can commence. Even more important will be the need to get the commitment of major and regional powers to providing the financial assistance to start the process.

Refugee Return

At present, majority of the refugees in Turkey are unlikely to be accepted by any western country. At the same time, President Erdogan has used them as a tool to delay the Syrian–Russian military operation in Idlib. Smaller numbers of refugees in Lebanon and Jordan have had a more favourable response from the EU and the United States although the EU countries are unlikely to have the capacity to take in all the refugees. Primarily the issue of return to Syria would apply to those refugees in camps in Turkey (3.1 million) and Jordan (85,000) since those outside the camps have made a life for themselves outside. The commencement back of the internally displaced to their habitual place of residence would create conditions to re-establish viable infrastructure, hospitals, and local security.

The EU's financial offer to the Turkish authorities to resettle the refugees back in Syria has become yet another political tool that Erdogan has exploited. The Turkish government has sought a more tangible movement towards their membership before they accept the financial incentive alone. Most Syrian refugees in Lebanon, and a good number in Jordan, have settled in the big cities making it unlikely that they would return to

Syria in the near future. The cash-strapped Jordanian government is keen to see the refugees from camps return to Syria to obviate the continuing need for international assistance to operate the camps. They are also conscious that the presence of a large number of dispossessed Syrians in the camps could lead to infiltration by ISIS or other radical Islamic groups.

The availability of massive international assistance is imperative and will need a mandate from the UN Security Council. In this sense, it would represent the acceptance by the UNSC members, involved in Syria, that no further political gains are possible by continuing the conflict. The next round of UN-sponsored talks needs to focus on this aspect given that the expected price tag is so high that neither the Syrian government nor its allies can foot the bill. The cost of reconstruction has been variously estimated between US $250–350 billion. Russia would like to see the West participate, but the West has long insisted that Assad must step down first. 'Money is the West's last remaining bargaining chip'.[8] The consideration of a bargain between a finite end to Assad's presidency after 2025 in return for a unanimous UNSC resolution to providing financial and other resources for re-construction is one possibility. A coalition composed of one NGO from each UNSC permanent member could be the instrument for disbursal of humanitarian and other assistance. A World Bank study estimated that from 2011 to end of 2016 the cumulative losses in gross domestic product (GDP) was $226 billion, about four times the Syrian GDP in 2010.[9,10]

'The conflict has inflicted significant damage to the Syrian Arab Republic's physical capital stock (7% housing stock destroyed and 20% partially damaged), led to large numbers of casualties and forced displacement (between 400,000 and 470,000 estimated deaths and more than half of Syria's 2010 population forcibly displaced), while depressing and

[8] Christopher Reuter, Fritz Schaap & Christian Werner, 'Syria's Uncertain Future under Bashar Assad', Spiegel Online, August 16, 2018, http://www.spiegel.de/international/world/the-future-of-syria-under-bashar-assad-a-1223178.html.

[9] The World Bank, 'The Toll of War: The Economic and Social Consequences of the Conflict in Syria', July 10, 2017, https://www.worldbank.org/en/country/syria/publication/the-toll-of-war-the-economic-and-social-consequences-of-the-conflict-in-syria.

[10] The World Bank, 'The Toll of War: Economic and Social Impact Analysis(ESIA) of the Conflict in Syria-Key Facts', July10, 2017, https://www.worldbank.org/en/country/syria/brief/the-toll-of-war-economic-and-social-impact-analysis-esia-of-the-conflict-in-syria-key-facts.

disrupting economic activity'.[11] The World Bank concluded that subsequent losses to the economy would be greater than the damages directly caused by the violence. Many of the country's cities lie in ruin, making reconstruction a decisive question—particularly when it comes to who will pay for it.

With the diverse tasks that ten years of the civil war have imposed, the imperative is to move towards the re-establishment of normalcy in the country by refashioning its political structure.

Political Structure

The UN has already taken on board the need for Syria to have a new constitution[12] that would bring in a functioning democracy. At their meeting in Istanbul on October 26, 2018 President Putin, Chancellor Angela Merkel, President Erdogan and President Macron stated that a committee must convene by the end of 2018 to write a new Syrian constitution. US and Jordan among seven other nations have also urged the UN to begin the constitutional process.[13] At the same time, the Syrian government has been stalling on any such initiative.[14] Eventually the Syrian Constitutional Committee—comprising opposition, civil society and government members—began its work on November 20, 2019 in Geneva but saw the withdrawal of the government for non-acceptance of its proposals.

The UN Special Envoy is presently negotiating its resumption. The Assad government may be stalling given that it is on the threshold of taking complete territorial control of the country. It sees this as an advantage in order to impose a favourable constitutional solution. It has also stated that a constitution drafted outside the country will not be acceptable. Russia's role will be crucial in overcoming President Bashar al-Assad's opposition to work of the constitutional committee.

[11] Ibid.

[12] Financial Times, 'Leaders Demand Progress on New Syria Constitution', October 27, 2018, https://www.ft.com/content/025a23e8-da19-11e8-9f04-38d397e6661c.

[13] Mathew Lee, 'US, Jordan Among 7 Nations Urging UN to Begin Constitution Process', The Times of Israel, September 28, 2018, https://www.timesofisrael.com/us-jordan-among-7-nations-urging-un-to-begin-syria-constitution-process/.

[14] Edith M. Lederer, 'UN Says Syria Is Blocking Efforts to Draft New Constitution', AP, October 26, 2018, https://www.apnews.com/1adbdb5ec56c4f40880894348e211e29.

The committee will require strong support from the United States and EU for its work to be seen to be effective.

Any constitution-drafting exercise must nevertheless lay down the guiding principles for its work including a comprehensive set of articles that address the conflict's root causes and the elimination of threats to a stable and peaceful Syria.[15] Possible, though not inclusive, guidelines towards this end could be:

1. Basic working documents for the committee:

   There is continuing lack of clarity on the earlier Syrian constitutions as acceptable basis for start of discussions. Possibly, the Syrian constitutions of 1950 and of 2012 would encapsulate the constitutional developments since Syrian independence. In addition, the Egyptian constitution of 2014,[16] and for specific provisions, the Turkish constitution of 1982[17] would be equally useful;
2. Acceptance as the majority community of the Sunnis who number 76.9% of the Syrian population;
3. A multi-party system, including the Syrian Arab Ba'ath party (ABSP), eschewing 'deba'athification'[18] as in Iraq after Saddam Hussein's fall;
4. Consociational democracy[19]: would allow sectarian passions to cool before a more broad-based system to be established. Political scientists define a consociational state as one with major internal divisions along ethnic, religious, or linguistic lines, with none of

[15] Ibid., Emma Beals.

[16] Holger Albrecht, 'Egypt's 2012 Constitution', US Institute of Peace, January 25, 2013, https://www.usip.org/sites/default/files/PB139-Egypt%E2%80%99s%202012%20Constitution.pdf.

[17] Selin Esen, 'The 2017 Constitutional Reforms in Turkey: Removal of Parliamentarism or Democracy', IACL-AIDC Blog, March 17, 2017, https://blog-iacl-aidc.org/test-3/2018/5/26/analysis-the-2017-constitutional-reforms-in-turkey-removal-of-parliamentarism-or-democracy.

[18] Paul Bremer, 'I Ran Iraq in 2003. Washington Had'nt Prepared for the Aftermath of the War', *The Guardian*, July 6, 2016, https://www.theguardian.com/commentisfree/2016/jul/06/iraq-war-aftermath-paul-bremer.

[19] Christalla Yakinthou, 'Consociationalism in Theory and Practice', Political Settlements in Disordered Societies, pp. 10–34, 2009, Palgrave Macmillan, https://link.springer.com/chapter/10.1057/9780230246874_2#citeas.

the divisions large enough to form a majority group, yet nonetheless manages to remain stable, due to consultation among the elites of each of its major social groups. The goals of consociationalism are governmental stability and the survival of the power-sharing arrangement.

5. An alternative could be confessional democracy[20] as practiced in Lebanon. Over the years, since Hafez al-Assad's 'state capture', the government has gone beyond in creating power brokers in a transactional state thus reducing the power of the state.[21]
6. General elections based on a proportional system, like in Turkey,[22] requiring each party to secure at least 10% of vote in any election for representation in Parliament.
7. Introduce a prime ministerial system with limited powers for the president.
8. Secularism would remain the organizing principle of the state and society and maintain the division between the political and the religious authority.[23,24]
9. Reform of Syria's legal system: It is a patchwork of conflicting ideologies and, by extension, legal frameworks. Such legal systems as exist in rebel-held areas are typically subject to a strict interpretation of Sharia. 'If Syria does not receive an accountable justice system, the costs will be devastating', Abou el-Dahab said. 'Without accountability, with-out legal redress, without access to

[20] Brief, 'Lebanon's Confessionalism: Problems and Prospects', US Institute of Peace, Thursday March 30, 2006, https://www.usip.org/publications/2006/03/lebanons-confessionalism-problems-and-prospects.

[21] Lina Khatib and Lina Sinjab, 'Syria's Transactional State: How the Conflict Changed the Syrian State's Exercise of Power', October 2018, Chatham House Research Paper, https://www.chathamhouse.org/publication/syrias-transactional-state-how-conflict-changed-syrian-states-exercise-power.

[22] AJ Impact, 'Explainer: How Turkey's Election System Works', Al Jazeera, May 26, 2011, https://www.aljazeera.com/indepth/spotlight/turkeyelection/2011/05/201152613439511649.html.

[23] Sunniva Rose, 'Syria's New Religious Bill Angers Assad Loyalists', *The National*, October 4, 2018, https://www.thenational.ae/world/mena/syria-s-new-religious-bill-angers-assad-loyalists-1.777378.

[24] Joseph Daher, 'Secularists, Secularism and the Syrian Uprising (Part1/2)', Syria Untold, August 18, 2018, http://syriauntold.com/2018/08/secularists-secularism-and-the-syrian-uprising-part-1-2/.

an independent legal and judicial system, social grievances and violations of civil and political rights will continue to be perpetrated without any consequences'.[25]

10. The legal system will also provide, as at present, for Muslim personal law administered under the grand Mufti of Syria.[26] Similarly, the heads of Christian and other religions will exercise personal law jurisdiction.
11. Constitution will guarantee all minorities both Islamic and non-Islamic. It will also recognize a special political and strategic status for the Syrian Alawi community.
12. Accountability: The setting up of a legal system that provides full legal redress with access to an independent legal and judicial system and guarantees against social grievances and violations of civil and political rights.
13. Security concerns of the people: Syrian families lack necessities, such as food, shelter and medical care. Children cannot go to school. The war is being fought in towns and on the streets with the result that infrastructure and housing in most Syrian cities, except Damascus, has been destroyed. This includes hospitals and conservancy facilities. In the settled areas of many cities, the exodus of people from the rural areas to the major cities has created security problems especially for women.
14. Detainees and Missing Persons: It is abundantly clear that no progress is possible in reaching a political settlement and lasting peace is Syria without tackling the justice-based needs of Syrian victims and survivors. One of the main challenges is to overcome the 'impunity gap', between the perpetrators and their victims. The issue of the detainees and the missing requires accountability for the crimes and immediate tangible forms of justice. In particular, learning the whereabouts of their missing and, if alive, obtaining their release. Equally, receiving reparation for the horrific abuses endured in detention; to bring closure where deceased relatives are

[25] Suddaf Choudary, 'Syria's Justice System: Working Without a Written Law', The Arab Weekly, December 10, 2017, https://thearabweekly.com/syrias-justice-system-working-without-written-law.

[26] Eva Bartlett, 'Syria's Grand Mufti Hassoun Discusses Peaceful Co-existence, Love and an inclusive Nonsectarian Syria', Mintpress, December 7, 2018, https://www.mintpressnews.com/interview-grand-mufti-ahmad-badr-al-din-hassoun-syria/252590/.

buried and perhaps even ceremonially reburying them. Eventually, ensuring secret places of detention are closed down.[27]

15. Issues of citizenship and right of return: As the international community pushes for the return of refugees to Syria, there is need to keep a close watch on the various obstacles, fears and instability factors that can prevent or discourage refugees from returning. In addition, till the military operations in Idlib are completed new waves of refuges and displaced will swell the ranks.[28] The Syrian government has called for all refugees to return home to highlight its confidence after getting nearly 90% of the territory back.[29] At the same time, changes in the property law have virtually shut out some refugees. Unless the refugee can prove ownership in 30 days, a new housing law passed by the Syrian government in April 2018 makes it certain that the refugees will have no homes to return. Law 10 of 2018 will introduce widespread redevelopment areas in the country, allowing the government to demolish residential communities where houses are uninhabited and make them over to real estate companies for redevelopment. As the Syrian government looks to the international community to fund these projects, human rights organizations are worried about the implications of this law for displaced Syrians.[30] The government's intention is clearly to keep out those Syrians who fled after being involved in military action against the regime. Clearly, the peace talks will have to address denial of return to all refugees and displaced.
16. Reform of the police and intelligence services: The re-establishment of security is an essential condition to the restoration of trust between different sections of society. In such contexts, the

[27] NYU Center on International Cooperation, 'Tacking the Impunity Gap in Syria: Detainees and Disappearances', https://cic.nyu.edu/publications/Tackling-the-Impunity-Gap-in-Syria-Detainees-and-Disappearances, September 13, 2018.

[28] Alessandria Masi, 'Syria 2018: The Major Issues for the Year Ahead', Syria Deeply, January 18, 2018, https://www.newsdeeply.com/syria/articles/2018/01/18/syria-2018-the-major-issues-for-the-year-ahead.

[29] Hussein Malla, 'Syrian Government Calls on Refugees to Return Home', Associated Press, July 3, 2018, https://www.newsdeeply.com/syria/articles/2018/01/18/syria-2018-the-major-issues-for-the-year-ahead.

[30] Brennan Cusak, 'As Syria Plans to Rebuild New Law Makes It Difficult for Refugees to Have a Say in How', Forbes, June 26, 2018, https://www.forbes.com/sites/brennancusack/2018/06/26/will-syria-rebuild-without-its-refugees/#744f1c625c1f.

reconstruction of security institutions is a major issue in diverse societies. Syria's military and security apparatus, one of the most powerful in the region, has been responsible for the regime's survival. Their 'involvement in the country's system of management, oppression and interrogation' makes it certain that 'the question of systemic, functional change will be on the agenda of the parties in the conflict'.[31] The dilemma in security reform is that while security is absolutely important in the context of the transition process, the dismantling of existing security forces will lead itself lead to insecurity. The approach in this regard must simultaneously initiate restructuring of the security apparatus under public and/or international scrutiny and allow existing structures to provide security. The enormous task of rebuilding trust between Syrian intelligence structures and the society is a corollary of the political process. It will inevitably require compromises.

Bashar Assad and Alawi

The fate of Syria's Alawi community in a post-civil war scenario is linked with that of Assad and his family. Alawi, despite representing a small proportion of the population, holds key positions in the bureaucracy, army and dominate the police. Since 2011 they have been the bedrock of the government and have contributed to the main fighting forces to defend the regime. It is equally true that a number of Alawi families opposed the Assad family.

However, almost every Alawi family is affected by the war. For them, it was as much about saving Assad as about preserving their very existence. There is a palpable fear in the Alawi mind that Bashar Assad's exit from power will unleash an unbridled assault against their community. It has played into the narrative that the Sunni Muslim majority, the source of opposing radical Islamic groups, wants to eradicate their community. It is a factor in the community keeping with Assad, despite their dissatisfaction with him on the military, political and economic front. It has enabled Assad to refuse the return of all those who left Syria at different times

[31] Alexey Khlebnikov, 'Major Challenges for Military and Security Services in Syria', RIAC (Russian International Affairs Council, February 15, 2018, http://russiancouncil.ru/en/analytics-and-comments/analytics/major-challenges-for-the-military-and-security-services-in-syria/.

during the civil war. This fear, more genuine than illusory, has militated against the efforts for national reconciliation, political change and free elections.

Assad's ability to keep the Alawi community with him remains vital to preserving his legitimacy, a fact recognized by both Iran and Russia. With Assad in control of almost the entire country, it is likely that he would oppose a constitution that abridges the president's current powers. It makes for increasing uncertainty in accomplishing a credible political set-up that ultimately leads to a Syria without Assad as head of state. 'How to better help the Syrian populations in need, without consolidating Assad's power is a difficult equation', French UN Ambassador François Delattre has said. The crux of the constitutional negotiations towards a democratic political framework rests on this dilemma.

Agenda of Foreign Forces

United States

US's approach to Syria has been confusing and erratic. Donald Trump has always claimed that he was 'committed' to defeating IS, which still has a small presence in Syria. Simultaneously, his administration pledged to pull out of Syria, with Trump criticizing his predecessors for taking military action in the first place. Trump ordered limited strikes on Syria in April 2017 and disclosed that 2000 US troops were on the ground. Yet it does not amount to a strong military presence in Syria. The contradictions have continued with successive announcements of increase or withdrawal of troops.

After the April 6, 2018 apparent chemical attack on civilians by the Syrian government (though Russia blamed the opposition for the attack), Trump again publicly castigated Russia's support. He first claimed that the United States would be sending over missiles, taunting Russia with a series of tweets, before lamenting that the relationship between the United States and Russia was at rock bottom. On April 8, 2018 limited missile strikes, in collaboration with US allies, targeted supposed chemical weapons productions and storage sites. Even as the US military appears to want to expand its role, Trump's preferences remain unpredictable.[32]

NATO Allies

A US-led coalition has been operating against IS in both Syria and Iraq since 2014. It includes several NATO allies: Belgium, Canada, France, Germany, The Netherlands and the UK. NATO countries on April 12, 2018 condemning the alleged chemical attack on Douma called for accountability of those responsible, full and unimpeded accesses to international medical assistance, and international monitoring. Yet only USA, UK and France, carried out the last airstrikes. Despite a semblance of unity between NATO members Syria has truly split the alliance by driving rifts between specific allies and between certain member states with Turkey. At one stage, Turkey even revealed the positions of French troops and US bases in northeast Syria. Turkey's president, Recep Tayyip Erdoğan, sharply criticized his French counterpart Emmanuel Macron, for meeting SDF Kurdish leaders in Paris and offering to mediate with Turkey. For Erdoğan they are terrorists. Some of the concerns of the naysayers stem from the belief that any missile attack could lead to a wider conflict in the Middle East, and potentially between Russia and the West.[33] NATO remains divided on further military action with Chancellor Merkel opting out.

Turkey

At the end of their trilateral Syrian summit on April 4, 2018, the leaders of Turkey, Syria and Iran put on a show of unity. Yet the three countries remain deeply divided over the Syrian war particularly on the fate of Afrin and Idlib, and on what sort of peace they would want to see. This was particularly visible when Iran's president, Hassan Rouhani, moved that the Afrin District, captured by Turkey and the Syrian Free Army from

[32] Natasha Edrow, 'Syria: Who's Involved and What Do They Want', The Conversation, April 13, 2018, http://theconversation.com/syria-whos-involved-and-what-do-they-want-95002.

[33] Simon Smith, 'Syria: Who's Involved and What Do They Want', The Conversation, April 13, 2018, http://theconversation.com/syria-whos-involved-and-what-do-they-want-95002.

Kurdish forces, be returned to the government. Russian foreign minister, Sergey Lavrov supported the view even though the military operation had received Russia's green light.

Turkey's precarious position in the Syrian conflict is not entirely dependent on its relations with Iran and Russia. Turkey's advantage against these two countries could also weaken if the US forces withdraw. Yet Turkey's motive to curb Kurdish moves to assert their independence will remain. Turkey's position will remain uncomfortable given that both Iran and Russia will work to secure their geopolitical interests in Syria's future. Just as its relationship with the United States over Syria is very tense, Turkey is realizing that warm handshakes from Iran and Russia do not necessarily imply lasting alliances.'[34] The eventual withdrawal of Turkish forces from Idlib needs to be assured.

Israel

The Israeli government faces serious security concern on the country's extremely tense northern border with Syria. It fears a dramatic regional escalation, and the possibility that Syria will become a theatre of open conflict between Russia and states like the USA, UK and France.[35] At the same time, Israel has made it known that it will continue aerial strikes on Iranian targets in Syria. Both Israel and the United States have come together on their goal of restricting Iran's presence in the area.

Russia

In the UN Security Council, Russia has been Syria's steadfast support consistently vetoing resolutions that could repeat the Libyan intervention in 2011, when a no-fly zone was liberally interpreted to justify regime change. Since September 2015, Assad's fate has been closely tied to Russian policy. Russia protects the Syrian government to, firstly, to ensure its re-asserted role as 'the geopolitical interlocutor for the rest of

[34] Alpaslan Ozerdem, 'Syria: Who's Involved and What Do They Want', The Conversation, April 13, 2018, http://theconversation.com/syria-whos-involved-and-what-do-they-want-95002.

[35] Beverley Milton-Edwards, Queens University, Belfast, 'Syria: Who's Involved and What Do They Want', The Conversation, April 13, 2018, http://theconversation.com/syria-whos-involved-and-what-do-they-want-95002.

the world';[36] Second, to ensure the integrity of Syria's governance structure as a bulwark against radical Islamist alternatives; and lastly, to hold on to its first naval base in the Mediterranean in the port of Tartous.

Iraq

'A US-led airstrike or intervention in Syria could profoundly affect security inside Iraq. There is real concern in Iraq that an escalation in Syria could create a dangerous security vacuum, strengthening the position of holdout IS militants who are already present near the Iraqi-Syrian border'.[37] Iraqi Prime Minister, Haider al-Abadi, stressed that Iraqi forces are doing their best to 'secure all Iraqi lands' and revealed that he had told President Trump that to defeat IS in eastern Syria, Iraq will coordinate with its partners including Russia and Syria.

Iran

'On first sight, Iran and Syria make strange bedfellows. One is perhaps the world's preeminent theocracy and the other a secular Arab-nationalist state—and yet their alliance is one of the most enduring in the Middle East'.[38] Their strategic outlook encompasses key regional issues like Palestine and on the Hezbollah in Lebanon. Iran and Syria have ideological commonality on countering both Israel and the West's goals in the Middle East.

Iran vitally needs a friendly government in Damascus to safeguard its strategic clout in the region and facilitate a conduit for Iranian military and other support to Hezbollah. The debt is even greater with the Hezbollah since 2015 serving alongside Iranian forces as a key Assad ally. Iran has also helped to corral volunteer fighters from across the Shi'a

[36] Moritz Pieper, University of Salford, 'Syria: Who's Involved and What Do They Want', The Conversation, April 13, 2018, http://theconversation.com/syria-whos-involved-and-what-do-they-want-95002.

[37] Balsam Mustafa, University of Birmingham, 'Syria: Who's Involved and What Do They Want', The Conversation, April 13, 2018, http://theconversation.com/syria-whos-involved-and-what-do-they-want-95002.

[38] Edward Wastnidge, The Open University, 'Syria: Who's Involved and What Do They Want', The Conversation, April 13, 2018, http://theconversation.com/syria-whos-involved-and-what-do-they-want-95002.

initially as defenders of sacred Shia shrines in Syria. While Iran with Russia and Turkey has established the de-escalation zones in Syria continuing Israeli air strikes against Iranian targets, and the threat of Western action against Assad, bring in the real possibility of direct clashes on Syrian soil.

Hezbollah

Following Iran's entry in 2013 in support of Bashar al-Assad that of the Lebanese Hezbollah was inevitable. It transformed their role from a recipient of Iranian military hardware, sent through Syria, to a participant in the long-running civil war. Hezbollah, considered a terrorist organization by Washington, has gained extensive battlefield experience in Syria, and it claims to be prepared for another war with Israel if necessary.

From the Hezbollah's point of view, their active role in supporting the Syrian Army established a more intensive bond with the Syrian government. Hezbollah had deployed since 2013 several thousand fighters in Syria and by 2015 lost up to 1500 fighters in combat. The group's 'decisive and essential' role in Syria has turned it into a major military force in the Middle East. Hezbollah has also been very active to prevent rebel penetration from Syria to Lebanon, being one of the most active forces in the Syrian conflict's spill over into Lebanon. In a sense, it was a payback for the assistance received from the Syrian army during its long presence in Lebanon. Hezbollah chief Hasan Nasrallah's position that 'we will be where we need to be' anticipated the recognition of the organization's growing ability to fight outside the country.[39]

Kurds

The US-led coalition's military and diplomatic support to 'the multi-ethnic, semi-autonomous Democratic Federation of Northern Syria (DFNS) will influence the Kurds' future in Syria.[40] US-led intervention will alone secure the Kurds negotiations with the Syrian government to

[39] Ali Harb, 'A Regional Power': How Fighting Assad's War Transformed Hezbollah, Middle East Eye, October 9, 2017, https://www.middleeasteye.net/news/regional-power-how-syria-civil-war-changed-hezbollah-lebanon-israel-1187885930.

[40] Cengiz Gunes, 'Syria: Who's Involved and What Do They Want', The Conversation, April 13, 2018, http://theconversation.com/syria-whos-involved-and-what-do-they-want-95002.

secure a better deal. Frequent US announcements that it will withdraw from Syria has raised the Kurd's worst fear: of US abandonment. On the other hand, if the United States attacks the government without a strong commitment to see a resolution of the conflict, Russia, Iran and the Assad government might be provoked into targeting the Kurdish-led entity as an 'enemy within'. In that scenario, Russia could even give the green light to Turkey to pursue its long-held objective of dismantling the Kurdish-led autonomous entity altogether, as it did with Turkey's invasion of Afrin in northwest Syria.[41]

Future of the Rebel Groups

Some figures estimate that Idlib, where the last major conflict is in limbo, hosts up to 70,000 militants ranging from moderate opposition forces to radical elements with former and current links to al-Qaeda, particularly the Hayat Tahrir al-Sham. With nine years of pent up animosity against the government and its allies, many of these militants may use the Turkish-Russian agreement to withdraw further and may try to wage a low-level insurgency with support and even sanctuary in Turkey. HTS the most influential in the besieged province has not moved to the cordon around the Idlib DMZ provoking in May 2019 the Syrian Army and Russian air assets to commence an attack. Its outcome could well drive HTS underground throughout Iraq and Syria to continue their activities. It raises questions regarding the future shape of the Salafi-jihadist movement in Syria.[42]

Their future would depend on the assimilation of reach, resources and support of foreign powers. For radical groups focused primarily on Syria (and, possibly Iraq) the possibility of bringing them back into the national mainstream is viable. Some success was seen in the Dara'a area when some opposition groups joined the government. Possibly Grand Mufti of Syria could be a valid interlocutor for the government to catalyze this initiative. On condition that they give up arms and swear an oath of allegiance to the constitution of the Republic they could be allowed to join any approved

[41] Cengiz Gunes, ibid.

[42] Maxwell B. Markusen, 'Idlib Province and the Future of Instability in Syria', CSIS (Center for Strategic and International Studies), September 21, 2018, https://www.csis.org/analysis/idlib-province-and-future-instability-syria.

political party; yet the option to convert the militant group into political party would not be available to them.

Future of ISIS

The problem arises with radical Islamic groups like the remnants of the Islamic state or the HTS that retain the ambition that transcend Syria. In their case, the larger issue of their disruptive goals would have to be addressed by the Organisation of Islamic Cooperation (IOC),[43] the legitimate forum to address these issues. Of the radical groups in Idlib some like the HTS appear to be counting on securing succour and sanctuary from Turkey.

It is not likely that Russian and US success, in separate military operations, in eliminating the ISIS will guarantee their physical eclipse from Syria. 'Even as the group is being decisively defeated on the battlefield after losing key territories including its de facto capital Raaqa in October 2017, the organization is far from being uprooted; and it is premature to claim ISIS has been extinguished from the face of the earth. In other words, ISIS switches from governing mode to insurgency mode'.[44] The collapse of ISIS has created a terrorist diaspora with the potential to carry out sophisticated attacks in the West and radicalize other Muslims in the Arab world. The challenge must counter their ideology, rather than only focus on a military and security approach.

Yet eliminating the force of their ideology will need a wider discussion within Islam not only through the OIC but more generally. Some suggestions[45] for a wider effort by the world's Islamic countries include:

1. Dealing with the imperative to establish security in previous ISIS-controlled areas of Syria (and Iraq) through adequate military forces.

[43] Web Desk, 'OIC 2019: All About the Islamic Summit Where India Was Invited for the First Time Ever', *India Today*, March 2, 2019, https://www.indiatoday.in/education-today/gk-current-affairs/story/oic-2019-islamic-summit-india-invited-first-time-sushma-swaraj-1468689-2019-03-02.

[44] Bendaoudi Abdelillah, 'After the 'Almost 100 Percent' Defeat of ISIS, What About Its Ideology?', Al Jazeera Centre for Studies, May 8, 2018, http://studies.aljazeera.net/en/reports/2018/05/100-percent-defeat-isis-ideology-180508042421376.html.

[45] Abdelillah, ibid.

The link between extremist terrorist groups and civil wars need to be cut.

2. De-radicalization through the provision of the human needs of the population and addressing their long-standing grievances.
3. There is a parallel need to counter the ISIS discourse that has been disseminated through social media by regularly deleting their content, exposing the atrocities of the group and disseminating moderate views of recognized Islamic scholars to de-bunk ISIS reinterpretation of Islam and finally to promote education programmes for the youth emphasizing co-existence in Islam.

Only a consistent effort over years would to achieve this change. It would only be successful in the backdrop of a political settlement in Syria that would win the trust of the Sunni community.

The Islamic Conference Organization is ideally placed to work on these suggestions both on its own and in cooperation with the countries involved. This would require the ICO to withdraw their suspension of Syria from the organization.

Need for UNSC Policy Change

The future direction of the interests of the regional and international powers in the Syrian conflict becomes of crucial importance. Assad's control over nearly 90 per cent of Syria's territory is evidence that the room for anti-Assad radical groups, hence for their foreign backers, has shrunk. It is an opportunity to get the Western powers, particularly the P-5, to focus in re-building the devastated country. Yet most of these powers feel that their economic muscle is the last remaining instrument to secure Assad's exit and they will use it. Russia, as the major player in Syria, remains the only UNSC permanent member in a position to persuade the other UN Security Council members. If this can be achieved the agreement of the regional powers would be possible by assuring them of adequate constitutional provisions to achieve Sunni majority status.

Russia's possible tactic to achieve this result could be to propose a trade-off between P-5 acquiescence to provide humanitarian and economic assistance and giving them 'guarantor status' on the proposed post-civil war constitutional arrangement. One possible model is the Cyprus Treaty of Guarantee between the Republic of Cyprus and Greece, the United Kingdom and Turkey (1960).[46] A successful conclusion would require harmonization of the long-term aims in Syria of Russia and Iran, on the one hand, and the major Western powers.

As stated above, Russia's intervention is not entirely about ensuring survival of Assad's family. It is as much to raise Russia's international profile as to 'keep Syria from becoming an Iranian vassal; Moscow and Tehran are, at best, frenemies, happy to try to marginalize the United States yet also fierce competitors seeking influence in the Middle East and South Caucasus'.[47]

Social Structure and Sectarianism

The constitutional recognition of the Sunni majority will be crucial to getting their support in building the new governance of the country. United Nations human right report has characterized the Syrian civil war as an 'overtly sectarian and ethnic conflict, raising the specter of reprisal killings and prolonged violence should the Assad government fall. Feeling threatened and under attack, ethnic and religious minority groups have increasingly aligned themselves with parties to the conflict, deepening sectarian divides, according to the UN report'.[48]

The sharpest split is between the ruling minority Alawi sect, a Muslim sect from whom President Assad and his most senior political and military associates are drawn, and the country's Sunni Muslim majority, mostly aligned with the opposition. The conflict equally has drawn in other minorities, including Armenian Christians, Assyrian Christians, Druze, Palestinians, Kurds, Yezidi and Turkmens.

The differences between Alawis and Sunnis in Syria have sharpened dangerously since the beginning of the 2011 uprising. The primary reason for the tensions is political rather than religious: Alawi officers hold top positions in Assad's army, while most of the rebels from the Free Syrian

[46] Costas M. Constantinou, 'Revising the Treaty of Guarantee for a Cyprus Settlement', Research Gate, June 21, 2017, https://www.researchgate.net/publication/320465293_Revising_the_Treaty_of_Guarantee_for_a_Cyprus_Settlement.

[47] Mark Galeotti, 'Putin in Playing a Dangerous Game in Syria', *The Atlantic*, February 15, 2018, https://www.theatlantic.com/international/archive/2018/02/the-costs-of-russian-intervention-in-syria-are-rising/553367/.

[48] Joby Warrick (20 December 2012), 'Syrian Conflict's Sectarian, Ethnic Dimensions Growing, U.N. Warns', *The Washington Post*. Retrieved 21 December 2012.

Army and other opposition groups belong to Syria's Sunni majority. Despite Bashar Assad's overt effort to increase his proximity to the Sunnis he has not been able to combat the relentless antagonism of their backers from the Gulf states, particularly Saudi Arabia, Oman, UAE and Turkey. It has ended up defining the root cause of the prolonged conflict.

Hafez al-Assad (1971–2000), had reserved top positions in the military and intelligence services for the people he most trusted: Alawi officers from his native area. The fact that historically the Alawis were the poorest and most discriminated community in Syrian society was a major binding force. However, Hafez Assad also drew the support of powerful Sunni business families, particularly from Aleppo. At one point in time, Sunnis did constitute the majority of the ruling Ba'ath Party and rank-and-file army and held high government positions.[49] Nevertheless, over time, the increase in the Alawi hold on the security apparatus and privileged access to state power generated Sunni resentment, particularly the religious fundamentalists who provided the fodder for the growing number of radical opposition groups.

Even among the Alawi there were dissidents critical of the Assad family. Yet most stayed with Bashar Assad either out of loyalty to the Assad family or fear that an elected government, inevitably dominated by the Sunni majority, would take revenge for the abuse of power by Alawi when in power. Thus while the Alawi veered towards the feared pro-Assad militias, known as the Shabiha, or the National Defense Forces and other groups, the Sunnis joined opposition groups such as Jabhat Fatah al-Sham, Ahrar al-Sham, and other factions.

It is this long-standing and pervasive animosity that needs to be defused starting with constitutional guarantees for the majority community. It would equally need to include guarantees for all minority communities in Syria as well as grant of constitutional protection for the Alawi minority. 'Islam's schism, simmering for fourteen centuries, doesn't explain all the political, economic, and geostrategic factors involved in these conflicts, but it has become one prism through which to understand the underlying tensions. Two countries that compete for the leadership of Islam, Sunni Saudi Arabia and Shia Iran, have used the sectarian divide to further their ambitions. How their rivalry is settled will likely shape the

[49] Premoz Manfreda, 'The Difference Between Alawites and Sunnis in Syria', ThoughtCo, June 21, 2018, https://www.thoughtco.com/the-difference-between-alawites-and-sunnis-in-syria-2353572.

political balance between Sunnis and Shias and the future of the region, especially in Syria, Iraq, Lebanon, Bahrain, and Yemen'.[50]

The time has come for the Organization of Islamic Cooperation and Islamic nations to unite to end the Syrian conflict. Given the sectarian underpinning of the long civil war, the OIC remains the only international organization in a position to tackle the roots of the internecine sectarian struggle within Islam. This effort has to go in parallel with the negotiations on bringing in a durable ceasefire leading to an acceptable political structure. Its absence will prolong the two proxy wars raging in Syria: the sectarian between Saudi Arabia and Iran and the great power between the United States and Russia.

At the same time, at the ground level, innovative and non-conflictual solutions need to be put in place that will assure to all Syrians adequate health, education, safety and other services regardless of their sect or religion. In this respect, a census of all Syrians that will mention their religion and sect will be crucial. It could generate for an individual a bar-coded identity card available to government agencies responsible for distributing subsidies and other constitutionally legislated benefits.

Economic Structure and Rebuilding of Infrastructure

Before the civil war, the two main pillars of the Syrian economy were agriculture and oil, which together accounted for about half the GDP. Agriculture, for instance, accounted for about 26% of GDP and employed 25% of the total labour force. However, poor climatic conditions and severe drought badly affected the agricultural sector, thus reducing its share in the economy to about 17% of GDP in 2008 down from 20.4% in 2007, according to data from the Central Bureau of Statistics. On the other hand, higher crude oil prices countered declining oil production, led to higher budgetary and export receipts.

The sanctions, destruction and dislocation associated with the civil war have devastated Syria's economy. By the end of 2013, the UN estimated total economic damage of the Syrian civil war at $143 billion. The total economic loss from the conflict reached $237 billion by the

[50] The Council on Foreign Relations, 'The Sunni-Shi'a Divide', November 6, 2017, https://www.cfr.org/interactives/sunni-shia-divide#!/.

end of 2015, according to the United Nations Economic and Social Commission for Western Asia, with the Syrian opposition's capture of the Nasib border crossing costing the government additionally a further $500–$700 million a year. In 2018, the World Bank estimated that about one-third of Syria's housing stock and one half of its health and education facilities had been destroyed by the conflict. According to the World Bank, a cumulative total of $226 billion in GDP was lost due to the conflict from 2011 to 2016.[51]

The social and economic impacts of the conflict are also large and growing. The lack of sustained access to health care, education, housing, and food have exacerbated the impact of the conflict and pushed millions of people into unemployment and poverty. In addition, a severe decline in oil receipts and disruptions of trade has placed even more pressure on Syria's external balances, resulting in the rapid depletion of its international reserves.[52]

The larger aim of post-conflict reconstruction must foster 'in place institutions, norms, and practices that address the causes of violence and provide a basis for effective governance and sustainable peace'.[53] Economic governance in pre-war Syria was perverse in that corrupt, predatory, crony capitalism had a field day with low accountability and transparency and a weak rule of law. Regime survival trumped concerns with economic and social development and continues even as Assad is poised to take full control of the country. The Syrian government, in a victorious mode, is advancing its own 'tried' conception of how to rebuild Syria's political economy. Under the circumstances, economic reconstruction will have to form part of the larger discussion to set agreed principles on which the Assad government will handle economic reconstruction.

[51] Raja Abdulrahman and Nazif Osserian, 'Reviving Syria's Economy Is an Uphill Battle for Assad After Years of War', *The Wall Street Journal*, January 31, 2020, https://www.wsj.com/articles/reviving-syrias-economy-is-an-uphill-battle-for-assad-after-years-of-war-11580497279.

[52] The World Bank, 'The World Bank in Syrian Arab Republic', October 11, 2018, https://www.worldbank.org/en/country/syria/overview.

[53] Stevan Heydemann, Smith College and The Brookings Institution, 'Reconstructing Authoritarianism: The Politics and Political Economy of Post-Conflict Reconstruction on Syria', POMEPS Studies 30 "Politics of Post-Conflict Resolution", https://pomeps.org/2018/09/10/reconstructing-authoritarianism-the-politics-and-political-economy-of-post-conflict-reconstruction-in-syria/.

The restoration of the Syrian economy will have to start with refurbishing its oil and gas sector and phosphatic fertilizer production. It will help to recommence the revenue stream for the massive expenditures expected. The reconstruction of major trunk roads and oil pipelines will have to go hand-in-hand. It could catalyze Syria's economic engagement with the region and the outside world.

The elimination of crony capitalism presents major difficulties stemming from the massive support that Bashar al-Assad has received from the handful of families who have ruled the economic roost. Even as Assad is consolidating his hold on the country there is information that in the building of new townships in and near Damascus the same group of capitalists have secured monopoly power. Under Decree No.66, properties in major cities have been appropriated and handed over to the favoured few for reconstruction of massive housing estates with all manner of amenities while the likely beneficiaries have been restricted.[54]

The need to widen economic opportunity is an essential ingredient since by promoting small scale industry democratic governance will gain firmer root. In particular, the government has to restrict certain areas for operation only by small-scale like local, citywide and inter-city bus transport.

The setting up of an economic advisory council is a priority to decide the economic growth and taxation plan for the country to promote industrial and agricultural growth. The need to exempt, for ten years, the agricultural sector from income tax and a system of incentives and subsidies for agriculture inputs will help to revive agriculture.

Reconstruction will require massive foreign funding, and possibly the first beneficiaries will be Iran, Russia and China that have most supported Bashar al-Assad regime. In February 2017, the Syrian Minister of Economy, Adib Mayaleh, declared that companies from Iran and other allied countries would be rewarded while European and American companies will first need to have their governments apologize before benefitting. Following the recapture of Eastern Aleppo, Aleppo, Governor Hossein Diyab also stressed that Iran was going to 'play an important role in reconstruction efforts in Syria, especially Aleppo'. The Iranian Reconstruction Authority publicized in March 2017 its renovation of 55

[54] Joseph Daher, 'Militia and Crony Capitalism to Hamper Syrian Reconstruction', Open Democracy NAWA, September 5, 2017, https://www.opendemocracy.net/north-africa-west-asia/joseph-daher/militias-and-crony-capitalism-to-hamper-syria-reconstruction.

schools across the Aleppo province. Iran also had the largest presence at the 2017 International Trade Fair in Damascus. In October 2015, a Russian delegation visiting Damascus announced that Russian companies would lead Syria's postwar reconstruction. Deals worth at least €850 m emerged from these negotiations. A Russian parliamentary visit to Syria in November 2016 resulted in Syrian Foreign Minister Walid Muallem reportedly offering Russia firms priority in rebuilding Syria.

The Chinese government, in early August 2017, hosted the 'First Trade Fair on Syrian Reconstruction Projects', during which a Chinese-Arab business group announced a $2 billion commitment from the government for the construction of industrial parks in Syria. China has demonstrated that its search for primary materials led it to being the first to move into mining a still-disturbed Afghanistan. Its credentials established by continuous support to Syria in the UNSC makes their entry into the country's oil and gas sector inevitable.

The other issues that will hamper Syria's economic resurgence, apart from the need to reduce the power of the crony capitalists, are the malign role of the paramilitary organization in the country. The illegal fees extracted by them at the checkpoints on all roads have become a negative feature of the economic sector. Despite official statements that this would be stopped progress on the ground is limited.[55]

Conclusion

The Syrian conflict, by comparison, is much more difficult to resolve, because 'Syria is partitioned by foreign powers, there are a lot of them, they're all pretty powerful, and many of them have a border with Syria', Itani said. (Syria borders five countries, Lebanon just two.) Compounding the challenge is that these foreign powers have staked out irreconcilable positions. Iran and Israel do not want the same thing in Syria, while Turkey cannot accept a [Kurdish]-run statelet on its border. If the United States stays on in Syria to keep ISIS out the end point is difficult to visualize. On the other hand, Trump could declare victory over the ISIS and withdraw US troops. If he holds to his commitment to push back against the Iran it will lend yet another complication to the Syrian conflict. Bashar

[55] Joesph Daher, ibid.

Assad has still to recover all his country and the grounds for a settlement are becoming tenuous.

'I can't think of a historical parallel, in the Middle East at least, with so many powerful external actors directly involved', said Phillips. Going forward, 'I would expect more conflict but [fewer] question marks about who's going to rule in Syria'. In his view, the answer is clearly trending in the direction of Russia and Iran, which have made the biggest investments in the war.[56] The Syrian conflict could go on for a very long time if the cycle is not broken.

The fate of Syria is no longer for Syria to decide. Its reunification or partition will largely depend on the regional and international consensus that emerges after the war and the decisions of the foreign powers that have intervened there. At the same time, with its near-control of the country's entire territory the Assad government now speaks as a victor. Thus, the tragedy is that there appears no incentive to change the systems that have proved useful in the difficult years of the conflict.

The Assad family and its government, and Syria itself, is caught in a double-edged dilemma. Only changes in the political, economic and social organisation of the country, howsoever incremental, will assure that the civil war does not re-ignite, yet the very fact of these changes would reduce the longevity of the Assad clan. After the end of military operations by all parties, at least for a decade, a situation where Assad remains in power, but with a restriction on presidential autonomy, will alone foster a process towards making Syria a more open and democratic state and in preserving its system of secular governance.

[56] Uri Friedman, 'Syria's War Has Never Been More International', *The Atlantic*, February 14, 2018, https://www.theatlantic.com/international/archive/2018/02/syria-civil-war-next/553232/.

Epilogue

Syria: The Tragedy of a Pivotal State

As it begins its tenth inconclusive year, the future of Syria has acquired a chimeral quality. No sooner had Bashar Assad gained confidence following his wresting the bulk of Syria from his adversaries, new factors, both external and internal, have projected an impression of impermanence. The cumulative effect of these factors could see a second incarnation of the Syrian conflict centred in the northwest of the country. Apart from Turkey which already is in military control of a part of Idlib and Afrin, it could provoke the entry of Saudi Arabia, UAE, France, and possibly, NATO and eventually the United States.

Idlib's strategic importance comes from its borders with Turkey to the north straddling as it does the highways running south from the city of Aleppo to the capital Damascus, and west to the Mediterranean city of Latakia. A long-standing bastion of opposition, Idlib has invited an attack by the Syrian army since 2015 when it came under the control of the extremist groups. The danger multiplied with the province became a dumping ground for militant groups ousted from other provinces as they fell to government forces. Turkey in vain gathered the various groups under the umbrella of the Syrian National Army (SNA) to bring them into the Astana process. In May 2018 factions outside the SNA formed a coalition, the National Liberation Front (NLF); together the SNA & NLF included 44 different factions.

R. M. Abhyankar, *Syria*,
https://doi.org/10.1007/978-981-15-4562-7

Yet the Hayat Tahrir al-Sham (HTS), formerly affiliated with Al-Qaeda and on UNSC's terrorist list, remained outside and continued to garner support of the other factions. A UN committee estimated in January 2020 that the group had between 12,000 and 15,000 fighters in Idlib and surrounding areas. In its military action against the government offensive HTS is supported by a variety of forces—including Chinese Uighur militants, a new al-Qaeda affiliate and the Turkey-backed SNA. By skilful public diplomacy it has facilitated Turkey's hold over opposition-held areas in northwestern Syria. While HTS remains averse to Turkey-backed groups gaining clout in Idlib, not the least because of Russian insistence that Turkey, in line with Sochi agreement, neutralize and isolate the HTS.

Syria and Russia determined to recapture Idlib and bring the Syrian war to a close, have waged a relentless and brutal offensive since May 2019 that has included hospitals and other civilian facilities.[1] The military action, in the main, has concentrated around the M-4 and M-5 highways linking Lattakia to Aleppo destroying towns like Saraqeb, at the junction of the two strategic highways, and others like Maarat al-Numan and Ariha. Both Ankara and Moscow expect the ceasefire announced by the March 5, 2020 agreement to hold longer. The agreement tamped down a conflict that had pushed the two countries to the brink of open war. 'The agreement included joint patrols by Russian and Turkish troops of a seven-mile wide corridor along a highway that runs through Idlib eastward from the Mediterranean coast toward the border with Iraq'.[2]

Idlib has seen intense fighting recently as the Russian-backed forces of Syria's president, Bashar al-Assad, have moved to expel the last rebels. In late February 2020, the fighting killed at least 34 Turkish soldiers sending hundreds of thousands of Syrian refugees fleeing towards the closed border with Turkey. For Bashar Assad, the long-running battle to secure Idlib has become a nuisance keeping him from claiming back the entire country. At the same time, he has to fall in line with President Putin's effort to keep the conflict over Idlib in check lest it involves

[1] Kareem Faheem, 'How This Closing Chapter of Syria's War Has Become Its Most Brutal', *The Washington Post*, 25 March 2020, https://www.washingtonpost.com/world/middle_east/how-this-closing-chapter-of-syrias-war-has-become-its-most-brutal/2020/03/24/250d4f5c-573e-11ea-8efd-0f904bdd8057_story.html.

[2] Andrew Higgins, 'Putin and Erdogan Reach Accord to Halt Fighting in Syria', *The New York Times*, 5 March 2020, https://www.nytimes.com/2020/03/05/world/europe/putin-erdogan-syria.

Russia with a NATO member and defeats his goal of using Turkey to break the organization. The third factor that Putin has to cater for is the growing domestic pressure to end the country's involvement in Syria. Even for Iran, with the pressure for US sanctions exacerbating the country's economic position, domestic lobbies are increasingly calling for reducing the Syrian commitment. The Iranian leadership has been miffed at not being involved by Russia in the battle for Idlib or in its agreements with Turkey. The possibility of Iran acting a spoiler cannot be excluded.

In spite of understandings between Turkey and Russia the situation remains unstable providing de facto legitimacy to Turkey's military presence in Idlib in utter disregard of cardinal UN principles of non-interference and sovereign equality. Yet it remains an open question whether and how Turkey, in accordance with its Sochi commitment, will get the armed groups in Idlib to toe the line.[3] The Russian-Turkish agreement of March 5, 2020, temporarily froze the conflict, without formalizing a Turkish buffer zone within Syria. Nevertheless, Russia has acquiesced to increased Turkish military presence in the province. The agreement gave Turkey more time to engage the West in seeking a solution for Idlib.[4] Yet, it allowed the Syrian forces to continue holding the areas re-captured in northwestern Syria to withdraw to the lines established by the September 2018 Sochi Agreement. In accepting the territorial gains made by Russian-backed government forces and allied militias it indicated that the goal of taking Idlib remains.

Nearly three million Syrians live in the province, a million of whom have been repeatedly displaced. Government air strikes and ground operations have driven almost a million civilians from their homes since December 2019—the biggest single displacement in Syria's nine-year war. They are again looking at the prospect of fleeing to Turkey or beyond. Syria, for its part, remains ambivalent about taking the population of the province whom it sees as hostile, neither do the people of Idlib want to move to territories under government control.[5] Syria would rather keep

[3] Fehim Tastekin, 'Turkey Plays Extra Time in Idlib Game with New "Army" Plan', Al-Monitor, 17 April 2020, https://www.al-monitor.com/pulse/originals/2020/04/turkey-syria-russia-idlib-new-army-plan-cleanse-jihadis-hts.html.

[4] Galip Dalay, 'How Long Will the Turkish-Russian deal on Idlib Last?', Al Jazeera, 16 March 2020, https://www.aljazeera.com/indepth/opinion/long-turkish-russian-deal-idlib-200316135110613.html.

[5] Ibid.

the strategic infrastructure in Idlib while pushing its population to Turkey or Europe.

Turkey, despite the acquisition of Russian's-400 system, has used the lull in the fighting to seek US Patriot air defence system through NATO to strengthen its position vis-a-vis Russia. There is no hope of a positive response from the United States. Neither has Turkey received support from the European Union. While the ceasefire of March 5, 2020 is still holds, there is an overall stalemate with Syria, Russia and Turkey holding strong suits that would make an all-out offensive by the Syrian Army and Russia a costly enterprise in material and human terms.[6] The Idlib stalemate is marked by:

1. Differences in the opposing positions on Idlib's future between Turkey and Russia. Turkey seeks to keep the Syrian regime out of Idlib pending a comprehensive political settlement of the Syrian conflict unmindful of the UN principles of non-interference and absence of any justification to exercise the right of self-defence. Russia supports Damascus in its objective of reclaiming all the country's territory—through negotiated deals if possible, or by force if the regime deems it necessary.
2. Hyat Tahrir al-Sham (HTS), the jihadist group that dominates the area, is neither covered by the existing ceasefire nor has it been reined in and eliminated by Turkey. Despite its obligation to do so, Ankara may have concluded that HTS is too strong locally to be eradicated militarily and to garner time to strengthen its forces in Idlib. Also by keeping HTS in place Turkey expects to forestall a Syrian offensive.
3. Russia's military superiority over the rebels gives the Syrian army the kind of military support it would need to press for total victory. Yet military action would significantly worsen the humanitarian crisis, and could paradoxically trigger even greater Turkish involvement. Turkey has already deployed advanced drones and surface-to-air missiles qualitatively enhancing its presence in Idlib.
4. The additional threat that COVID-19 poses to Idlib's over three million inhabitants, and in particular, to the tens of thousands of

[6] ICG, 'Silencing the Guns in Syria's Idlib', International Crisis Group, Report No. 213/Middle East & North Africa, 14 May 2020, https://www.crisisgroup.org/middle-east-north-africa/eastern-mediterranean/syria/213-silencing-guns-syrias-idlib.

> displaced civilians living in makeshift camps, underlines the urgency for all parties to achieve a coordinated international humanitarian response.

The Idlib situation does not augur well for the Syrian government. From what started as an offensive to take back the last outpost not under the government control, the situation has evolved with Turkey's entry as a belligerent and put pressure on Russia to continue its military support for the government. Neither side appears to be in a position to take decisive action. Decisive military onslaught by the Syrian Army backed by sophisticated Russian military assets could lead to final victory but mean direct conflict between Russia and Turkey. It would equally exacerbate the already monumental humanitarian crisis facing the country; on the other hand, decisive Turkish military action opens the possibility of Syria's de facto loss of its province of Idlib.

In either case, the continuing political uncertainty will rekindle efforts by the radical Islamic groups against Bashar Assad, re-introduce other international players and delay introduction of the political, constitutional and social reforms to initiate the process towards a secular, inclusive and democratic Syria.

On June 17, 2020, the most wide-ranging US sanctions ever applied against Syria went into effect expected to put Bashar Assad under pressure to show demonstrable progress towards achieving the goals of UN Security Council Resolution 2254. The US Caesar Syria Civilian Protection Act, passed into law as part of the most recent US National Defense Authorization Act,[7] dramatically expands the authority of the US government to sanction businesses, individuals and government institutions for economic activities that support the Assad regime's ability to wage war. It would restrict the ability of the Syria government to use Lebanon's economy for its purpose and restrict the ability of Gulf regimes like the UAE that have taken steps to normalize relations. The Act leaves the future of Bashar Assad open in deference to Russian interests. Expectedly, the Act has been criticized by the Syrian government as infringing its sovereignty. Nevertheless, it would have served a useful purpose if the Act provokes greater adherence to UNSCR 2254 particularly in regard to

[7] Steven Heydeman, 'The Ceasar Act and a Pathway out of conflict in Syria', Brookings Institution, 19 June 2020, https://www.brookings.edu/blog/order-from-chaos/2020/06/19/the-caesar-act-and-a-pathway-out-of-conflict-in-syria/.

a durable ceasefire and the provision of desperately needed humanitarian assistance to the population.

Absent progress towards attaining goals of UNSCR 2254 the country could well face a Gaza-like situation in northwestern Syria. A 'no man's land' in Syria, comprising over a 1000 sq.km strip bordering Turkey, controlled by HTS and other the terrorist groups with more than half a million Syrians in the small pocket bringing together refugees and radical groups not wanted by either Turkey or Syria.[8] The Caesar Act could well debilitate the Syrian government and reverse the gains so far.

An inability of the Syrian government to settle the situation in northeast Syria would become a festering sore in Syria's body politic and equally prove a running sore for Turkey. The best option would appear to be a durable ceasefire to avoid a massive humanitarian catastrophe by adhering to UNSCR 2254 and curtail associated political costs that would follow an all-out assault on Idlib.

[8] Fabrice Balanche, 'Idlib May Become the Next Gaza Strip', The Washington Institute for Near East Policy, POLICYWATCH 3288, 26 March 2020, https://www.washingtoninstitute.org/policy-analysis/view/idlib-may-become-the-next-gaza-strip.

Appendices

Appendix A

Zaatari Refugee Camp Visit
Zaatari, near Amman, Jordan
Interviews
29 June 2017
NB: *Translation of interviews from Arabic to English*

Interview #1
Name: Mr. Adel Toukan and his wife

Q1: Where are you from in Syria?
A: Daraa (Dara'a, Deraa, Dera'a) part of historically ancient Houran Region South of Syria.

Q2: When did you came to Zaatari?
A: Since 2013 with family including wife and two kids.

Q3: What are the reasons that made you decide to leave becoming refugee?
A: Different reasons are

R. M. Abhyankar, *Syria*,
https://doi.org/10.1007/978-981-15-4562-7

1. Fear from being arrested by the regime or other fighting parties. The situation was big mess that arrests where arbitrary and no neutral investigation guaranteed.
2. Fear from being forced to serve in fight/military operations by either party
3. Fear of fate of his wife and the two kids in case he's been taken away or themselves being injured by war.
4. His wife added that women were very much worried of being raped in light of all mess surrounding and absence of law.

Q4: What is your date of marriage, How many kids you had at the time of leaving Syria as refugees for Jordan?
A: Marriage in 2009. The crisis started Mar. 2011 and at the time of leaving they had two kids.

Q5: Currently how many kids do you have?
A: Now 4 kids, 2 kids were born in the camp in the period 2013-2017 (total 2 boys 2 girls).

Q6: What were your future dreams before the crisis?
A: We shared our parents' house and planned to have our own new home where we would enjoy independence and privacy plus offering our kids better place to grow. In addition we were dreaming of growing financially which would facilitate other projects assure a better future for our kids and us as well.

Q7: What are your dreams for future after being refugees at Camp in light of surrounding conditions?
A: Current situation led to a desperate feeling of no hope of the future. They find going back home is becoming impossible through feedback received either from Media or by relatives still in Syria. On the one hand the Media confirms that it is unsafe there while the feedback from the people who remained in Syria is that Media is exaggerating and the big

problem is lack of food and weak economic conditions. Neither feedback was encouraging us to go back home.

Q8: How, in your opinion, is the Syria crisis could be resolved? And what things required to achieve peace again?
A: In his opinion, and references to several incidents he himself lived, the revolution against the regime is based on lies and a fabricated scenario which was adopted by media and spread over the world. He mentioned some incidents where children were brought dyed with red paints and taped like victims of regime. He sees that Syria should not be divided and all external parties have to stop interfering with Syrian business.

Q9: What was your work before leaving Syria?
A: Technician of furniture like bedroom, sitting rooms and others.

Q10: Where you were working before leaving for the Zaatari Camp?
A: I was working in Beirut in the same field (Furniture Technical) for 7 years.

Q11: Why did you choose to refuge in Jordan rather than Lebanon having been working there for long period?
A: I was not sure how far Syrians will be welcomed by people in Lebanon in light of latest events including PM Hariri assassination which led to anger toward Syrian people by considerable part of Lebanese community and gave opportunity to raise hatre speech against Syrians.

Q12: You said you were sharing parents' house, so where are your parents now?
A: They left to Lebanon as Father already had work there with residence permit hence my Mother joined my Father and they are now settled there.

Q13: Currently, What are working?
A: Inside the camp, as furniture technician with one of NGOs (IRC: International Rescue Committee).

Q14: Are refugees allowed to work out the camp?

A: Yes, through permissions either on monthly or yearly basis.

Q15: Why you don't go and work out of the camp for better opportunities?
A: I preferred to work inside camp as it is near my wife and kids. I am available the time they need me. In addition, here I don't have to rent a place where additional cost required while here we have free water and electricity.

Interview #2
We entered into mini market (small Grocery shop) and met the responsible person there, who appeared in late sixties or first of seventies. Also his wife was there through the interview with his sons. He refused to give his name being worried that he might be followed late in the future by authorities in his country.

Q01: Where are you from in Syria?
A: Countryside of Damascus (Eastern Ghouta).

Q02: When did you come to Zaatari?
A: On 12 Nov. 2013 with his wife and daughter leaving rest 4 sons who joined them later after he sent them money required for securing transfer to Jordan.

Q03: What are reasons made you decide to leave being refugee?
A: Different reasons as follows:

1. Direct reason was following killing his son (20 years) by one military plane attack.
2. Fear of being arrested by the regime or other fighting groups. The situation was big mess, arbitrary arrests and no neutral investigation guaranteed. As he's old man the major concern was arrest of his young sons.
3. Fear of being forced to serve in fight/military operations by either party.
4. Fear regarding the fate of his wife and daughter especially with incidences of rape.

Q04: What were your future dreams before crisis?
A: Were dreaming of bright future for sons and the only daughter in terms of education and work. Plus working to increase their family business in farming.

Q05: What are your dreams for future after being refugees at Camp in light all surrounding conditions?
A: Mostly depressed yet looking forward for the day of going back home when peace is achieved and crisis is eliminated. For the time being they suffer the "unknown" state which prevails as nothing is certain in political situation so far. Till the day of crisis being resolved they're living day-to-day.

Q06: How, in your opinion, the Syria crisis could be resolved? And what things are required to achieve peace again?
A: Political solution and not military one will work. Compromises by different parties are a must. Also, only Syrian people to decide and all external powers to move out of Syria. Leave Syria for Syrians. In conclusion, it needs a "miracle" by God.

Q07: What was your work before leaving Syria?
A: Farming at family owned business (about 25 donum/ 25000KM2) growing fruits, vegetables and winter crops plus raising cows in Eastern Ghouta (Harran Al-awameed).

Q08: Currently, what are you working?
A: Inside the camp, I invested all the money I brought with me in this small grocery shop (minimarket) which is owned by me.

Q09: Are refugees allowed to work out the camp?
A: Yes, through permissions either monthly or yearly basis.

Q10: Why you didn't decide to invest your money out of the camp where better opportunities might be available?

A: I preferred to be near my family wife, sons and daughter all the time plus other facilities provided for free like water, electricity and residence.

Q11: what are your sons working at currently?
A: Not working, just sometimes helping at the shop. Before in Syria we were all sharing the farming work, we are farmers.

Q12: Did you think of immigration?
A: No! I will be waiting here till the crisis resolved and get back home.

Q13: What about your sons, who are young men, don't they think of immigration or at least working out of the camp?
A: No. I am against this idea. I want the family to stay together as we always used to be in our home. Being distracted is not acceptable to me. [At that point, his sons confirmed that they will not do anything against their father's desire].

Appendix B: Timelines—How Different Interest Groups Participated in the Syrian Crisis (2011–2014)*

2011: Syria time lines

Month	*Syrian government*	*Opposition forces/rebels*	*US, UK, Europe*	*Middle East*	*International organizations*	*Russia*
January						
February						
March 11/3	The security forces shot dead protesters in Dera'a who were demanding the release of political prisoners (teenagers arrested for anti-regime graffiti). This triggered nationwide animosity at the regime's atrocities President Assad announces conciliatory measures, releasing political prisoners, dismissing the government and lifting the 48-year old state of emergency Faisal Kalthoum the governor of Dera'a is sacked by Assad The government resigns In his first speech since the protest Assad blames foreign conspirators for the unrest but declines to elaborate on major reforms					
April 11/4	Assad appoints a new cabinet. Adel Safar is prime minister in the new government Security forces raid a sit-in protest in Homs		The US imposes new sanctions on Syria's intelligence agency and two relatives of Assad			

(continued)

(continued)

2011: Syria time lines

Month	*Syrian government*	*Opposition forces/rebels*	*US, UK, Europe*	*Middle East*	*International organizations*	*Russia*
	More than 221 are missing following the government crackdown of protesters in Damascus, Aleppo, Deraa and Homs Syrian troops backed by tanks begin and 11-day siege of Dera'a Assad tries to win support among the Kurds by restoring citizenship to up to 300,000 stateless Kurds					
May 11/5	The Army enters Dera'a, Banyas, Homs and the suburbs of Damascus to crush the anti-regime protests	The opposition calls for nationwide strike—call ignored by the people of Damascus and Aleppo	The US and Europe tighten the sanctions			
June 11/6	The police and soldiers in Jisr al-Shughour in the north-eastern Syria join protesters they were ordered to shoot	The Uprising takes control of the town However within a few days the government retakes the town	Britain, France, Germany and Portugal circulated in the UNSC a draft resolution that would condemn the crackdown and demand an immediate end to the violence	Turkey's prime minister Erdogon condemns Syria's crackdown on anti-government protesters and indicates Ankara could support a UN resolution against Damascus Erdogan presses al-Assad—a personal friend—to initiate reform but did not stress his departure	The IAEA Nuclear watch dog reports on Syria to the UNSC over its covert nuclear reactor program The structure housing the alleged reactor was destroyed in an Israeli air raid in 2007 European powers increase pressure on the UNSC to break silence on events in Syria	

(continued)

(continued)

2011: Syria time lines

Month	*Syrian government*	*Opposition forces/rebels*	*US, UK, Europe*	*Middle East*	*International organizations*	*Russia*
				Many Syrian refugees cross over to Turkey and Turkey host Syrian refugees in tents at the border. More than 3000 Syrians have fled to Turkey		
July 11/7	President Assad removes the governor of the northern province of Hama following mass demonstrations. Army troops are sent in to restore order, many are killed in this process The government adopts a draft law authorising the creation of political parties alongside the ruling Baath party	Following the crackdown by the Syrian Government, the opposition becomes more organized and militarized Military defectors establish the Free Syrian Army (FSA) The main opposition groups boycott talks with the government and say they will not negotiate till Assad stops the violent crackdown and frees the political prisoners	The US secretary of State Hillary Clinton declares that Assad has lost legitimacy	Qatar closes its embassy in Syria		
August 11/8			President Barack Obama and the European Union call on Assad to resign and orders the freezing of Syrian government assets	Turkey and the Arab League condemn the attack—Syrian government's crackdown on protesters Arab foreign ministers meeting in Cairo urges the Syrian government to restore peace and order		

(continued)

(continued)

2011: Syria time lines

Month	*Syrian government*	*Opposition forces/rebels*	*US, UK, Europe*	*Middle East*	*International organizations*	*Russia*
				A group of 'revolutionary blocs' announces the formation of a coalition called the Syrian Revolution General Commission Saudi, Kuwait and Bahrain recall their Ambassadors from Syria		
September 11/9	Syria accuses the US of inciting violence against its security forces and assures will confront their attempts to interfere in its domestic affairs	A group of Syrian activists form a Syrian National Council (SNC) in Istanbul, Turkey, representing a united front in opposition to the Syrian government				
October 11/10	Assad warns against western intervention in Syria	The SNC forges alliance with internal and exiled opposition activist Syrian opposition groups meet in Istanbul and reject foreign intervention urges international action to stop the indiscriminate killings of civilians by the authorities		Many residents flee to neighbouring Jordan to escape the unrest, some crossing legally at Al-Ramtha border crossing while others entering illegally. The authorities have detailed the illegal refugees but not sent them back to Syria	The UNSC condemns the widespread violations of Human rights and use of force against the civilians by the Syrian authorities	Russia and China Veto a resolution threatening sanctions, Veto a European-drafted UN Security Council resolution condemning Syria Russian President Dmitry Medvedev says Syria's leaders should step down if they cannot enact reforms, but warns the West not to oust President Assad from power

(continued)

(continued)

2011: Syria time lines

Month	*Syrian government*	*Opposition forces/rebels*	*US, UK, Europe*	*Middle East*	*International organizations*	*Russia*
November 11/11	Syrian officials do no participate in the dialogue initiated by the Arab League	The FSA launches high profile attack on the military base near Damascus The Muslim Brotherhood in Egypt hinted a preference of Turkey's intervention over western intervention	France calls for western military intervention in Syria The US and the European Union have imposed major sanctions, including an oil embargo, on the Syrian leadership US and Germany calls for the UN Security Council to finally take 'decisive action' against Syria's atrocities	The Arab League votes to suspend Syria, accuses it of failing to implement the Arab Peace Pan and imposes sanctions Lebanon not willing to impose economic sanctions on Syria	Arab and European countries circulate UNSC resolution condemning rights violations A draft resolution, circulated by European countries to the General Assembly's human rights committee was backed by Saudi Arabia, Qatar, Jordan, and Morocco. It gave Assad's Government three days to halt the violence, that the UN estimates has killed more than 3500 people, and accept an observer mission UN investigators release a new report accusing senior Syrian government officials and leaders of the country's military and security forces of ordering mass atrocities in efforts to crush anti-government protests since March UN General Assembly's Human Rights Committee condemns Syria for the crackdown, with 122 votes in favour, 13 against and 41 absentions	Russia continues to arm the regime Russia and China veto the resolution, while Brazil, India, South Africa and Lebanon abstained

(continued)

(continued)

2011: Syria time lines

Month	*Syrian government*	*Opposition forces/rebels*	*US, UK, Europe*	*Middle East*	*International organizations*	*Russia*
					NATO Secretary-General Anders Fogh Rasmussen rules out the possibility of military intervention in Syria	
December 11/12	Syria says it has conditionally approved an Arab League peace plan. Syria rejects foreign interference and demands the annulment of sanctions plus reinstatement in the regional bloc		US officials indicate the involvement of al-Qaeda following the bomb blast in Damascus	An Arab league observer mission enters Syria Iraq sends a delegation to the meet the officials and discuss the 'Iraqi Initiative' to end the Syrian crisis and convince the Syrian government and the opposition to meet in Iraq and discuss Jordon backs out of the embargo against Syria		Russia and China submit a draft resolution to the UNSC

2012: Syria

Month	*Syrian government*	*Opposition forces/rebels; external—militant outfits*	*US, UK, Europe*	*Middle East and Israel*	*International organizations*	*Russia*
January 12/1		A new rebel faction al-Qaeda affiliated to 'al-Nusra front' is formed. Since then it has been described as 'one of the most effective rebel forces' in Syria. The group has been designated as a terrorist organisation by the UN, US, UK, Australia and Turkey Fierce fighting escalates between the Free Syrian Army and government troops in the suburb of Damascus		The Arab league mission withdraws, citing increasing violence European and Arab nations have pressed for UNSC backing for an Arab League plan calling on Bashar al-Assad, Syria's president, to stand down		
February 12/2	Hundreds of casualties reported in a major assault by government forces on Homs' Khalidiyah district Syria holds referendum on a new constitution, a gesture by Assad to placate the opposition. If passed, it would restrict the president to serving a maximum of two terms of seven years and introduce a pluralistic party system. The West dismisses the vote as a sham	The FSA and the Government contend for control in Homs, Damascus and other major cities	'Group of Friends of Syrian People'—an amalgamation of more than 60 countries including France, Britain, Saudi Arabia, Turkey and the US proclaim the SNC a legitimate representative of Syrian people The United States strongly back the call by the Arab League and Qatar for 'rapid and decisive' action	Arab League urges the UNSC to adopt a clear resolution to support the league's efforts in ending the 11-month-old conflict in Syria. They oppose foreign military intervention to achieve the objective	The UNGA votes 137-12 for Assad to resign Former UN Secretary General Kofi Annan appointed the UN-Arab League Special Envoy to Syria	Thirteen countries vote for the resolution proposed by European and Arab nations to give strong backing to the Arab League's plan to end the violence in Syria, Russia and China veto a resolution in the UN Security Council

(continued)

(continued)

2012: Syria

Month	*Syrian government*	*Opposition forces/rebels; external—militant outfits*	*US, UK, Europe*	*Middle East and Israel*	*International organizations*	*Russia*
	The government is pushing ahead, trying to firm-up its control all over the country, particularly in the rebellious areas, like Homs, Deraa and the suburbs of Damascus		EU announces new sanctions The United States vows to block funding and arms supplies to Syria after Russia and China veto UN resolution condemning the government's crackdown on dissent US pulls out diplomats and UK recalls its Ambassador from Damascus	In its current form, the resolution calls on Assad to halt the government crackdown on protests and implement an Arab League peace plan calling for him to hand over power to his deputy. If Assad fails to comply within 15 days, the council would consider 'further measures', a reference to a possible move to impose economic or other sanctions Iranian warships cross the Suez Canal and dock in Syria's port of Tartous		
March 12/3	Syrian troops take control of shattered Bab Amr in Homs after a government assault that raged for weeks	The main opposition group, the SNC, forms a military council to organise and unify all armed resistance The FSA fighters are regrouping in northern Lebanon to plan alternative military tactics				
April 12/4		'Friends of Syria' pledges economic support for opposition forces		Saudi and the gulf states announce new funds for the FSA	A ceasefire brokered by Annan does not stem violence	

(continued)

(continued)

2012: Syria

Month	*Syrian government*	*Opposition forces/rebels; external—militant outfits*	*US, UK, Europe*	*Middle East and Israel*	*International organizations*	*Russia*
	Syria promises to comply with a UN-brokered ceasefire but carves out an important condition—that the regime still has a right to defend itself against terrorists that it says are behind the uprising. The agreement ultimately fails to hold					
May 12/5	A massacre in Houla village in Homs leave more than 100 killed, nearly half of them children				The UNSC condemns the use heavy weapons in Houla The UNHRC later releases a report accusing Assad's forces and pro-government militiamen of war crimes during the bloodbath	
June 12/6			The White House condemns the attacks on civilian in Syria	The head of the Arab League asks the UNSC to boost the size of the UN mission in Syria and give it expanded powers to protect people	UN observers suspend patrols in Syria due to escalating violence	Putin's visit to China is aimed at bolstering crucial ties between the powerful neighbours who have aligned at the United Nations to block tougher international action against Syria despite widespread condemnation of the government's deadly crackdown

(continued)

(continued)

2012: Syria

Month	*Syrian government*	*Opposition forces/rebels; external—militant outfits*	*US, UK, Europe*	*Middle East and Israel*	*International organizations*	*Russia*
July 12/7	There is intense fighting between the government forces and the opposition forces in Idlib, Damascus, Deir Ezzor, Homs, Hama and Dera'a Following the opposition's act of blowing up the government security headquarters—severe fighting breaks out in Aleppo The Syrian Army and Airforce attack the rebels in Aleppo The intense fighting that follows, daily barrel bombs are dropped on the poorer and more densely populated rebel-held east, causes estimated 1 million civilians to flee The Syrian air force continues to target populated urban areas north of Hama City Syria threatens to unleash chemical and biological weapons if the country faces a foreign attack, the country's first acknowledgement that it possesses weapons of mass destruction	Rebel fighters seize eastern Aleppo, dividing the city The rebel forces bomb the capital's National Security Headquarters killing and injuring many senior officials including the defence minister and the deputy defence minister, Assad's brother-in-law. The interior minister is also wounded Opposition fighters have seized control of many of Syria's border crossings with Iraq	The US and the UK announce sanctions against the Syrian government US Secretary of State Hillary Clinton expressed outrage and demanded that UNSC take action to stop the violence	Iraq asserts that al-Qaeda fighters are streaming out of the country to carry out attacks across the border in Syria Qatar and Saudi Arabia have been transferring arms to Syria's increasingly militarised opposition	The International Committee of the Red Cross declare a serious situation in Syria The UNHRC makes appeals for Syria conflict to be referred to the International Criminal Court as arming of the government and the opposition is escalating the conflict	Russia and China Veto the Security Council Chapter VII resolution Russia, condemned the Tremseh killings, but blamed the opposition Russia and Iran are among the Syrian government's key suppliers

(continued)

(continued)

2012: Syria

Month	*Syrian government*	*Opposition forces/rebels; external—militant outfits*	*US, UK, Europe*	*Middle East and Israel*	*International organizations*	*Russia*
August 12/8	The regime suffers high level of defections. Prime Minister Riad Hijab defects	The Kurds control the northeastern belt of Syria under an agreement with the Syrian Government The opposition SNC has warned of a 'humanitarian catastrophe' in Homs, saying it had been under siege for 80 days and was in desperate need of food and medical supplies	President Obama indicates that the use of chemical weapons is the redline which may trigger US intervention through military action	The number of Syrians now sheltering in Turkey to more than 78,000	The UNGA by resolution denounces Assad's use of heavy weapons in Aleppo and Damascus The UN Humanitarian Mission pulls out of Aleppo due to heavy fighting Kofi Annan resigns as international envoy. Annan cited 'finger-pointing and name-calling' in the 15-nation UNSC as one of the reasons for his decision to step down Algerian diplomat and former foreign minister Lakhdar Brahimi takes his place United Nations claims that the number refugees fleeing the violent uprising has risen beyond 200,000 A Norwegian peacekeeper is heading to Damascus to take charge of a UN mission overseeing a shaky ceasefire	

(continued)

(continued)

2012: Syria

Month	*Syrian government*	*Opposition forces/rebels; external—militant outfits*	*US, UK, Europe*	*Middle East and Israel*	*International organizations*	*Russia*
September 12/9	The ancient Omayyad Mosque is destroyed by fire and shelling Syrian troops assisted by tanks and helicopters resist a rebel attack in Aleppo Syrian Government declares the rebels as terrorist and affirms its position of going after them till the entire city of Aleppo is liberated of them The Syrian army retook Darayya, near Damascus after three days of heavy bombardment Air strikes by Syrian government forces have targeted rebel-held police stations inside Aleppo city, as visiting peace envoy Lakhdar Brahimi met with opposition groups in the capital Damascus	The FSA launches a major offensive in Aleppo The opposition in possession of heavy weapons including tanks in Aleppo, the rebels have captured a number of tanks, and some armoured units have defected with their vehicles		The Druze community in the Golan Heights still consider themselves Syrian, even though Israelis have occupied their land for more than four decades. They have been supporting the Syrian government for years, but as the conflict between forces loyal to President Bashar al-Assad and rebels continues to intensify, division appear among them Turkey, which serves as headquarters for the FSA Free hosts members of the political opposition group, the SNC, has accused its southern neighbour of 'state terrorism' Lebanon deported 14 Syrians despite the violence over the border, drawing criticism from human rights activists	The UN says more than 100,000 people fled their country in August—the highest monthly total since the uprising began The United Nations and Human Rights Watch allege that the armed opposition and government in Syria have both committed war crimes and had performed summary executions but Assad's troops and militia loyal to the president had committed many more offences than the rebels Lakhdar Brahimi, the UN-Arab League Envoy warns the unrest threatens regional stability and that Syria was too far gone for reform and there could be no winners in the conflict The World Food Programme sends food assistance for distribution to 28,000 people in Aleppo The UN estimates that more than 18,000 people have been killed since the uprising in March 2011	

(continued)

(continued)

2012: Syria

Month	*Syrian government*	*Opposition forces/rebels; external—militant outfits*	*US, UK, Europe*	*Middle East and Israel*	*International organizations*	*Russia*
October 12/10	Fire in Aleppo destroys much of the historic market (souk) as fighting and bomb attacks continue in various cities	Syrian opposition fighters are close to capturing a strategic city in Idlib province	The US Secretary of State dismisses the SNC as lacking a base inside Syria and no longer reflects the visible leader of Syria	Conflict spills over with deaths in Turkey, Lebanon and Jordan. Wissam Al-Hassan, the intelligence chief for Lebanon's Interior Security Forces, assassinated in Beirut Tensions escalate between Syria and its northern neighbour Turkey	The U.N. negotiates a short-lived truce for the whole city of Aleppo during the Muslim Eid al-Adha holiday	
November 12/11		Syrian opposition groups including the SNC establish the National Coalition for Syrian Revolutionary composed of Opposition Forces, a new opposition leadership that will include representatives from the country's disparate factions fighting to topple Assad's regime, responding to repeated calls from their Western and Arab supporters to create a cohesive and representative leadership National Coalition for Syrian Revolutionary and Opposition Forces formed in Qatar, excludes Islamist militias	US President Barack Obama signs a secret order authorising US support for rebels seeking to depose Syrian President Bashar al-Assad and his government	Israel fired warning shots toward Syria after a mortar shell hit an Israeli military post. It was the first time Israel fired on Syria across the Golan Heights since the 1973 Yom Kippur War European and Arab foreign ministers are meeting at the Arab League headquarters in Cairo, Egypt, to discuss the Syrian crisis The Gulf Co-operation Council recognises the National Coalition as the legitimate representative of the Syrian people		

(continued)

(continued)

2012: Syria

Month	*Syrian government*	*Opposition forces/rebels; external—militant outfits*	*US, UK, Europe*	*Middle East and Israel*	*International organizations*	*Russia*
		Syrian rebels claim that they captured a helicopter base near Damascus after a battle with government forces. This is the second military facility on the outskirts of the capital to fall into opponents control				
December 12/12	All flights from Aleppo airport are suspended after al-Qaida-linked fighters threaten to shoot down civilian planes	Rebels launch an offensive and expand their presence in Aleppo province and secure supply lines to the Turkish border. They seize a number of military and air bases, increasingly isolating government forces Following heaving fighting the opposition forces take control of most of the Yarmouk Palestinian refugee camp in Damascus	USA declares the Nusra Front a terrorist group US also accuses Assad of using 'Scud Missiles'	France, US, UK, Turkey and the Gulf states recognize the National Coalition as Syria's legitimate representative		

2013: Syria

Month	*Syrian government*	*Opposition forces/rebels*	*US, UK, Europe and other countries*	*Middle East*	*International organizations*	*Russia*
January 13/1	Assad declines to stepdown despite increasing international pressure Bodies begin washing up on the banks of Aleppo's Queiq River, in the rebel-held Bustan al-Qasr neighbourhood. The victims were most likely killed in government-controlled areas		Nearly 200 Australians in Syria, either doing humanitarian work or fighting alongside the rebels. The government issues a statement that such activities amount to breaking the Australian Law	Around 200,000 Syrians have entered Jordan legally since the start of the revolution Jordan is concerned about this large influx in light of little assistance provided from the international community		Russia sends two planes to Lebanon to evacuate more than 100 of its citizens from Syria Russia carries on one of the largest naval exercises in the Mediterranean sea and the Black sea including Syria's coast
February 13/2			Finnish authorities launch an investigation into an alleged attempt to smuggle arms to Syria from Russia from the port of Helsinki, Finland's capital			Russian ships have been stopped repeatedly in international waters for trying to transport weapons to Syria in breach of an EU arms embargo
March 13/3		The opposition forces/rebels capture al-Raqqa	The US and UK promise non-military aid to the rebels The United States and Saudi Arabia present a united stance to Iran and Syria			

(continued)

(continued)

2013: Syria

Month	*Syrian government*	*Opposition forces/rebels*	*US, UK, Europe and other countries*	*Middle East*	*International organizations*	*Russia*
April 13/4	The Syrian Army and the Hezbollah launch major offensive to retake the strategic town of Qosair Aleppo's ancient Citadel, used by government forces as a base, comes under rebel fire. The government targets the Umayyad mosque minaret, suspecting rebels were using it as a base	Abu Bakr al-Bhagdadi, the self proclaimed emir of al-Qaeda in Iraq claims responsibility for establishing the Nusra Front and announces the groups merger as the Islamic State in Iraq and Levant(ISIS), however the leaders of the Nusra Front and al-Qaeda's al-Zawahiri reject the move There is division and infighting among the ranks of the self-labelled jihadists	The United States has approved providing Syrian rebels with \$123 miilion in new non-lethal aid that may include body armour and other types of supplies that have not been part of the assistance package in the past			
May 13/5	The government forces capture Qosair—a major strategic victory	The opposition meeting in Istanbul, is disappointing and they destroy any goodwill or support the National Coalition had among Syrians and the international community	EU ends its embargo of arming the rebels	The conflicts continue to reverberate in Lebanon as two rockets strike a Hezbollah stronghold in Beirut Israeli officials have confirmed that the country's air force carried out a strike against Syria The al-Zaatari refugee camp in Jordan is transforming into the largest refugee camp in the world		

(continued)

(continued)

2013: Syria

Month	*Syrian government*	*Opposition forces/rebels*	*US, UK, Europe and other countries*	*Middle East*	*International organizations*	*Russia*
June 13/6	Backed by thousands of Lebanese Hezbollah fighters, Assad's forces re-capture the strategic town of Qusair from rebels, near the border with Lebanon	Abu Bakr al-Baghdadi reaffirms commitment to merging with Syrian opposition al-Nusra Front. There are growing tensions between the Islamic State of Iraq and al-Qaeda's central command	Obama authorises sending weapons to Syrian rebels after White House discloses that US has conclusive evidence Assad's government used chemical weapons on a small scale against opposition forces			
July 13/7		ISIS kills two FSA commanders, the divide between the rebel groups widens The Pakistani Taliban's first batch of fighters arrived in Syria to fight alongside rebels		Turkey supports Syria's territorial integrity and will not tolerate the creation of a 'de facto' Syrian Kurdish entity on its borders		
August 13/8	The Assad regime is accused of using chemical weapons in the Damascus suburbs to kill hundreds of civilians, including many children as they slept. The government denies using chemical weapons	The Islamist forces including the Nusra Front and ISIS attack Alawite villages in Latakia province Opposition forces capture a military airport north of Aleppo and the towns of Ariha and Khanasir severing regime supply lines to Aleppo Insurgents gain control of the Aleppo-Damascus highway, tightening the siege on the government part of the city	Obama announces that the US will bomb Syria after Congressional approval The British Parliament votes against military intervention in Syria The UK and US have dispatched planes and warships to the eastern Mediterranean	About 35,000 refugees, believed to be mainly Syrian Kurds, have entered Iraq	The number of child refugees that have fled Syria has now reached one million-UNHCR and UNICEF, children made up half of all refugees from the Syrian conflict and most have arrived in Lebanon, Jordan, Turkey, Iraq and Egypt	Russia and Iran have given fresh warning to the United States and its allies against a military intervention in Syria

(continued)

(continued)

2013: Syria

Month	*Syrian government*	*Opposition forces/rebels*	*US, UK, Europe and other countries*	*Middle East*	*International organizations*	*Russia*
			France urges the international community to react forcefully if the charges of using chemical weapons by the Syrian government are proved to be true			
September 13/9	A chemical weapons attack in the Damascus suburbs kills hundreds. The government denies using chemical weapons Syria welcomed a suggestion to move all of the country's chemical weapons under international control	Opposition Forces including the Nusra Front seize the Christian town of Maalula, but it is lost to the Syrian government forces soon	The US administration backs down from attacking Syria		UN Inspectors report the use of chemical weapons in Damascus The environmental, chemical and medical samples provide clear and convincing evidence that surface-to-surface rockets containing the nerve agent sarin were used in the Ghouta area of Damascus UNSC unanimously adopts resolution requiring the Syrian regime to dismantle its chemical weapons arsenal	Vladimir Putin, the Russian president, has warned the US against taking one-sided action in Syria, but Russia 'doesn't exclude' the possibility of supporting a UN resolution authorising military strikes Russia agrees to help guard Syrian chemical weapons sites and destroy President Bashar al-Assad's stockpiles but will not ship any of the chemical arms to Russia for destruction
October 13/10	Assad permits international inspection to begin the process	Al-Zawahiri ordered the dismantling of ISIS, Baghdadi rejects this proposal		Arab League chief Nabil el-Araby said on Sunday that international envoy Lakhdar Brahimi informed him that the talks will convene on November 23	Officials from OPCW arrive in Damascusto monitor the dismantling of Syria's chemical weapons arsenal The number of Syrian refugees registered with the U.N. tops 2 million	Russia and China have vetoed three UNSC resolutions since October 2011. The resolutions would have condemned the Syrian governments and warned it with sanctions

(continued)

(continued)

2013: Syria

Month	*Syrian government*	*Opposition forces/rebels*	*US, UK, Europe and other countries*	*Middle East*	*International organizations*	*Russia*
	The regime launches two major offensive which help them gain control in Damascus and Aleppo Syria destroys its chemical weapons production equipment The Syrian Government uses starvation as a war tactic, blocking food and medicine from entering and people from leaving besieged areas	Poor coordination and infighting weaken the rebels' ranks. Islamic State militants clash with the rebels, establishing a presence in the eastern part of the city				
November 13/11	Syrian forces have launched a fierce offensive in the rebel-held Qalamoun hills, thousands of people to flee to neighbouring Lebanon Military air strikes hit the town of Qara, in the strategic Qalamoun region Syrian troops have recaptured parts of a military base seized by rebels, near Aleppo international airport Rebel forces had seized control of Base 80 in February	Al-Qaeda and Sunni fighters see the Kurds as their second enemy after President Bashar al-Assad's regime, threatening the minority group's aspirations in both Syria and Turkey Four bombings in Qalamoun area Islamic State of Iraq and the Levant (ISIL) and Al-Nusra Front, two Al-Qaeda-affiliated groups claim responsibility			More than 120,000 people have been killed, according to the UN The United Nations has set a date of January 22, for talks between the Syrian government and opposition at Geneva, but the rebels insist the removal of Assad as a precondition for talks	

(continued)

(continued)

2013: Syria

Month	*Syrian government*	*Opposition forces/rebels*	*US, UK, Europe and other countries*	*Middle East*	*International organizations*	*Russia*
	The base's garrison was responsible for securing Aleppo international airport and the adjacent Nayrab military airfield, which both remain under regime control					
December 13/12	The government begins an unprecedented campaign of dropping barrel bombs on Aleppo city and surrounding areas, driving more people out of eastern Aleppo	IS expands its presence in the eastern part of city The leader of al-Qaeda's branch in Syria states that the battle is coming to an end with the rebels having an upper hand Leader of Ahrar al-Sham, Syria's most powerful rebel group unwilling to recognise any agreement reached in the Geneva peace conference planned for January intense battles between Kurdish forces, known as the People's Protection Units (YPG), and the al-Qaeda offshoot Jabhat al-Nusra	The US and the UK suspend 'non-lethal assistance' to rebels on northern Syria after jihadist seize FSA bases Britain's Foreign Office has said it will help the international mission to destroy Syria's chemical weapons arsenal by destroying 150 tonnes of industrial-grade stockpiled chemicals at a commercial facility. UK joins the United States, Russia, China, Denmark, Norway and Finland, who are committed to the mission	Six people are killed in Lebanon's Tripoli, as the country gets dragged into the civil war raging in neighbouring Syria. Sectarian tension in Tripoli, is picking up again with politicians of diverse sects siding with rival parties in the Syrian dispute	The United Nations in its report cited 'credible evidence' which prove the probable use of chemical weapons' in Ghouta, Khan al-Assal, Jobar, Saraqeb and Ashrafieh Sahnaya The United Nations sent its first delivery of humanitarian aid by air to Syria from Iraq The United Nations has appealed for $6.5 billion for Syria	Russia has airlifted to Syria 75 vehicles and other equipment to help in the multinational operation to remove and destroy the country's chemical weapons Russia has supported India's decision to take part in an international conference—Geneva-II (to bring to the table all the conflicting parties, domestic and international, to stabilise Syria)

(continued)

(continued)

2013: Syria

Month	*Syrian government*	*Opposition forces/rebels*	*US, UK, Europe and other countries*	*Middle East*	*International organizations*	*Russia*
			India offers to help destroy Syrian chemical weapons arsenal and related facilities. it was also interested in contributing $1 million to the Trust Fund for use in the destruction of the chemical weapons and other related equipment by the Organisation for the Prohibition of Chemical Weapons (OPCW)			

2014: Syria

Month	*Syrian government*	*Opposition forces/rebels*	*US, UK, Europe*	*Middle East*	*International organizations*	*Russia*
January 14/1		The Islamist Front coalition of Salafist rebel groups and the FSA forces launch offensive against the ISIS	USA and Russia have made a joint call for Syria's regime and rebels to agree to ceasefires ahead of their peace talks	The report, commissioned by the government of Qatar states that the Syrian government systematically tortured and killed thousands Donors meeting in Kuwait pledged nearly $2.4 billion in humanitarian aid for victims of the Syrian war. 70 nations and 24 international organisations participated in The second International Humanitarian Pledging Conference for Syria	UN Secretary-General Ban Ki-moon convenes the first round of peace talks in Geneva involving the Syrian government and Syrian National Coalition	
February 14/2		AL-Zawahiri distances al-Qaeda from ISIS The al-Nusra joins the fray			A second round of the Geneva talks is held; representatives of government and opposition fail to agree on agenda; Joint Special Envoy Lakhdar Brahimi apologises to the Syrian people for lack of progress in the talks. UN-brokered peace talks in Geneva fail, largely because Syrian authorities refuse to discuss a transitional government	Russia said it will veto a U.N. resolution on humanitarian aid access in Syria, claiming that the draft is an effort to prepare for military strikes against President Bashar al-Assad's government

(continued)

(continued)

2014: Syria

Month	*Syrian government*	*Opposition forces/rebels*	*US, UK, Europe*	*Middle East*	*International organizations*	*Russia*
March 14/3	Syrian Army and Hezbollah forces recapture Yabroud, the last rebel stronghold near the Lebanese border The Syrian army shelled the Kurdish-held neighbourhood of al-Msheirfah in Al-Hasakah city	Jihadist groups and FSA members from Turkey conquer the Syrian Armenian town of Kessab	The US expelled all the Syrian diplomats from the United States	International pressure compels Turkey to declare the Nusra Front a terrorist group The Israeli Air Force launched several air strikes on Syrian military		
April 14/4	Syrian Army drives the Jihadi's out, the inhabitant return to the town of Kessab Chemical weapons are used again in Syria, on the town of Kafr Zita, Hama			Lebanon's parliament has failed to elect a new president, as no candidate succeeded in getting the minimum 86 votes, or a two-thirds majority, needed to win the presidency Iraqi helicopters reportedly destroy an ISIL convoy inside Syria	Two rounds of Geneva Talks convened by the UN Secretary-General reveal nothing According to the UN, the number of Syrian refugees registered in Lebanon has exceeded one million	
May 14/5	The Syrian Army gains control over Homs, and the rebel forces are permitted to evacuate the city The government's barrel bomb campaign on eastern Aleppo intensifies	The rebels tunnel beneath a hotel used as a government command and control center and blow it up Rebels withdraw from the besieged city of Homs in accordance with the U.N.-brokered deal between them and the Syrian government		Lebanon's General Security department has forcibly deported 41 Palestinian refugees back to Syria	By a unanimous vote the UNSC demands that all the parties to the conflict cease the attacks on civilians, especially the use of barrel bombs in populated areas	Russia and China veto a U.N. Security Council resolution that would have asked the International Criminal Court to investigate war crimes in Syria

(continued)

(continued)

2014: Syria

Month	*Syrian government*	*Opposition forces/rebels*	*US, UK, Europe*	*Middle East*	*International organizations*	*Russia*
		Syrian rebels secure, the Khan Shykhun and its surrounding areas in the Idlib offensive and also captures the al-Salam checkpoint west of the town				
June 14/6	Syria holds a presidential election in government-held areas. More than one person could stand as a presidential candidate for the first time since the Assad family came to power more four decades ago Assad, wins nearly 90% of the vote Syrian government helicopters have dropped barrel bombs on opposition-held districts of the northern city of Aleppo	ISIS captures Mosul and Tikrit, it renames itself Islamic State and proclaims global caliphate Islamic State of Iraq and Syria militants declare 'caliphate' in territory from Aleppo to eastern Iraqi province of Diyala			International inspectors complete the removal of chemical weapons Lakhdar Brahimi resigns from his position as the UN-Arab League envoy for Syria, largely out of frustration at Syrian President Bashar al-Assad's plans to hold an election in June Staffan de Mistura is appointed the successor to Brahimi's role of the UN special envoy for Syria	
July 14/7	Syrian government troops retook the Shaar gas fields in Homs province Severe water cuts hit Aleppo province	Islamic State group takes control of Syria's largest oil field, al-Omar, after battles with the Nusra Front, al-Qaida's branch in Syria			The UNSC unanimously approve a resolution on Syria allowing aid convoys to go into rebel-held areas without government approval	

(continued)

(continued)

2014: Syria

Month	*Syrian government*	*Opposition forces/rebels*	*US, UK, Europe*	*Middle East*	*International organizations*	*Russia*
August 14/8	Syrian army loses Tabqa airbase to the ISIS	The Nusra Front captures the Quenitra Crossing into Israel-occupied Golan Heights The Islamic State kills hundreds in Deir Ezzor province The ISIS seizes the Syrian military airfield of Tabqa—after this ISIS completely controls Raqqa Province Al-Qaeda linked Syrian rebels have been accused of seizing 43 UN soldiers in the Israeli-occupied Golan Heights and trapped another 81 in the region ISIS loots and destroys antiquities in Syria and Iraq The Islamic State group has an army of more than 50,000 fighters in Syria Rebel militants withdrew from the Lebanese town of Arsal after a ceasefire with the Lebanese army	The US intervenes through air strikes in the region of Sinjar hills. Kurdish fighters also join in US officials ask the Syrian opposition to call on the international community to hit positions belonging to the Islamic State group and help rebels eliminate the self-declared jihadists The US begins arming the Iraqi-Kurdish forces and along with the coalition of international forces begins air strikes on ISIS in Iraq There is a shift in the US attitude of condemning Assad to bombing the regimes opponents	In Iraq, ISIS captures the towns of Zumar, Wana and the Sinjar Hills	Two groups of UN peacekeepers evade capture by Syrian rebels in the Golan Heights	

(continued)

(continued)

2014: Syria

Month	*Syrian government*	*Opposition forces/rebels*	*US, UK, Europe*	*Middle East*	*International organizations*	*Russia*
September 14/9	The Syrian Army presses north of Aleppo until it controls the major supply lines to the city The Syrian government has warned that any foreign intervention in the country would be an act of aggression unless it is approved by Damascus	ISIS attacks the Kurdish town of Kobani in Syria The Kurdish fighters aided by international air strikes repel the IS forces from a major part of the town The rebels say they have captured more territory on Quneitra	The United States is prepared to strike against Islamic State fighters in the country US and five Arab countries launch air strikes against Islamic State around Aleppo and Raqqa			
October 14/10	The Army captures the town of Morek				UN peace envoy Staffan de Mistura proposes an action plan to 'freeze' fighting in local areas to allow for aid deliveries and to lay the groundwork for talks, he suggested the city of Aleppo would be a good starting point Despite a UN resolution authorising cross-border aid delivery without Syria's consent, UN agencies are 'still unable to deliver sufficient quantities of aid to people in the hardest to reach areas	

(continued)

(continued)

2014: Syria

Month	*Syrian government*	*Opposition forces/rebels*	*US, UK, Europe*	*Middle East*	*International organizations*	*Russia*
November 14/11	The regime air strikes in Raqqa kills dozens	The Nusra-Front captures Nawa from the Syrian Army ISIS shoots down Syrian Airforce fighter jet		Hassan Nasrallah has declared 'victory' for his Hezbollah movement against self-declared jihadists in Syria. The Shia group has sent thousands of fighters into neighbouring Syria to fight alongside the troops of President Bashar al-Assad	Polio, eliminated in Syria in 1995, re-emerged last year and spread across large swaths of the country's opposition-held north The World Health Organisation (WHO) and UNICEF responded by launching a mass polio vaccination campaign across the region	
December 14/12	There is a consensus that the opposition will not be able to topple the regime Syria is ready to participate in a preliminary and consultative meeting in Moscow with the Rebels					

*Prepared by Farhana Khan, Research Assistant, O'Neill School of Public and Environmental Affairs, Indiana University, Bloomington

Appendix C: Timelines Syrian Crisis—How Different Interest Groups Participated (2015–2018)*

2015: Syria

Month	*Syrian government*	*Opposition forces/rebels*	*US, UK, Europe*	*Middle East*	*International organizations*	*Russia*
January 15/1	The Syrian Regime strikes kills people in Damascus, rebels are executed in Ratyan which is located north of Aleppo Heavy losses were reported in the ranks of the pro-Assad security forces and militants of Hezbollah The YPG clashes with Syrian government forces in Al-Hasakah city in northeast Syria	The Kurdish forces retake the city of Kobane in the Northern Syrian region from IS. They also advance into Raqqa Province The FSA and al-Nusra Front launch an offensive against Hezbollah strongholds in the Jirud Fleita area, of western Kalamun, near the Lebanese border	The Combined Joint Task Force combating ISIL conducts ten air strikes in Syria, eight of them targeting the contested city of Kobani, the air strikes destroy fourteen ISIL fighting positions		U.N. estimates Syria's conflict has killed at least 220,000 people	
February 15/2	Aerial bombardment by the pro-regime warplanes in the eastern Ghouta of Damascus countryside kills many	ISIS releases a video of a Jordanian pilot Moath Youssed al-Kasasbeh being burnt alive Kurdish fighters reconquer villages near Tel Hamis in the northeast forcing IS to retreat The jihadist group launched offensive in the western part of the country attacking the Tadmur airbase in the Homs governorate		Jordan reacts in retaliation leading to a series of air strikes by the Jordanian Air Force		

(continued)

(continued)

2015: Syria

Month	*Syrian government*	*Opposition forces/rebels*	*US, UK, Europe*	*Middle East*	*International organizations*	*Russia*
March 15/3	The rebel-aligned Liwaa Sham Al-Rasoul brigade surrendered to the Syrian government-backed National Defense Forces The northwestern city of Idlib falls to Islamist groups led by the Nusra Front	Abu Homam al-Shami, the military chief of the Nusra Front is killed in regime led air strikes Nusra-led Jaish al-Fatah captures the city of Idlib Rebels recapture the village of Hardatnein near Aleppo Rebels set off a large quantity of explosives in a tunnel running underneath or near Air Force Intelligence's headquarters in the Jamiat al-Zahra district of Aleppo			The UNSC has adopted a US-drafted resolution condemning the use of chlorine as a weapon in Syria	
April 15/4		ISIS captures large parts of the Yarmouk refugee camp on the outskirts of Damascus after clashes with the anti-Assad Palestinian Militias The Kurdish people's Protection Units (YGP) and the FSA capture territories and towns near Kobane		The Palestine Liberation Organization will not be drawn into military action in a Palestinian refugee camp in Syria that has been overrun by fighters from ISIL	The UNSC has heard first-hand accounts from Syrian doctors of alleged chemical weapons attacks in a closed-door meeting in New York	

(continued)

(continued)

2015: Syria

Month	*Syrian government*	*Opposition forces/rebels*	*US, UK, Europe*	*Middle East*	*International organizations*	*Russia*
		IS captures the town of al-Sukhnah in Homs province The Jisr al-Shughur offensive in the northwest was launched by the rebel group leading to the capture of city of Jisr al-Shughur				
May 15/5	President Bashar Assad acknowledges serious setbacks for his military	IS captures the historic site of Palmyra from the government troops and destroys the ancient statues, invokes great international condemnation IS is successful in pushing back the regime army and advances within 35 Kms of Homs Jaish al-Fatah takes over Ariha which was the last regime held town in Idlib province. This poses a serious threat to the regime heartland of Latakia The Islamic State group parts of the town of Al-Sukhnah and its surroundings in the Homs province			The UNICEF participates in two missions to provide humanitarian assistance to families recently displaced from Yarmouk camp	

(continued)

(continued)

2015: Syria

Month	*Syrian government*	*Opposition forces/rebels*	*US, UK, Europe*	*Middle East*	*International organizations*	*Russia*
June 15/6		IS resume its effort to retake Kobane IS suicide bomber kills many in Hasakeh, an important city in the northeast Syria FSA and the Islamic Front seize Brigade 52 base from government forces, located east of the town of Al Hirak The Qalb Loze massacre of Syrian Druze was carried by the al-Nusra Front YPG and Asayish forces clashed with the regime in Qamishli, capturing several regime held institutions ISIL launches attacks on the cities of Kobani and Hasakah				
July 15/7	The Syrian Army and the Hezbollah enter the strategic town of Zabadani off the Beruit-Damascus highway held by the Nusra Front and other rebel groups Regime forces make gains while pushing back IS from Palmyra	IS initiated mass execution of regime soldiers in Palmyra amphitheatre The FSA and Jasih al-Fatah gain the vital area of al-Ghab Plain. This area lies on the highway connecting Latakia and Aleppo and it is vital for the government's efforts to hold Latakia		Turkey launches air strikes against ISIL		

(continued)

(continued)

2015: Syria

Month	*Syrian government*	*Opposition forces/rebels*	*US, UK, Europe*	*Middle East*	*International organizations*	*Russia*
	The Syrian Airforce continues to use barrel bombs in Douma a suburb near Damascus	Rebels captured a former Syrian Scientific Research Center in Aleppo				
August 15/8		The IS fighters attack the southern outskirts of Damascus. ISIS fighters launch an assault on Qadam and Asali in the southern outskirts of Damascus from their base in Al-Hajar al-Aswad, clashing with Jaysh al-Islam fighters in Qadam and those of Ajnad al-Sham in Asali				
September 15/9	The government forces continue to drop barrel bombs in Aleppo and Bosra. Air strikes are also conducted against the IS-held Raqqa The government forces recapture a number of villages around Hama Pro-Assad forces targeted al-Shaar neighbourhood in eastern Aleppo city with surface-to-surface missiles	Anti-government violence erupted in the town of Sweida, a stronghold of the Druze minority sect, following the killing of Druze leader Sheikh Wahid Al-Balous	France launches its first air strike against the IS training camp The United States has suspended the 'train and equip' program for Syrian Rebels also known as New Syrian Forces	Israeli Prime Minister Benjamin Netanyahu refuses to accept Syrian refugees Iraq's military officials are engaged in intelligence and security cooperation in Baghdad with Russia, Iran, and Syria to counter the threat from the ISIL		Rumours circulate that Russia had conducted air strikes and also that Russian troops are conducting training in the regime territory Putin supports the United States' stand of terming the rebels illegal according to the UN resolution Russia soon begins its air strikes Russian President Vladimir Putin branded US support for rebel forces in Syria as illegal under the UN charter

(continued)

(continued)

2015: Syria

Month	*Syrian government*	*Opposition forces/rebels*	*US, UK, Europe*	*Middle East*	*International organizations*	*Russia*
October 15/10	The regime with the help of Iranian and Russian support begins another offensive to retake Hama. though FSA put up an intense resistance, the regime gains control in parts of the Idlib province capturing the villages of Atshan and Om Hartein Syrian troops launch an offensive around Aleppo Regime forces conducted air strikes that dropped many barrel bombs on the town of Darayya in multiple raids	IS captures Mheen and Hawwarin, west of Al-Qaryateyn city	US and Russia's relationships are strained as US officials claim that the Russian led air strikes targeted the CIA trained rebels instead of the IS President Obama announces that US special forces will be sent to Syria in an advisory role The United States has disclosed plans to station the first American boots on the ground in Syria in the war against the ISIL fighters Military officials of Russia and the US signed a 'memorandum of understanding' to avoid clashes in air over Syria Prime Minister of Canada, Justin Trudeau announced that his nation will no longer provide jets fighters for the fight against ISIS	Egyptian President Abdel Fattah el-Sisi supports Russian intervention Iran is invited for the first time to participate in the Vienna talks Iraqi, Lebanese and Iranian militias also throw their weight behind the government An Iranian Revolutionary Guards General Hossein Hamadani has been killed near Aleppo, where he was advising the Syrian army	International talks to resolve the crisis held in Vienna There are disagreements between nations on the future of President Assad	Russia begins launching air strikes to bolster Assad's forces Russia is ready to support the Free Syrian Army (FSA) with air strikes and cooperate closely with the United States in fighting ISIL group and other factions

(continued)

(continued)

2015: Syria

Month	*Syrian government*	*Opposition forces/rebels*	*US, UK, Europe*	*Middle East*	*International organizations*	*Russia*
November 15/11	The Army advances into the Marj Al-Sultan Military Airbase in Damascus, after heavy clashes with Jaysh al-Islam. In Aleppo the Lebanese Group Hezbollah and Syrian Army Units capture Jabal Al-Eiss from Harakat Ahrar Al-Sham rebels Government forces and its allies capture 408 sq.kms of Territory in Southern Aleppo Syrian armed forces gain control from Homs Governorate at Mahaden, Northern Latakia and strides towards the Aleppo-Lattakia highway A regime helicopter dropped barrel bomb on a populated area of Zafaraneh town near the city of Homs	Large-scale terror attacks masterminded by the IS kills many in Paris, France Jaysh al-Islam a major rebel group near the capital Damascus, use civilian captives as 'human shields' rebel forces seized control of Murak, following clashes with pro-government forces Massive desertions in the Free Syria Army (FSA) forces located in Aleppo, due to lack of payment	French President Hollande vows to create a grand coalition to defeat the IS Seventeen nations meet in Vienna to adopt a timeline for a transition plan in Syria that includes a new constitution as well as U.N.-administered parliamentary and presidential elections within 18 months	Turkish Airforce shoots down a Russian fighter get in their airspace close to the Syrian border	The UNSC drafts a resolution to completely destroy the group by any means necessary	Putin accuses Turkey of aiding the IS and warns about serious consequences Russian air strikes on areas in the town of Maaret al-Numan, Idlib

(continued)

(continued)

2015: Syria

Month	*Syrian government*	*Opposition forces/rebels*	*US, UK, Europe*	*Middle East*	*International organizations*	*Russia*
December 15/12	Government Forces capture land in the Province of Latakia from FSA and other rebel forces Government fighter jets launched several raids on the opposition-held district of Hammuriyah in southeastern Damascus A series of rebel leaders are targeted across the country in Syria-Russian air strike coordinated with Syrian government intelligence	Western media reports of low morale, desertions, and distrust of leaders by the Free Syria Army (FSA) fighters Buses and ambulances head to Zabadani to evacuate 126 civilians and wounded fighters from the besieged rebel bastion. The evacuation is part of a truce in which rebels and civilians are taken from the besieged town and transported to Beirut	United Kingdom fighters restart bombing operations in Syria against Islamic State militants Germany's parliament approved government plans to join the military campaign against Islamic State in Syria. German air strikes will operate independently that those of France, Britain, United States and Russia	Israeli Prime Minister Benjamin Netanyahu admitted for the first time that Israeli forces have been operating in Syria A Kurdish-Arab coalition fighting the (ISIL) group has announced the creation of a political wing after a two-day conference in Syria's northeastern town of al-Malikiyah	The UN Security Council adopts resolution 2254 endorsing the Vienna road map for a transitional period in Syria The number of 'refugees and migrants' arriving by land and sea to the European Union passed the one million mark	Russian announced its intentions to open a second airbase in Homs Russian warplanes strike a residential area in Aleppo's Azaz district Russian warplanes carry air strikes on residential buildings in rebel-held town of Jisr al-Shughour

2016: Syria

Month	*Syrian government*	*Opposition forces/rebels*	*US, UK, Europe*	*Middle East*	*International organizations*	*External—militant outfits*
January 16/1	The Syrian government has allowed humanitarian workers access to an opposition-held town near the border with Lebanon The regime also allowed aid to Madaya and two Shia towns that have been cut off by rebels in the province of Idlib The town of Zabadani near the Lebanese border continues to suffer under siege despite a deal between pro-government forces and rebels to ease the blockade Wounded rebel fighters and their families allowed leave the town in deal brokered by Iran and Turkey last month. In exchange, pro-government forces and Lebanese Shia Hezbollah fighters were allowed safe passage back from rebel-dominated areas in northern Syria	The Islamic State of Iraq and the Levant (ISIL) group has carried out a massacre in Syrian government-held districts in the eastern city of Deir Ez Zor	The United States and Russia fail to find agreement on the participants in the peace talks to be held in Geneva US troops have taken control of Rmeilan airfield, in northern province of Hasakah, to support Kurdish fighters against the Islamic State of Iraq and the Levant (ISIL)	Iran recruits Afghan Shia fighters to step up the Islamic Republic's efforts in the Syrian war, and offers them salaries to join the fight to save the government of President Bashar al-Assad	The meetings in Switzerland, part of a process outlined in a UNSC resolution envisages an 18-month timetable for a political transition, including the drafting of a new constitution and elections in Syria UN Special Envoy for Syria Staffan de Mistura, said that Syria will push for a nationwide ceasefire for all parties other than the ISIL and al-Nusra Front armed groups	

(continued)

(continued)

2016: Syria

Month	*Syrian government*	*Opposition forces/rebels*	*US, UK, Europe*	*Middle East*	*International organizations*	*External—militant outfits*
February 16/2		The Syrian Opposition High Negotiations Committee (HNC), the major opposition bloc involved in negotiations, agreed that it would accept the terms of the negotiation	Russia and the U.S. broker a ceasefire that excludes extremists. The agreement called on all sides to sign up to the agreement by midday on February 26 and to stop fighting by midnight	Turkish forces have shelled Kurdish-held areas, including an air base, in Syria's northern province of Aleppo	ISIL and the al-Nusra Front are not included in the agreement as they are listed as terrorist groups by the UN Security Council The ceasefire in Syria that took effect on February 27 2016 was part of a negotiated deal, based on UNSC Resolution 2254, passed in December 2015 UN special envoy announces a temporary suspension of talks in Geneva between the opposition and the government The UN-backed Commission of Inquiry on Syria presented a 25-page report on Monday on killings of detainees by President Bashar al-Assad's government The Council adopted a resolution drafted by the United States and Russia that endorses the ceasefire deal. Syrian peace talks to reconvene on March 7, 2016, if the ceasefire holds	Russian Prime Minister Dmitry Medvedev has warned that the deployment of foreign ground troops in the Syrian conflict could result in a world war

(continued)

(continued)

2016: Syria

Month	*Syrian government*	*Opposition forces/rebels*	*US, UK, Europe*	*Middle East*	*International organizations*	*External—militant outfits*
March 16/3	Syrian government forces retake Palmyra from Islamic State with Russian air assistance The Syrian Government negotiator does not want United States and Russia to interfere in Syrian peace talks Syria's foreign minister stated that the government delegation would reject any attempt by the UN envoy to include presidential elections on the agenda at the peace talks	Kurdish-controlled areas of northern Syria are expected to declare a federal system imminently	The United States and France accused the Syrian government of trying to disrupt the upcoming peace talks in Geneva as Syrian government delegation, which has arrived in Geneva, insists that removing Assad is a 'red line'	The declaration by Syria's Kurds of a 'federal democratic system' in the north is condemned	The UN special envoy to Syria Staffan de Mistura, has hinted on the possibility of federalism as a possible solution for the upcoming peace talks in Geneva	Putin ordered a pull out of 'the main part' of his troops fighting in Syria. Russia's bases in Tartous and Khmeimim will continue their normal operations

(continued)

(continued)

2016: Syria

Month	*Syrian government*	*Opposition forces/rebels*	*US, UK, Europe*	*Middle East*	*International organizations*	*External—militant outfits*
April 16/4	The ceasefire collapses, bombing resumes, and the Castello road, the only road out of eastern Aleppo, becomes a death trap The Syrian army and its allies launched a counteroffensive to recapture a village south of the city of Aleppo	Syria's main opposition group, the High Negotiations Committee (HNC), has threatened to boycott the next round of peace talks unless the government stops its bombing campaign Syrian rebel groups have announced a new offensive against the government in a move they said was a response to ceasefire violations from the forces of President Bashar al-Assad	US President Barack Obama has said he plans to send 250 more troops to Syria to support the local forces fighting ISIL. The forces are deployed on a 'counter-terrorism' mission The German chancellor has sought the creation of 'safe zones' to shelter refugees inside Syria		The UNSC rejected Israeli Prime Minister Benjamin Netanyahu's claim that the annexed Golan Heights in Syria would 'for ever' remain under Israeli control. The 15-member council agreed the status of the Golan, which Israel seized from Syria in 1967, 'remains unchanged' and Israel's imposition of its laws, jurisdiction and administration in the occupied Syrian Golan Heights was null and void and without any international legal effect	
May 16/5				Hezbollah's military commander Mustafa Badreddine died because of artillery shelling by a Sunni armed group in Damascus	A first-aid convoy organized by the International Committee of the Red Cross (ICRC), the United Nations and the Syrian Arab Red Crescent—was prevented from reaching the city of Daraya, Syria, by forces loyal to President Bashar al-Assad	

(continued)

(continued)

2016: Syria

Month	*Syrian government*	*Opposition forces/rebels*	*US, UK, Europe*	*Middle East*	*International organizations*	*External—militant outfits*
June 16/6	At least 224 people were killed in the first week of Ramadan in Syria, in bombings by Syrian and Russian warplanes Syria announced that it gave the UN and the Red Cross permission to send humanitarian aid convoys into at least 11 of the 19 besieged areas as a response to the call for humanitarian airdrops		The United States has reportedly dropped weapons to rebel fighters in Syria. The weapons supplies were airdropped to rebels in Marea, a town in the northern province of Aleppo	Jordanian soldiers are killed on the Syrian border bomb attack	The United Nations is seeking permission from the Syrian government to airdrop or airlift humanitarian aid to civilians in besieged areas	Russia contemplating to deploy special operations forces on the ground in Syria
July 16/7	The government and allied forces impose a full siege on eastern Aleppo, home to an estimated 250,000 people The Syrian government and Russia agree to open up a route to give besieged civilians, and rebels willing to surrender, a way out of the northern city of Aleppo	The Islamic State of Iraq and the Levant (ISIL, also known as ISIS) claimed responsibility for the attack on the Kurdish town of Qamishli in northern Syria The leader of al-Nusra Front confirms the Syria-based armed group's split from al-Qaeda and the formation of a new group operating under the name 'Jabhat Fath al-Sham'	Dozens of civilians have been killed in US-led air strikes against areas in Syria held by the Islamic State of Syria and the Levant The United States lead on the suburbs of the northern Syrian city of Manbij kills 28 and injures several people	Turkey has launched more air raids against the Islamic State of Iraq and the Levant (ISIL) in Syria and against Kurdish fighters in Iraq The Palestinian refugee camp of Khan Eshieh in the Damascus area is severely damaged during a major offensive between the Syrian government and the opposition rebels Egypt's prime minister blamed foreign intervention in the region for the rise of groups such as the ISIL at Arab League summit in the Mauritanian capital	According to the UN 300,000 residents are trapped in the eastern part of Aleppo Staffan De Mistura urges Moscow to let the UN take charge of any humanitarian corridors created in the divided city of Aleppo UNRWA, the United Nations agency for Palestinian refugees, confirmed the increase in bloodshed in Khan Eshieh. The regime has prevented the entry of medicine into the camp for more than two months	Russian jets also fire into the Palestinian refugee camps

(continued)

(continued)

2016: Syria

Month	*Syrian government*	*Opposition forces/rebels*	*US, UK, Europe*	*Middle East*	*International organizations*	*External—militant outfits*
				Yemen's president called on his country's Houthi fighters to surrender their weapons and withdraw from territories they control as Arab coalition air raids continue to strike the armed group's positions Saudi in addressing the conflict in Syria, maintained that there could be no solution while President Bashar al-Assad was still in power	UN appeals for greater humanitarian access and the resumption of peace talks	
August 16/8	The government drops cluster bombs in rebel held areas of Aleppo Helicopters dropped containers of toxic gas overnight on a town in Syria's Idlib province The Syrian government controls Aleppo's west as well as a northern corridor connecting it to government territories	The rebels control a swath of territory that includes the city's eastern and southern areas, as well as the surrounding countryside Free Syrian Army (FSA) fighters, along with Turkish special forces and tanks, and supported by Turkish and US air power, took control over the ISIL-controlled town of Jarablus	The Obama administration is set to meet its goal of admitting 10,000 Syrian refugees a month ahead of schedule	Turkish troops cross into Syria to help rebel groups push back so-called Islamic State militants and Kurdish-led rebels from a section of the two countries' border Turkey sent more tanks into northern Syria and demanded Kurdish fighters retreat within a week as it seeks to drive out ISIL from the border region. This is Turkey's first major incursion into Syria	Syria's war has claimed at least 400,000 lives and forced millions from their homes	Russian jets based in Iran struck targets inside Syria, in Aleppo, Idlib and Deir ez-Zor provinces Russia maintains that its use of an Iranian airbase to carry out bombing missions in Syria does not violate a UN resolution that forbids supplying fighter jets to Tehran

(continued)

(continued)

2016: Syria

Month	*Syrian government*	*Opposition forces/rebels*	*US, UK, Europe*	*Middle East*	*International organizations*	*External—militant outfits*
	Buses evacuated residents and rebel fighters from the Damascus suburb of Daraya under a deal that was agreed on after a four-year siege by government forces	US-backed opposition fighters have almost recaptured all of Manbij, a Syrian city northeast of Aleppo, from the Islamic State of Iraq and the Levant		Iran has reportedly formed what it calls the 'Liberation Army' whose units will be deployed in Arab countries, Qassem Soleimani will lead the liberation army in Syria		
September 16/9	Syria's army and opposition forces have agreed on a truce in the besieged neighbourhood of al-Waer in the central city of Homs. Under the agreement, signed by the local reconciliation committee and government officials, President Bashar al-Assad's forces are to end the siege on the area and stop bombardments in return for the withdrawal of rebel groups Syrian government forces backed by Moscow continued their offensive to retake the eastern part of the city of Aleppo from opposition fighters	A group of US-trained Syrian fighters has handed over ammunition and equipment to al-Nusra Front in exchange of safe passage Rebel groups make advances in the province of Hama, in the centre of the country They captured the towns of Tayyibat Al-Imam and Suran in Hama's northern suburbs after taking over several government-controlled villages and checkpoints in the area	A ceasefire negotiated by Russia and the United States holds for a few days, but talks to bring in aid fail The United States and Russia reach an agreement to put Syria's peace process back on track, including a nationwide ceasefire US-led coalition air raids reportedly killed dozens of Syrian soldiers, endangering a US-Russian brokered ceasefire and prompting an emergency UNSC meeting as tensions escalate between the United States and Russia The United States has threatened to suspend cooperation with Russia over Syria, after the bombardment of two hospitals in rebel-held areas of Aleppo		An air strike hits a humanitarian aid convoy north of the city	

(continued)

(continued)

2016: Syria

Month	*Syrian government*	*Opposition forces/rebels*	*US, UK, Europe*	*Middle East*	*International organizations*	*External—militant outfits*
October 16/10			A US-led coalition air strike killed senior leader of Jabhat Fateh al-Sham, the former Syrian branch of al-Qaeda, near Idlib			Russia announces it is suspending its air strikes on eastern Aleppo and designates humanitarian corridors, urging the rebels and residents to leave the eastern enclave
November 16/11	Syrian government forces continued to advance in the rebel-held part of the city of Aleppo, thousands have left the city Syria's military announced a new commando force, calling on volunteers to apply		The US-backed Syrian Democratic Forces (SDF) have declared their intention to launch an assault on ISIL-held Raqqa US legislators have passed a bill that would sanction the government of Syria and its supporters, including Russia and Iran, for war crimes and crimes against humanity in the country	More than 14,000 Iraqis fleeing the offensive against ISIL in Mosul have crossed the border into Syria Turkish jets hit 15 'targets' in the al-Bab area of northern Syria		
December 16/12	Government troops, backed by Russian air power and Iranian-sponsored militias, recapture Aleppo, the country's largest city, depriving the rebels of their last major urban stronghold	ISIL has recaptured the Syrian city of Palmyra after thousands of its fighters launched a multi-pronged assault on the ancient city	UK conducts air raids on suspected ISIL targets in Syria President elect Trump has agreed to cooperate more closely with Russia on counterterrorism measures	Turkey and Russia have agreed on a countrywide ceasefire plan for Syria, except for areas where government forces are battling armed groups declared terrorist organizations by the United Nations	The UNSC with Russia's backing, voted to quickly deploy UN observers to Aleppo to monitor evacuations and report on the fate of civilians who remain in the besieged Syrian city	Russia has urged the UNSC to permit the ceasefire in Syria, it is the third truce this year Russia has said the United States could join a fresh peace process once Donald Trump takes office as president on January 20

(continued)

(continued)

2016: Syria

Month	*Syrian government*	*Opposition forces/rebels*	*US, UK, Europe*	*Middle East*	*International organizations*	*External—militant outfits*
	The evacuation of the eastern part of the war-torn Syrian city of Aleppo begins with ambulances and buses carrying the wounded and sick leaving the rebel-held territory in the city under a fragile exit deal. The convoy travelled from Al-Amiriyah district and crossed into government-held Ramussa According to the Syrian government the agreement for truce does not include the ISIL group; fighters from al-Qaeda's former branch, al-Nusra Front; and factions linked to these armed groups The Syrian government along with its ally Hezbollah,, has stepped up its efforts to take control of rebel-held Wadi Barada on the outskirts of the capital Damascus		The annual defence policy bill signed into law by US President Barack Obama gives the next US administration under Donald Trump the authority to send Syrian rebels surface-to-air missiles			Russia and China blocked a draft resolution at the UNSC demanding a seven-day truce in Aleppo to evacuate the sick and wounded, and to provide humanitarian aid workers time to get food and medicine in the rebel held areas Suspected Russian air strikes on several areas of Idlib province in northwest Syria UNSC unanimously endorses a ceasefire currently in effect in Syria, as well as plans for peace talks to be held in the Kazakh capital next month Russia and the United States will continue talks on Aleppo

2017: Syria

Month	*Syrian government*	*Opposition forces/rebels*	*US, UK, Europe*	*Middle East*	*International organizations*	*Russia*
January 17/1	Syrian Army forces seize the Air Defence Battalion Base, near Hazrama, from Jaysh al-Islam militants in the Eastern Ghouta region of rural Damascus The Syrian Army takes full control of Wadi Barada, The government will fix the Ein-Fijeh Springs thus restoring the water supply to 5 million people who reside in Greater Damascus	Syrian opposition halted peace negotiations in Astana, Kazakhstan, because of government ceasefire violations	US air strikes struck the former Syrian Army Sheikh Suleiman military base in western Aleppo used by Jabhat Fatah al-Sham and the Nour al-Din al-Zenki Movement	Russia, Iran and Turkey agree to enforce a ceasefire between the government and non-Islamist rebels, after talks between the two sides in Kazakhstan	The first day of Syria talks in Kazakhstan hit a snag as direct negotiations between rebels and the government	
February 17/2	Syrian government forces used chemical weapons in rebel-held areas of Aleppo during the final weeks of assault to retake the city	SAA and SDF forces seize other towns from ISIS control in the Aleppo countryside		Israel cancels a plan to accept 100 Syrian child refugees due to opposition within its government The Turkish-backed Free Syrian Army forces, take full control of the city of al-Bab Kazakhstan invited the government and rebels for February 15–16 talks	A new round of UN-backed peace talks are due to begin in Geneva Amnesty International report states that the government had executed up to 13,000 prisoners in mass hangings at a military jail near Damascus	

(continued)

(continued)

2017: Syria

Month	*Syrian government*	*Opposition forces/rebels*	*US, UK, Europe*	*Middle East*	*International organizations*	*Russia*
March 17/3	The Syrian Army with Russian support recaptures Palmyra from ISIS forces Syrian Forces capture Deir Hafer in Eastern Aleppo	Arima buffer zone along part of the border is established between the SDF-aligned Manbij Military Council and the Free Syrian Army (FSA) forces within the Turkish occupied zone is established Hundreds of SDF soldiers are airlifted by United States across the Euphrates to begin their advance to capture Tabqa Dam and cut off ISIS reinforcements from Raqqa	U.S. Marine units are deployed at the Northern Districts of Raqqa Governorate to help SDF forces take control of Raqqa from ISIL The Syrian Arab Army launches anti-aircraft interceptor missiles, which targeted Israeli jets on the Israeli-controlled side of the Golan Heights prompting Israeli anti-missile response	Iran and Qatar reach a deal to allow civilians and combatants to leave the besieged towns of Al-Fou'aa-Kafrayain, Madaya and Al-Zabadani in Idlib and Damascus governorates	Turkey announces the end of its military operations in Syria	
April 17/4	The Syrian government launches a chemical weapon attack on Khan Shaykhun The Syrian Army expands the buffer zone around Palmyra West Damascus district of Zabadani is declared free of 'militants' by the regime	Al-Qaeda leader Ayman al-Zawahiri has called on the armed Syrian opposition to wage guerrilla warfare against the government of Bashar al-Assad and its allies	The United States fired 59 Tomahawk cruise missiles from two warships in the Mediterranean at the Shayrat airfield—a government-controlled airbase, in Homs province, in retaliation for a suspected chemical weapons attack on a rebel-held town			Russia, a key military ally of the Assad government, strongly condemned the strikes by the United States

(continued)

(continued)

2017: Syria

Month	*Syrian government*	*Opposition forces/rebels*	*US, UK, Europe*	*Middle East*	*International organizations*	*Russia*
May 17/5	Syrian government forces retake the Damascus–Palmyra highway from ISIL	Tahrir al-Sham and other rebel fighters, family members and supporters relocate from Qaboun, Barzeh and Tishreen in the Damascus suburbs to Idlib Governorate SDF forces have completed the capture of the town of Tabqa and the adjacent Tabqa Dam from Islamic State forces	The United States decides to arm the YPG Kurdish Popular Protection Units. These fight alongside the main opposition Syrian Democratic Forces A US-led Coalition bombing reportedly kills over 108 civilians in Al Mayadeen Syria	At peace talks in Astana, the presidents of the Russian Federation and Turkey announced their support for the creation of 'safe zones' in Syria Troops report captures of Muhammad Hassan Hasweh, who they describe as a senior Tahrir al-Sham commander, in the frontier town of Arsal		
June 17/6	Government forces and allies captured areas of Al-'Alb, Bi'r Dahlon and Sharat Dahlon in Eastern Homs Governorate from ISIL Air strikes also intensified in the eastern Ghouta as the 2017 Jobar offensive began		United States shoots down Syrian fighter jet near Raqqa after it allegedly dropped bombs near US-backed rebel Syrian Democratic Forces (SDF) The Australian Department of Défense reported that the Royal Australian Air Force (RAAF) halted its aerial military support in Syria. Within a few days the Royal Australian Air Force announced a resumption of military air operations in Syria	Israeli air force attacks Syrian government positions in the Quneitra province after fighting between rebels and the Syrian government spilled over the Israeli controlled Golan Heights	The first aid convoy to Harasta in besieged rebel-held eastern Ghouta, jointly organized by the International Committee of the Red Cross, the Syrian Arab Red Crescent and the United Nations, attacked by pro-government forces	

(continued)

(continued)

2017: Syria

Month	*Syrian government*	*Opposition forces/rebels*	*US, UK, Europe*	*Middle East*	*International organizations*	*Russia*
			The United States send a civilian team of State Department officials and security team to help stabilize areas that have been captured from ISIL by American-backed forces British troops had left Syria in and halted their FSA training program			
July 17/7	Syrian Army forces fully recaptures the quarries area west of Baath City in Quneitra Syrian government carried out several air strikes in Eastern Ghouta, in violation of the cessation of hostilities The Syrian government dropped 244 barrel bombs in July, in the 'de-escalation zones', targeting Daraa governorate, the Damascus suburbs, Suwayda, Hama and Homs	Abu Bakr al-Baghdadi, the Caliph of the Islamic State and the Levant is killed The FSA and Tahrir al-Sham (HTS) in Southern Syria reject the US-Russia ceasefire A FSA military commander of the Syrian Revolutionaries Front, Bashair al-Numairi, targeted and killed between the towns of Zimrin and Um Al-Uosaj in northern Daraa Fighters formerly linked to al-Qaeda took control of Idlib in Syria		The Lebanese militant group Hezbollah and the Syrian army launch a military operation to dislodge jihadist groups from the Arsal area, near the Lebanese-Syrian border A fifth round of talks organized by Russia, Turkey and Iran takes place in Astana, on the implementation of safe zones in Syria		Russian General Staff announced the introduction of new 'de-escalation zones' in Syria, including in the north of the city of Homs and in East Ghouta region

(continued)

(continued)

2017: Syria

Month	*Syrian government*	*Opposition forces/rebels*	*US, UK, Europe*	*Middle East*	*International organizations*	*Russia*
August 17/8	The Syrian government shells rebel towns in Eastern Ghouta: Ein Tarma town targeted with 10 ground-to-ground local FIL missiles	ISIL forces agree to withdrawal from Qalamoun to Abu Kamal in Idlib 600 rebels are bused under Syrian army escort into ISIL-controlled territory in a deal negotiated by Hezbollah, the Lebanese and Syrian Forces to gain control of their borders	Former US ambassador to Syria Robert Ford stated that the Syrian President Assad's victory in Syria and the Iranian role in the region are realities	8000 Syrian refugees and fighters arrived in rebel-held central Syria from Lebanon as part of a ceasefire deal between Hezbollah and Fateh al-Sham		
September 17/9	Syrian Army forces captured the city of Uqayribat from ISIL, the last stronghold of the group in Hama Governorate The Syrian Army, aided by Iranian-backed militias, as well as by Russian advisers and Russian air strikes, break the three-year siege of the city of Deir ez-Zor by ISIL by reaching the Brigade 137 desert base Pro-government forces regained full control of the highway from Deir ez-Zor to Damascus Russian and Syrian warplanes launch air strikes in the south of Idlib	Syrian Democratic Forces (SDF) have seized full control of the Old City in Raqqa from ISIL Representatives of the Syrian government and opposition groups meet once again in the capital of Kazakhstan	US air forces allowed a convoy carrying ISIL fighters to reach al-Mayadin in ISIL-held territory in eastern Syria as part of an evacuation agreement brokered by Hezbollah and the Syrian government A United States coalition spokesman stated that US-backed SDF forces will not enter Deir Ezzor city, but will leave it clear to Russian and government forces	Israeli jets bomb a suspected chemical weapons depot near the city of Masyaf, Hama Governorate The representatives of Iran, Russia and Turkey reached an agreement for the implementation of a 'de-escalation zone', in the Idlib Governorate	Staffan de Mistura, the U.N special envoy for the Syrian conflict indicated that Syrian opposition must accept it has 'failed to win the war', but that the government 'cannot announce victory' The sixth round of talks in Astana—brokered by Russia, Turkey and Iran—is aimed at implementing lasting ceasefire in so-called de-escalation zones in Syria	The Russian Aerospace Forces destroyed a large convoy of twelve ISIL trucks with ammunition and weapons in Deir ez-Zor province Russian President Putin holds talks with Turkish President Erdogan in Ankara, to discuss the set-up and monitoring of a combat-free zone in Syria

(continued)

(continued)

2017: Syria

Month	*Syrian government*	*Opposition forces/rebels*	*US, UK, Europe*	*Middle East*	*International organizations*	*Russia*
	Agreement between the Syrian Army and ISIL militants on the East Hama region. The truce includes the evacuation of ISIL members and their families out of the villages they control Representatives from the Syrian government and armed opposition groups meet in the Kazakh capital Astana for the sixth round of the Astana The government forces conduct air raid on four hospitals in Syria's northwestern province of Idlib				The UN has met to discuss the humanitarian crisis in Syria. It's alleged that Russian-led air raids have destroyed hospitals and killed dozens of civilians	
October 17/10	The Islamic State seizes the town of Al-Qaryatain in the province of Homs The Syrian Army captures Al-Mayaden, intense fight takes place between the East Deir Ezzor city and the countryside of Deir Ezzor province	The Islamic State group is driven from Raqqa, its de-facto capital in Syria Jaysh al-Islam militants launch a successful attack on the East Ghouta region in Damascus, regaining territory they lost to the Syrian government The Syrian Democratic Forces have captured the Islamic State capital Raqqa		The Turkish Army, along with Turkish-backed Free Syrian Army, launch an operation to remove Tahrir al-Sham from Idlib Israeli jets destroy an anti-aircraft battery outside of Damascus after its planes were fired upon in Lebanese airspace	Representatives of the Syrian government and some armed opposition groups are meeting in the Kazakh capital, Astana, with the goal of implementing a lasting ceasefire agreement	

(continued)

(continued)

2017: Syria

Month	*Syrian government*	*Opposition forces/rebels*	*US, UK, Europe*	*Middle East*	*International organizations*	*Russia*
		Syrian Democratic Forces have captured the al-Omar oil field, from Islamic State forces The Syrian opposition wants the three main rebel factions in northern Syria to reunite as one army				
November 17/11	The Syrian Army captures Deir ez-Zor from ISIL Syrian Army captures Abu Kamal in Deir ez-Zor Governorate which was the last stronghold of ISIL	Forced conscription of young men by the Syrian Democratic Forces causes civil unrest in Manbij, Al-Thawrah and western Raqqa		The Israeli Defense Minister, declares Assad 'victorious' in the Syrian civil war	Amnesty International releases a report confirming that forces loyal to Bashar al-Assad have committed crimes against humanity through their 'starve or surrender' strategy and sieges that devastated areas controlled by the opposition A UN inquiry team investigating the use of chemical weapons in Syria will be disbanded	The Atarib air strikes by the Russian Air Force on the public market of the town of Atarib, Syria kills many civilians Russia vetoed a resolution to extend its mandate

(continued)

(continued)

2017: Syria

Month	*Syrian government*	*Opposition forces/rebels*	*US, UK, Europe*	*Middle East*	*International organizations*	*Russia*
December 17/12	Government troops, with Russian support, continue reclaiming areas from rebels in the north-western Idlib province					Russian President Putin visits, declaring mission accomplished for his forces in the battle against Islamic State Russian President Putin announced the beginning of the withdrawal the Armed Forces of the Russian Federation Russia started establishing a permanent presence at its two military bases at Tartus and Lattakia

2018: Syria

Month	*Syrian government*	*Opposition forces/rebels*	*US, UK, Europe*	*Middle East*	*International organizations*	*Russia*
January 18/1	The Syrian Army, Hezbollah and Iranian-backed militias took control of the Beit Jinn area in western Ghouta The Syrian Army captures the Harasta vehicle base from the rebels Syrian forces capture the Abu al-Duhur airbase in Idlib governorate Syrian government's intensified attacks on rebel-held areas in the Damascus suburb Syrian National Dialogue Congress ends. Final statement calls for the creation of a Constitutional Commission comprising government, opposition and Syrian civil society members			Turkey launches an assault on northern Syria to oust Kurdish rebels controlling the area around Afrin and subsequently Manbij from Kurdish forces (Rojava) Turkey has mobilized thousands of Free Syrian Army (FSA) rebels to a border province with Syria, as part of a planned offensive against Kurdish fighters	UN's humanitarian chief, deeply worried about civilians in Idlib and Eastern Ghouta A new round of Syria talks is starting on Wednesday in Vienna in what officials said may be the 'last hope' for a resolution to conflict	Russian air strikes killed civilians in Eastern Ghouta

(continued)

(continued)

2018: Syria

Month	*Syrian government*	*Opposition forces/rebels*	*US, UK, Europe*	*Middle East*	*International organizations*	*Russia*
February 18/2	Government launches a ferocious assault on Eastern Ghouta, the final rebel-held enclave near Damascus Shelling by Syrian forces with the aid of Russian forces intensified on Idlib, after the fighters from the Hay'et Tahrir al-Sham group shot down a Russian warplane SAA forces reported the capture towns in the north eastern part of Hama; Buyud al-Saffaf, Abu al-Kheir, Abu Khanadiq, Rasm al-Kibar, Tell al-Shur, Malihah Saghirah, Rasm al-Mafkar, and Khirbat Umm, from ISIL Pro-government fighters entered Syria's Afrin region on Tuesday to support Kurdish fighters battling Turkey's military		Tensions escalate between United States, Turkey and NATO nations after Turkey launches assault on Syria	Turkish President Erdogan claimed a total of 2021 YPG militants were 'neutralized' since the launch of the Afrin intervention The Turkish government uses the term 'neutralized' to refer to enemies both captured and killed The draft UNSC resolution, sponsored by Kuwait and Sweden, is aimed at implementing a ceasefire to allow aid delivery and the evacuation of civilians from the besieged suburb	UN High Commissioner for Human Rights Zeid Ra'ad Al Hussein calls for international action after 'one of the bloodiest periods of the entire conflict', mainly in Eastern Ghouta and Idlib The UN Human Rights Office received reports indicating that at least 277 civilians were killed between 4 and 9 February—230 in pro-government air strikes—with a further 812 civilians injured Health officials in the rebel-held enclave of Eastern Ghouta are accusing Syrian government forces of using chlorine gas in their aerial bombardment campaign in the Damascus suburb The UN was unable to reach an agreement on a ceasefire resolution, due to Russia's veto	Russia vetoed the vote as they has disagreements on the wording

(continued)

(continued)

2018: Syria

Month	*Syrian government*	*Opposition forces/rebels*	*US, UK, Europe*	*Middle East*	*International organizations*	*Russia*
March 18/3	The Syrian army captures 59% of the rebel-held eastern Ghouta pocket and divides it into three separate pockets. Tens of thousands of people leave the region There is renewed government bombing of Daraa, which is a 'de-escalation zone' Syrian and Russian warplanes launch attacks on Eastern Ghouta, in parts of rebel-controlled Syria many civilians are killed		President Donald Trump announced that the United States will be leaving Syria 'very soon' France hold a meeting with the represents of the Democratic Federation of Northern Syria and plans to send soldiers to the SDF held areas on the Euphrates river France warns of intervention measures if claims of a fresh Syrian government chemical attack in Eastern Ghouta prove to be true	Turkey gains control of the town near Afrin Israel confirms bombing Syria's nuclear reactor in 2007	UN investigators have accused the Syrian Democratic Force (SDF), together with other warring parties, of human rights violations and attacks on civilians in Syria UN Commission of Inquiry on Syria, the SDF is accused of conscripting children, including girls and 13-year-olds, against their will	Russian air raid on the besieged Syrian enclave Bombs hit a market in the town of Kafar Batna, within rebel-held Eastern Ghouta
April 18/4	The Syrian government uses chemical weapons in Douma Syrian and Russian forces take complete control of Douma in Eastern Ghouta. Syrian forces promptly began mine-clearing operations in the city Government gains control in the former rebel enclave of Jayrud	100 buses evacuated the last batch of rebels and civilians from Douma As a part of an evacuation deal, rebels in East Qalamun surrendered their weapons to the SAA in exchange for safe evacuation to rebel-held northern Syria Fighters in Dumayr, a rebel-held district northeast of Syria's capital Damascus, agreed to surrender	Claims of a new chemical attack in Eastern Ghouta's main town of Douma prompt the United States, Britain and France to carry out a wave of punitive strikes on Syrian Government Oil prices soar with the possibility of US air strikes on Syria	The SAA and allied Palestinian militias launch an offensive to dislodge ISIL from their pocket in southern Damascus	Investigators from the Organization for the Prohibition of Chemical Weapons have arrived in Syria to probe into the Douma attacks	Russia sponsored deal that requires the Jaish al-Islam rebel group surrender all prisoners before leaving. The deal came up due to increasing international pressure following the chemical attack in Douma Russia, Iran and Turkey see themselves as guarantor states in negotiations between the Syrian opposition and government

(continued)

(continued)

2018: Syria

Month	*Syrian government*	*Opposition forces/rebels*	*US, UK, Europe*	*Middle East*	*International organizations*	*Russia*
			The United States, UK and France against targets in Syria in response to a suspected chemical weapons attack in the former rebel stronghold of Douma The targeted sites are: Syria's Scientific Research centre in Damascus' Barzeh district, weapons storage facility west of Homs and Command post and storage facility near Homs			
May 18/5	In pursuance of an evacuation deal with the rebels the Syrian Army gains territories in north Homs-south Hama region under control of the rebels The government forces regain full territorial control over Damascus suburbs and countryside	The deal entailed that the evacuation towards the Eastern Syrian Desert by ISIL forces would be allowed	The US government announced the US-led coalition's 'operations to liberate the final ISIS strongholds in Syria'	The Israel Defence Forces (IDF) launched 'extensive' air strikes against alleged Iranian military installations in Syria in the Western Golan Heights	The United States freezes funding for the White Helmets	Russia says there is an agreement to hold a three-way meeting between Russia, the United States and Jordan to discuss the de-escalation zone in southern Syria

(continued)

(continued)

2018: Syria

Month	*Syrian government*	*Opposition forces/rebels*	*US, UK, Europe*	*Middle East*	*International organizations*	*Russia*
June 18/6	The Syrian government launches an offensive in the eastern part of the southern province of Daraa A temporary truce has taken effect in Syria's Deraa province between the government and the rebel group, Free Syrian Army (FSA), following Russian-led talks in Jordan		Air raids by the U.S.-led coalition in Tal al-Shayer kills civilians most of them were women and children The United States government warned rebel forces in Daraa not to expect military support		The UN says the fighting has also cut off vital cross-border relief and aid supply routes Dera'a	Representatives from Russia, Iran and Turkey are meeting in Geneva on Tuesday to discuss the establishing a committee tasked with drafting Syria's new constitution Russia has no plans to pull its military out of Syria
July 18/7	The Syrian Army backed by Russian forces reached the border with Jordan and captured the Nasib Border Crossing Syrian government forces and their Russian allies have raised the national flag over Deraa province's capital The Syrian government issues thousands of official death certificates for their missing relatives. But the government has not released their bodies or any evidence of the cause of death	US-backed Kurdish forces, which control more than a quarter of Syrian territory, will likely push for regional autonomy	In a US-led coalition air strike in Deir al-Zor province in eastern Syria many civilians are killed	The Royal Jordanian Army attacked Islamic State militants near the Jordanian border at the Yarmouk Valley Israel was also on high alert as Syrian President Bashar al-Assad's forces regained ground from the southern rebels, bringing his troops close to the Israeli occupied Golan Heights Displaced Syrians along the border with Jordan have started heading back to the areas they fled from	Attacks by the government forces on Deraa rebels has displaced 270,000 people in Syria's south, with thousands stuck at Jordan border. UN Calls this the largest displacement in the Syrian war	Russia holds urgent talks with Israel

(continued)

(continued)

2018: Syria

Month	*Syrian government*	*Opposition forces/rebels*	*US, UK, Europe*	*Middle East*	*International organizations*	*Russia*
August 18/8	The Syrian government launches an offensive in the Suwayda and Rif Dimashq Governorates against Islamic State of Iraq and the Levant Syria and Iran sign a deal for military cooperation	With the collapse of rebel factions in south Syria, multiple north Syria FSA factions announce a new coalition, the National Liberation Front		Israel to take strong and determined action against Iran's attempts to station forces and advanced weapons systems in Syria Iran's top defence official and Syria's President Bashar al-Assad and the country's defence minister meet in Damascus, to reach an agreement to contribute towards reconstruction in Syria		Russia criticized United States for not helping to fight against terrorist group ISIL in Syria Russia lashed out at Western countries, accusing them of blocking UN aid for Syria's reconstruction and prevent the return of refugees
September 18/9	The Nasib Border Crossing, the main crossing for Syrian exports to Jordan and the GCC countries, is officially reopened Syrian government forces backed by their Russian allies have stepped up their bombardment of rebel-held territories in northwest Syria	The northwest province of Idlib, the last rebel stronghold in the country hosts around three million people, and adjacent areas Thousands protest in Idlib against the potential full-fledged offensive by government forces and their allies	The French Foreign Minister, Jean-Yves Le Drian indicates d that 'Assad won the war, we have to state this. But he hasn't won the peace' The Netherlands halts funding of the Syrian opposition and police forces The White House has warned that the United States and its allies would respond 'swiftly and vigorously' if government forces used chemical weapons in Idlib	Russia and Turkey announced a demilitarized zone in Idlib Governorate and rules out any immediate military operations Israeli Air Force launches missiles from the sea at the coastal city of Latakia Turkey continues to deploy troops and heavy weaponry to its southwestern border with Syria in anticipation of a major offensive by the Syrian government and its allies on opposition-held territory	Netherlands also plans on stopping the funding of white helmets in December 2018 The UN has expressed concern that the offensive on Idlib would trigger a new wave of displacement that could uproot an estimated 800,000 people	Russia rejects Turkey's call for ceasefire in Idlib province

(continued)

(continued)

2018: Syria

Month	*Syrian government*	*Opposition forces/rebels*	*US, UK, Europe*	*Middle East*	*International organizations*	*Russia*
				Turkey' says no civilians will be removed from Syria's north western Idlib province under a deal signed by Ankara and Moscow to create a demilitarized zone in the area Iran welcomes the Russia-Turkey agreement on demilitarized zones		
October 18/10	Syrian President Bashar al-Assad has granted a general amnesty for men who deserted the army or have avoided military service	The National Liberation Front (NLF), an umbrella organization of Turkey-backed rebels that includes the Free Syrian Army, is withdrawing from Idlib Fighters in Syria's Idlib have failed to meet a deadline to leave a planned buffer zone around the country's last rebel bastion as set out under a Russian-Turkish deal		Israel to continue conducting strikes into Syria despite the recent arrival of Russia's S-300 anti-missile system Turkey says a planned buffer zone in the northwestern Syrian province of Idlib has been cleared of heavy weapons as part of a deal reached between Moscow and Ankara Turkey will not leave Syria until a general election is held in Syria Iran's Revolutionary Guard has said it launched ballistic missiles into eastern Syria	The Quneitra border crossing between the Israeli-controlled Golan Heights and Syria reopens for United Nations Disengagement Observer Force (UNDOF) personnel The UN special envoy for Syria, Staffan de Mistura, to step down at the end of November	Russia delivered S-300 surface-to-air missile system to the Syrian military as part of new security measures
November						
December						

*Prepared by Farhana Khan, Research Assistant, O'Neill School of Public and Environmental Affairs, Indiana University, Bloomington

Appendix D

United Nations S/RES/2254 (2015)

Security Council

Distr.: General
18 December 2015

Resolution 2254 (2015)

Adopted by the Security Council at its 7588th meeting, on 18 December 2015

The Security Council,

Recalling its resolutions 2042 (2012), 2043 (2012), 2118 (2013), 2139 (2014), 2165 (2014), 2170 (2014), 2175 (2014), 2178 (2014), 2191 (2014), 2199 (2015), 2235 (2015), and 2249 (2015) and Presidential Statements of 3 August 2011 (S/PRST/2011/16), 21 March 2012 (S/PRST/2012/6), 5 April 2012 (S/PRST/2012/10), 2 October 2013 (S/PRST/2013/15), 24 April 2015 (S/PRST/2015/10) and 17 August 2015 (S/PRST/2015/15),

Reaffirming its strong commitment to the sovereignty, independence, unity and territorial integrity of the Syrian Arab Republic, and to the purposes and principles of the Charter of the United Nations,

Expressing its gravest concern at the continued suffering of the Syrian people, the dire and deteriorating humanitarian situation, the ongoing conflict and its persistent and brutal violence, the negative impact of terrorism and violent extremist ideology in support of terrorism, the destabilizing effect of the crisis on the region and beyond, including the resulting increase in terrorists drawn to the fighting in Syria, the physical destruction in the country, and increasing sectarianism, and *underscoring* that the situation will continue to deteriorate in the absence of a political solution,

Recalling its demand that all parties take all appropriate steps to protect civilians, including members of ethnic, religious and confessional communities, and *stresses* that, in this regard, the primary responsibility to protect its population lies with the Syrian authorities,

Reiterating that the only sustainable solution to the current crisis in Syria is through an inclusive and Syrian-led political process that meets the legitimate aspirations of the Syrian people, with a view to full implementation of the Geneva Communiqué of 30 June 2012 as endorsed by resolution 2118 (2013), including through the establishment of an inclusive transitional governing body with full executive powers, which shall be formed on the basis of mutual consent while ensuring continuity of governmental institutions,

Encouraging, in this regard, the diplomatic efforts of the International Syria Support Group (ISSG) to help bring an end to the conflict in Syria,

Commending the commitment of the ISSG, as set forth in the Joint Statement on the outcome of the multilateral talks on Syria in Vienna of 30 October 2015 and the Statement of the ISSG of 14 November 2015 (hereinafter the "Vienna Statements"), to ensure a Syrian-led and Syrian-owned political transition based on the Geneva Communiqué in its entirety, and *emphasizing* the urgency for all parties in Syria to work diligently and constructively towards this goal,

Urging all parties to the UN-facilitated political process to adhere to the principles identified by the ISSG, including commitments to Syria's unity, independence, territorial integrity, and non-sectarian character, to ensuring continuity of governmental institutions, to protecting the rights of all Syrians, regardless of ethnicity or religious denomination, and to ensuring humanitarian access throughout the country,

Encouraging the meaningful participation of women in the UN-facilitated political process for Syria,

Bearing in mind the goal to bring together the broadest possible spectrum of the opposition, chosen by Syrians, who will decide their negotiation representatives and define their negotiation positions so as to enable the political process to begin, *taking note* of the meetings in Moscow and Cairo and other initiatives to this end, and *noting* in particular the usefulness of the meeting in Riyadh on 9-11 December 2015, whose outcomes contribute to the preparation of negotiations under UN auspices on a political settlement of the conflict, in accordance with the Geneva Communique and the "Vienna Statements", and *looking forward* to the Secretary-General's Special Envoy for Syria finalizing efforts to this end,

1. *Reconfirms* its endorsement of the Geneva Communiqué of 30 June 2012, *endorses* the "Vienna Statements" in pursuit of the full implementation of the Geneva Communiqué, as the basis for a Syrian-led and Syrian-owned political transition in order to end the conflict in Syria, and *stresses* that the Syrian people will decide the future of Syria;

2. *Requests* the Secretary-General, through his good offices and the efforts of his Special Envoy for Syria, to convene representatives of the Syrian government and the opposition to engage in formal negotiations on a political transition process on an urgent basis, with a target of early January 2016 for the initiation of talks, pursuant to the Geneva Communiqué, consistent with the 14 November 2015 ISSG Statement, with a view to a lasting political settlement of the crisis;

3. *Acknowledges* the role of the ISSG as the central platform to facilitate the United Nations' efforts to achieve a lasting political settlement in Syria;

4. *Expresses its support*, in this regard, for a Syrian-led political process that is facilitated by the United Nations and, within a target of six months, establishes credible, inclusive and non-sectarian governance and sets a schedule and process for drafting a new constitution, and *further expresses its support* for free and fair elections, pursuant to the new constitution, to be held within 18 months and administered under supervision of the United Nations, to the satisfaction of the governance and to the highest international standards of transparency and accountability, with all Syrians, including members of the diaspora, eligible to participate, as set forth in the 14 November 2015 ISSG Statement;

5. *Acknowledges* the close linkage between a ceasefire and a parallel political process, pursuant to the 2012 Geneva Communiqué, and that both initiatives should move ahead expeditiously, and in this regard *expresses its support* for a nationwide ceasefire in Syria, which the ISSG has committed to support and assist in implementing, to come into effect as soon as the representatives of the Syrian government and the opposition have begun initial steps towards a political transition under UN auspices, on the basis of the Geneva Communiqué, as set forth in the 14 November 2015 ISSG Statement, and to do so on an urgent basis;

6. *Requests* the Secretary-General to lead the effort, through the office of his Special Envoy and in consultation with relevant parties, to determine the modalities and requirements of a ceasefire as well as continue planning for the support of ceasefire implementation, and *urges* Member States, in particular members of the ISSG, to support and accelerate all efforts to achieve a ceasefire, including through pressing all relevant parties to agree and adhere to such a ceasefire;

7. *Emphasizes* the need for a ceasefire monitoring, verification and reporting mechanism, *requests* the Secretary-General to report to the Security Council on options for such a mechanism that it can support, as soon as possible and no later than one month after the adoption of this resolution, and *encourages* Member States, including members of the Security Council, to provide assistance, including through expertise and in-kind contributions, to support such a mechanism;

8. *Reiterates* its call in resolution 2249 (2015) for Member States to prevent and suppress terrorist acts committed specifically by Islamic State in Iraq and the Levant (ISIL, also known as Da'esh), Al-Nusra Front (ANF), and all other individuals, groups, undertakings, and entities associated with Al Qaeda or ISIL, and other terrorist groups, as designated by the Security Council, and as may further be agreed by the ISSG and determined by the Security Council, pursuant to the Statement of the ISSG of 14 November 2015, and to eradicate the safe haven they have established over significant parts of Syria, and *notes* that the aforementioned ceasefire will not apply to offensive or defensive actions against these individuals, groups, undertakings and entities, as set forth in the 14 November 2015 ISSG Statement;

9. *Welcomes* the effort that was conducted by the government of Jordan to help develop a common understanding within the ISSG of individuals and groups for possible determination as terrorists and will consider expeditiously the recommendation of the ISSG for the purpose of determining terrorist groups;

10. *Emphasizes* the need for all parties in Syria to take confidence building measures to contribute to the viability of a political process and a lasting ceasefire, and *calls on* all states to use their influence with the government of Syria and the Syrian opposition to advance the peace process, confidence building measures and steps towards a ceasefire;

11. *Requests* the Secretary-General to report to the Council, as soon as possible and no later than one month after the adoption of this resolution, on options for further confidence building measures;

12. *Calls on* the parties to immediately allow humanitarian agencies rapid, safe and unhindered access throughout Syria by most direct routes, allow immediate, humanitarian assistance to reach all people in need, in particular in all

besieged and hard-to-reach areas, release any arbitrarily detained persons, particularly women and children, *calls on* ISSG states to use their influence immediately to these ends, and *demands* the full implementation of resolutions 2139 (2014), 2165 (2014), 2191 (2014) and any other applicable resolutions;

13. *Demands* that all parties immediately cease any attacks against civilians and civilian objects as such, including attacks against medical facilities and personnel, and any indiscriminate use of weapons, including through shelling and aerial bombardment, *welcomes* the commitment by the ISSG to press the parties in this regard, and *further demands* that all parties immediately comply with their obligations under international law, including international humanitarian law and international human rights law as applicable;

14. *Underscores* the critical need to build conditions for the safe and voluntary return of refugees and internally displaced persons to their home areas and the rehabilitation of affected areas, in accordance with international law, including applicable provisions of the Convention and Protocol Relating to the Status of Refugees, and taking into account the interests of those countries hosting refugees, *urges* Member States to provide assistance in this regard, *looks forward* to the London Conference on Syria in February 2016, hosted by the United Kingdom, Germany, Kuwait, Norway and the United Nations, as an important contribution to this endeavour, and *further expresses* its support to the post-conflict reconstruction and rehabilitation of Syria;

15. *Requests* that the Secretary-General report back to the Security Council on the implementation of this resolution, including on progress of the UN-facilitated political process, within 60 days;

16. *Decides* to remain actively seized of the matter.

Index

R. M. Abhyankar, *Syria*,
https://doi.org/10.1007/978-981-15-4562-7